OUTCOMES

SPLIT **B** EDITION

PRE-INTERMEDIATE

STUDENT'S BOOK and WORKBOOK

HUGH DELLAR
ANDREW WALKLEY

Split Edition A

Split Edition B

Contents   5

9

IN THIS UNIT YOU LEARN HOW TO:

- describe common illnesses and their symptoms
- give advice and understand medical advice
- ask and answer common questions about illness
- give instructions
- understand instructions on medicines

SPEAKING

1   Work in groups. Look at the photo and discuss:

- where you think the people are.
- what time of year you think it is.
- what's happening – and why.
- whether you think this is a good idea or not.

2   Work with a new partner. Discuss these questions.

- Do you feel physically / mentally different at different times of the year?
- What time of year do you usually feel happiest? Why?
- What time of year do you usually feel healthiest? Why?
- Which illnesses / health problems are connected to different times of the year?
- What solutions can you think of for these problems?

MIND
AND BODY

UNDER THE WEATHER

VOCABULARY
Illnesses and health problems

1 **Match the health problems in the box to the pictures (a–i) they relate to.**

an allergy	hay fever	a sore throat
asthma	a headache	a temperature
the flu	a nosebleed	an upset stomach

a an inhaler   **b** a cat   **c** flowers

d a thermometer   **e** some aspirin   **f** honey & lemon

g oysters   **h** a bed   **i** tissues

2 **Work in pairs. Compare your answers and explain your choices.**

3 **Work in groups. Discuss the questions.**
   - Which of the health problems in Exercise 1 do you think is the most / least serious? Why?
   - Do you know anyone who suffers from hay fever, asthma or an allergy? How does it affect them?
   - Can you remember the last time you had any of the other health problems in the box?

4 **Check you understand the words and phrases in bold. Then match the symptoms to a health problem in Exercise 1.**

   1 It happens every spring. It's horrible. **My eyes get red and sore** and I **sneeze** all the time.

   2 I think it's because of something I ate. **I was sick** three times last night – and I still feel awful today.

   3 If I eat any kind of chocolate, I **get a horrible red rash** all over my body.

   4 I **get out of breath** very easily and I **cough** a lot at night.

   5 I've had it all morning. I **can't concentrate on** anything. I took some aspirin earlier, but they **didn't work**.

   6 I feel awful. I've got a temperature, my **whole body aches**, I've got a horrible cough and I've **lost my appetite**.

   7 It hurts when I **swallow** – and I'm **losing my voice** as well.

   8 I sometimes just suddenly get them. I don't know why. On bad days, they can **last** for up to 20 minutes!

   9 It was 38 degrees the last time I checked. I feel hot and cold and I'm **sweating** a lot as well.

5 **Work in pairs.**

   Student A: close your book.

   Student B: explain, act or draw five of the words / phrases in bold from Exercise 4.

   Student A: guess the word or phrase.

   Then change roles.

   B: *This means you don't want to eat, you don't feel hungry.*

   A: *I've lost my appetite.*

   B: *Right.*

LISTENING

6 ▶ **53** Listen to two conversations where people talk about how they are feeling. Answer the questions for each conversation.

1 What problems do they have?

2 What extra information do you hear about the problems?

3 What advice are they given?

4 Do they take the advice?

7 ▶ **53** Listen again and complete the sentences with three words in each space. Contractions like *don't* count as one word.

Conversation 1

1 Oh no! _____ . Are you sure it's not just a cold?

2 I just feel really _____ all the time.

3 No-one will thank you if you _____ it.

4 Well, you take it easy and _____ .

Conversation 2

5 I always get like this at this _____ .

6 I really want to rub them, but that just _____ .

7 That's not _____ , actually.

8 You never know. It might _____ .

GRAMMAR

Giving advice

We use three main structures to give advice – to say what we think is the best thing to do. They all mean basically the same thing.

8 Complete the sentences from the conversations with one word in each space. The first letters are given.

1 Maybe you s_____ go home and get some rest.

2 W_____ d_____ y_____ get some sunglasses to protect your eyes a bit?

3 Maybe you o_____ t_____ try it.

 Check your ideas on page 86 and do Exercise 1.

9 Complete the sentences with one word in each space.

1 That leg looks really bad! I think you _____ see a doctor about that.

2 Maybe you _____ to just go to bed early tonight and get some rest.

3 You really _____ make an appointment. _____ don't you call the doctor now and see if you can go in tomorrow?

4 I don't think you _____ go out if you're not feeling very well.

5 It's a big decision. Why _____ you think about it for a few days?

6 What _____ we do about the cat? If you have an allergy to him, maybe we _____ think about finding him another home.

7 That cough doesn't sound good. Maybe you ought _____ take something for it.

8 A: It's not right, the way he talks to you. You _____ to complain about it.

  B: I know I _____ , but I'm worried everything will just take longer if I do.

  A: Well, if you feel like that, why don't _____ just change your doctor?

10 Work in pairs. Decide what advice to give in each of the situations below.

1 I'm really unfit.

2 I'm really tired. I'm not sleeping well at the moment.

3 I feel quite depressed for some reason.

4 My knee really hurts.

5 I'm really worried about my exams.

6 My parents don't give me enough money.

G For further practice, see Exercise 2 on page 86.

DEVELOPING CONVERSATIONS

Common questions about illness

When someone isn't very well, we often ask them common fixed questions. Usually the answers people give are also quite fixed.

11 Match each question (1–3) with two possible answers (a–f).

1 Are you OK?

2 Have you been to the doctor's about it?

3 Are you taking anything for it?

a Yes. The doctor gave me some tablets the other day.

b No, not really. I've got a terrible headache.

c No, not yet, but I've got an appointment this afternoon.

d No, not really. I'm just drinking lots of water. That's all.

e Yes, I went yesterday. He just told me to go home and take it easy.

f No, not really. I've got a bit of a cold.

12 Work in pairs. Think of two more possible answers to each question.

CONVERSATION PRACTICE

13 You are going to roleplay two conversations similar to those you heard in the listening. First, imagine you have a health problem. Decide how serious it is, what the symptoms are, if you've been to the doctor's or taken anything for it, etc.

14 Work in pairs. One student should start the conversation by asking: *Are you OK?* Use as much language from this lesson as you can. Then change roles and repeat.

▶ 17 To watch the video and do the activities, see the DVD-ROM.

THE POWER OF THE MIND

READING

1 Work in groups. Read the introduction to the article on page 11. Then discuss these questions.

- In your country, is healthcare paid through tax or do people have private health insurance?
- Is the cost of healthcare a problem in your country? Why? / Why not?
- Why do you think the cost of healthcare is increasing in some countries?
- How can the power of the mind help good health?
- Have you heard of any of the following? Say what you know about them.

hypnotherapy	meditation	nocebos	placebos

2 Read the rest of the article. Find out how the following can affect health.

emotional reactions	hypnotherapy	nocebos
exercise in old age	meditation	placebos

3 Read each sentence and decide whether it is an argument the writer makes.

1 Asthma sufferers don't need drugs.
2 With a placebo, there can be changes in the body.
3 All side effects of drugs are caused by the nocebo effect.
4 Some people can change their body temperature by thinking about it.
5 How well you deal with pain depends completely on your character.
6 Using hypnotherapy instead of drugs can mean operations are more successful.
7 You are as old as you feel.
8 As you get older, you are more likely to get injured playing sport.

4 Complete the second phrase with the correct form of the word in bold. All the missing words are in the article.

1 several **different** solutions   see a big _____
2 provide **treatment** for free   _____ cancer
3 study **science**   become a _____
4 **experience** difficulties   no previous _____
5 control my **emotions**   give _____ support
6 **operate** on his leg   the _____ went well
7 make a good **recovery**   _____ from the flu
8 get **injured** playing football   a bad knee _____

5 Work in groups. Discuss the following.

- Give other examples of some of the six suggestions in the article. Think about your own experience, knowledge, people you know or stories in the news.
- Say how each of the six suggestions could reduce the cost of healthcare.

UNDERSTANDING VOCABULARY

Phrases with *mind* and *matter*

In the article, you saw the quote: '*Age is a question of* **mind over matter. If you don't mind, it doesn't matter!**' Some words like *mind* and *matter* are mainly used as part of fixed phrases. You need to learn the phrases rather than just the single words.

6 Complete the sentences with *mind* or *matter*.

1 You say *It's just a question of mind over* _____ to explain that you can do something very difficult or horrible by concentrating and using your thoughts.
2 You ask *What's the* _____ ? if you think someone looks worried or ill and you want to know the reason.
3 You say *I don't* _____ when you are happy with all the choices and want someone else to decide.
4 You say *It doesn't* _____ when what you said or did is not important and you don't want to continue to talk about it.
5 You say *Never* _____ when you are telling someone not to worry or be sad.
6 You say *To make* _____ *s worse* when you're telling a story about a problem and want to say something caused extra problems.
7 You ask *You don't* _____ ? or *Would you* _____ ? to check that someone is sure they are happy to do something.
8 You say *I've got a lot on my* _____ to say you have problems you are worrying about.
9 You say *That's a* _____ *of opinion* when you disagree with what someone said.

PRONUNCIATION

7 ▶ 54 Listen and notice which sounds are stressed. Then listen again and repeat.

8 Complete these short dialogues with phrases from Exercise 6.

1 A: So I was already late and then _____ , the bus broke down.
   B: Well, _____ . At least you're here now.
2 A: How could you make such a silly mistake?
   B: Sorry. _____ at the moment.
3 A: What do you want to eat tonight?
   B: _____ .
4 A: They don't spend enough on healthcare.
   B: Well, _____ . I pay enough in taxes already!
5 A: _____ ?
   B: Oh, nothing really. I just have a bit of a headache.
   A: Shall I go to the shop and get some aspirin?
   B: _____ ?
   A: No, of course not.

MIND OVER MATTER

In many countries, the cost of healthcare is increasing, but people don't want to pay extra taxes to pay for it. Perhaps because of this, interest is growing in how the power of the mind can help us stay fit, prevent illness and even treat ourselves when we are ill. Here are six ways that mind power could make a difference.

PLACEBOS

If you give asthma sufferers 'medicine' and tell them it will help their condition, many of them will report that they feel better after taking it, even when that 'medicine' wasn't actually real – it was a placebo. Sometimes doctors can measure physical changes after patients take a placebo. For example, their blood pressure may fall. So it seems the placebo effect is not just a trick of the mind.

NOCEBOS

The nocebo effect is a kind of opposite of the placebo effect. You get an illness because you believe you will. When doctors give a patient a drug to treat a serious illness, they tell them about problems (or side effects) that the drug might cause, like a headache or a rash. Experiments show that a percentage of people get these side effects even when the drug they receive is just a sugar pill.

MEDITATION.

Scientists have studied monks who have learned to control their bodies by meditating. In one experiment, a monk sat in a cold room with a wet sheet over his shoulders. Most people would get very very cold, but the monk concentrated and increased his body temperature to 40°C. He actually dried the sheet!

THE PAIN'S NOT SO BAD

Scientists have shown that when some people experience pain, for example in a marathon or at the dentist's, they deal with it better for two reasons. Firstly, they prepare themselves beforehand – they imagine the pain. Secondly, when they feel the pain, their reaction is less emotional: they think 'Oh I notice there's a pain in my tooth', rather than 'Ahhh! That hurts so badly! Help me!' The psychologist Dr Martin Paulus has also shown that people can learn how to do this with training.

HYPNOTHERAPY

In 2014, the singer Alama Kante had a successful operation on her throat in France. She was hypnotised before it, so she did not need any drugs and she could sing during the operation. This way her voice was not damaged and she recovered more quickly. Hypnotherapy has also been successful in other areas, such as helping people give up smoking.

DON'T GIVE UP

There is a quote that 'age is a question of mind over matter. If you don't mind, it doesn't matter!' In the past, many people stopped playing sport, not because of injury, but because they *thought* they were too old. However, science is discovering that our bodies can work well into old age, if we don't stop practising. Like Fauja Singh: he ran his first marathon when he was 89 and continued to run after he was 100!

DON'T WORRY. YOU'LL BE FINE.

VOCABULARY Parts of the body

1 Label the photos with the words in the box.

arm	eye	hair	lip
back	face	hand	mouth
chest	foot	knee	shoulder
ear	finger	leg	stomach

2 Complete each group of collocations with a part of the body from Exercise 1.

1 have a bad ~ / a pain in my lower ~ / have his ~ to me

2 my ~ are wet / have big ~ / wipe your ~

3 cut my ~ shaving / bite my ~ / ~-read

4 long straight ~ / brush your ~ / have my ~ cut

5 a pretty ~ / pull a ~ / have a big smile on your ~

6 work on an empty ~ / have an upset ~ / take something to settle my ~

3 Work in pairs.

Student A: imagine you are a doctor. Say instructions 1–5 below to your partner.

Student B: close your book. Listen and do what your partner tells you.

Change roles for instructions 6–10.

1 Stand up and then bend your knees.

2 Put your feet together.

3 Bend forwards and touch the floor with your hands.

4 Sit down and lift your leg straight.

5 Open your mouth and say 'ahh'.

6 Take a deep breath so I can listen to your chest.

7 Turn your head so I can look in your ear.

8 Relax your face, shoulders and arms.

9 Raise your arm above your head.

10 Follow my finger with your eyes, don't move your head.

LISTENING

4 ▶ 55 Listen to three conversations. Decide where the speakers are in each one.

a at the dentist's

b in a hospital

c in a restaurant

d in someone's house

e in a chemist's

5 ▶ 55 Listen again and answer these questions.

1 What problem does the woman have in conversation 1?

2 What did she do to cure the problem?

3 Which problem does the customer have in conversation 2: diarrhoea, indigestion or vomiting?

4 What instructions is she given?

5 What two problems does the man have in conversation 3?

6 How did each one happen?

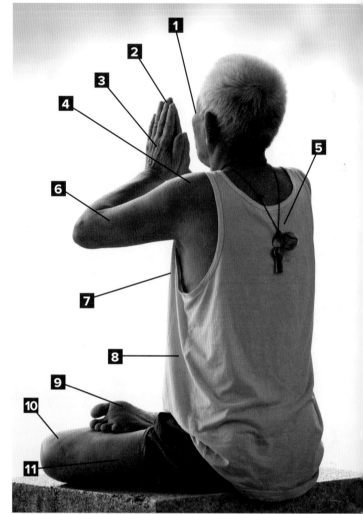

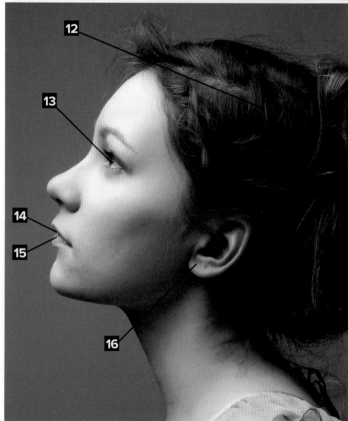

6 Work in groups. Discuss these questions.

- What's your cure for hiccups? For indigestion?
- Have you ever had any stupid accidents? Has anyone you know? If yes, what happened?
- Do you think the hospitals in your country are good? Why? / Why not?
- Have you ever been to hospital? Why? What was the service like?

GRAMMAR

7 Read the information and the sentences in the Grammar box. Then decide if the statements below are true (T) or false (F).

> ### Imperatives
> To make imperatives, we use the infinitive form of the verb (without *to*).
>
> ***Swallow*** *the water slowly.*
>
> *If they don't solve the problem,* ***talk*** *to your doctor.*
>
> To make negative imperatives, we use *don't.*
>
> ***Don't take*** *more than four tablets in a day.*

1 To make imperatives, we don't use a subject before the verb.

2 We only use imperatives to give instructions.

3 We often use conditional *if*-clauses with imperatives.

4 Imperatives always sound rude.

G Check your ideas on page 86 and do Exercise 1.

8 Choose the correct form.

1 *Take / Don't take* any more today! That's the third one you've had.

2 *Eat / Don't eat* something first and then take them.

3 *Put / Don't put* the bottle in the fridge. It'll go bad if you leave it out.

4 *Stop / Don't stop* taking them. You have to finish the prescription.

5 *Try / Don't try* to drink it or eat it.

6 *Wash / Don't wash* your hands after using it.

7 *Put / Don't put* it there in the sun. Put it in the cupboard.

8 *Let / Don't let* me drive if you're feeling sleepy.

9 Match the sentences in Exercise 8 to the warnings given with medication below.

a Store in a cool dry place.

b Keep refrigerated.

c May cause tiredness.

d Complete the full course.

e Don't take on an empty stomach.

f Don't exceed three doses in 24 hours.

g For external use only.

h Avoid contact with your eyes.

10 Work in pairs. Take turns adding an imperative ending to the conditional sentence starters below. Continue until one person can't think of another ending. Then play again using the next sentence starter.

A: *If you need any help, call me.*

B: *If you need any help, ask.*

A: *If you need any help, look on the internet.*

B: *If you need any help, … – I can't think! You win.*

1 If you need any help, …

2 If you've got a cold, …

3 If you're feeling stressed, …

4 If you see the teacher, …

5 If the alarm rings, …

6 If you can't sleep, …

G  For further practice, see Exercise 2 on page 86.

SPEAKING

11 You are going to tell someone about a scar you have. If you don't have one, use your imagination and invent one! Use the questions below to plan what you are going to say.

- How did you get the scar?
- When did it happen? How old were you?
- Where were you? What were you doing?
- Was anyone else with you?
- What did the other people do? Did anyone help you?
- Did you have to go to hospital or have stitches?
- Did you have to wait a long time to see a doctor?
- How long did it take for the cut to heal / for you to recover?

12 Work in groups. Share your stories.

SOUNDS AND VOCABULARY REVIEW

13 ▶ 56 Listen and repeat the sounds with /e/, /iː/ and /eɪ/. Are any of them difficult to hear or say?

14 ▶ 57 Work in groups. Listen to eight sentences using the words below. Together, try to write them down. Then listen again and check.

ache	bleed	feet	raise
bend	breath	pain	sweat

15 Work in teams. You have three minutes to write collocations or phrases for the words in Exercise 14.

my muscles ***ache***,

*have a head****ache****,*

*have awful tooth****ache***

PLACES TO STAY

IN THIS UNIT YOU LEARN HOW TO:

- describe places you stayed in
- book somewhere to stay
- apologise for bad news
- explain and deal with problems in hotels
- talk about imagined situations
- talk about past habits

SPEAKING

1 Work in groups. Look at the photo of a planned new resort and discuss the questions.

- Do you think it's a good place for a resort? Why? / Why not?
- Would you go there? Why? / Why not?
- What are the big resorts in your country? What can you do there?
- Have you been to any resorts? Where? Where did you stay? What did you do there?

2 Work in pairs. Discuss the questions.

- What do you look for when you choose somewhere to stay? Think about these things.

| entertainment | facilities | food | location | price |

- Which of these things are most important / least important to you? Why?

BOOKING A ROOM

VOCABULARY Places to stay

1 Complete the sentences with the collocations in the box.

babysitting service	provided meals
basic furniture	put up the tent
free wi-fi	real fire
heated pool	reduced rate
including breakfast	share a room
low season	shower block

1 It only cost €200 to rent for the week because it was still the _____ .

2 It was £50 a night for a double room _____ .

3 It normally costs $25 a night with electricity, but there was a _____ for groups.

4 They had a _____ , so we left the kids and went out on our own a couple of nights.

5 It was difficult to _____ because the ground was so hard.

6 There was a kitchen the guests could use, but they also _____ .

7 It had a _____ in the living room, which was nice.

8 We didn't have to _____ with lots of other people. They had some smaller family rooms.

9 There was a _____ which was shared by the whole block.

10 You had to walk a long way to get to the toilet and _____ , but at least there was plenty of hot water.

11 It had quite _____ , but the kitchen was OK and it was all very clean.

12 They charged a lot for internet access in the room, but there was _____ in the reception area.

2 Match each sentence in Exercise 1 to one of these places.

an apartment	a campsite	a hostel	a hotel

3 Work in groups. Can you think of:

1 two other things you can **share** in a hostel?

2 two other kinds of **room** in a hotel?

3 two other **services** a hotel or hostel **provides**?

4 two other things that can be **included in the price**?

5 two reasons you get a **reduced rate**?

6 the opposite of **putting up a tent**?

7 when the **low** and **high season** is in your country?

4 Work in pairs. Think of a hotel, apartment, hostel or camping site you stayed at. Tell your partner about it. Would you recommend it? Why? / Why not?

LISTENING

5 ▶ 58 Listen to a phone conversation. David is phoning a hotel for a friend who wants to visit Dublin with his wife and small child. Look at the questions David wants to ask. Then listen and note down the information.

> *Triple rooms?*
> *How much for everyone?*
> *With breakfast?*
> *Dates: Prefer 12th – 17th August*
> *Car hire cheaper from hotel?*
> *Parking available?*
> *Deposit?*

6 ▶ 58 Work in pairs and compare your notes. Then listen again and check.

7 Look at the audio script for Track 58 on page 99. Underline five words or phrases that you think are useful to learn. Compare what you chose with a partner.

DEVELOPING CONVERSATIONS

Apologising

We often say *I'm afraid* to apologise for giving bad news.

I'm afraid we're fully booked that weekend.

To reply to questions, we use *I'm afraid not / I'm afraid so*. We often also add a comment.

D: *And breakfast is included too?*

R: *I'm afraid not. It's 125 with breakfast.*

D: *So if, for whatever reason, they didn't come, they'd lose that money?*

R: *I'm afraid so. The complete payment is made on arrival.*

8 Work in pairs. Take turns asking these questions. Your partner should reply with *I'm afraid so* or *I'm afraid not* and add a comment.

1 Is there free wi-fi?

2 Do I need to pay a fee if I cancel?

3 Is the swimming pool heated?

4 Can we make a fire on the campsite?

5 Did it reject my credit card again?

6 Are there any tickets left for tonight's performance?

7 Is it going to rain again tomorrow?

8 Can't you do something about it?

9   Work in groups. You have three minutes to write as many things as you can that a hotel employee might say to guests using *I'm afraid*. Which group can think of the most sentences? Which group has the funniest ones?

I'm afraid we're full.

I'm afraid the air conditioning is broken.

10   ▶ 59 Listen to the receptionist taking another customer's credit card details. Complete the form below.

Name on the card:

Card number:

Security number:

Expiry date:

Contact number:

PRONUNCIATION

11   ▶ 60 Listen to the alphabet and put the letters next to the correct vowel sound.

/iː/	b	/eɪ/	a
/e/	f	/aɪ/	i
/əʊ/	o	/uː/	q
/aː/	r		

12   Invent some card details like the ones in Exercise 10 and write them on a piece of paper. Then work in pairs. Take turns asking for and giving these details. Note down your partner's details and compare them with what your partner wrote.

CONVERSATION PRACTICE

13   You are going to have two conversations similar to the ones you heard in Exercise 5.

Student A: read the role card in File 4 on page 95.

Student B: read the role card in File 12 on page 97.

Think about what information you need and write down the questions you want to ask.

14   Take turns being the receptionist and the customer ringing for information. Roleplay the conversations. The receptionist should apologise for at least two things using *I'm afraid*. Start like this:

A: *Hello, I'm ringing on behalf of some friends. They want some information about the hostel.*

B: *Sure. What would you like to know?*

🎥 18 To watch the video and do the activities, see the DVD-ROM.

WE'LL DEAL WITH IT RIGHT AWAY

SPEAKING

1 Work in groups. Discuss the questions.

- What problems might people have in a hotel? How many problems can you think of?
- Have you ever asked a hotel receptionist for anything? What happened?

VOCABULARY Solving hotel problems

2 Match the sentences (1–10) with the follow-up questions (a–j). Check you understand the words in bold in the sentences.

1 There's a lot of **noise outside** our room.
2 My room is **boiling**.
3 That's more expensive than I expected.
4 Are you sure you don't have a **record of my booking**?
5 I've forgotten my **toothbrush** and **toothpaste**.
6 I only have a **morning free for sightseeing**.
7 I have an **upset stomach**.
8 I have an **early flight**.
9 I have to leave before you start **serving breakfast**.
10 I **can't get** the air conditioning **to work**.

a Do you have any?
b Could you give me **a wake-up call** and **book a taxi**?
c Could I get something to take with me?
d Could you tell me what **the bill includes**?
e Could we **change rooms**?
f Could you **check again** please?
g Do you have anything that will help, or is there **a chemist** nearby?
h Is there any way I can **turn down the heating**?
i Could you **send someone up** to **have a look at it**?
j Where would you **recommend going**?

3 Spend a few minutes memorising the questions in Exercise 2. Then work in pairs and test each other.

Student A: say a sentence (1–10) from Exercise 2.

Student B: close your book. Say the follow-up question.

4 Work with a new partner. Choose four problems from Exercise 2 and roleplay the conversations. Take turns to be the guest and the receptionist.

G: *Excuse me. There's a lot of noise outside our room. Could we change rooms?*

R: *You can, but I'm afraid the only rooms available are more expensive.*

LISTENING

5 Work in pairs. Look at the photos. Discuss how they might be connected to problems with a hotel guest. What do you think the guest asks for?

6 ▶ **61** Listen to a conversation between a guest and a hotel receptionist. Check your ideas from Exercise 5. Can the receptionist give the guest what they ask for?

7 ▶ **61** Put the sentences in the order you heard them in the conversation. Then listen again and check your ideas.

a I'm afraid that's just not possible.

b We really didn't have much time to prepare them.

c I doubt I can find one.

d I'm calling on behalf of Lady Zaza.

e You've got hundreds of rooms in this place.

f I'm sure that if she was, she'd tell you exactly the same thing.

g There was no way we could stay in that last place.

h I'll make sure they're taken out.

8 Which of the adjectives below do you think describe Lady Zaza? Work in pairs and compare your ideas. Explain your choices.

| ambitious | demanding | lazy | selfish | tidy |

9 Work in groups. Discuss these questions.

- Can you think of any other adjectives to describe Lady Zaza? Do you know anyone else with these characteristics?
- Have you ever heard of anyone else making similar demands? What did they ask for?
- Why do you think people make demands like this?
- Why do you think people agree to these demands? Would you?

GRAMMAR

Second conditionals

Second conditionals are sentences of two parts. The *if* part uses past tenses to talk about imagined situations, or things that are unlikely or impossible; the *would* part gives the imagined results or further actions.

10 Look at the sentences from the conversation. Answer the questions below each one.

a *She**'d be** very ill **if she ate** one by mistake.*

1 Is she ill? Is it likely that she will eat a chocolate with nuts? Why not?

b *I **would move** them **if I could**.*

2 Does he want to move the people from the room below? Can he move them?

G Check your ideas on page 87 and do Exercise 1.

11 Complete the sentences with the correct form of the verbs in brackets.

1 I don't think I _____ so calm if I _____ deal with someone like Lady Zaza. I'd probably say something rude to them. (be, have to)

2 To be honest, I don't really like camping. I _____ it if I _____ the money to stay in hotels, but that's too expensive with a family. (never do, have)

3 The hotel was awful! Honestly, I _____ there again even if you _____ me! (not stay, pay)

4 A: The hotel was very noisy because of all the bars on the street.

 B: Really? I _____ a review on the web if I _____ you. It's good to warn other people. (post, be)

5 A: Which _____ ? Moscow or St Petersburg? We don't really have time to visit both. (you recommend)

 B: Difficult! They're both great, but if I _____ choose, I _____ to St Petersburg, just because the traffic isn't as bad. (have to, probably go)

6 A: If you _____ only visit one place in your country, where would it be? (can)

 B: Probably New York. There's so much to see and do there.

12 Complete each sentence 1–5 in two different ways using your own ideas. Then work in groups and share your ideas.

1 If I had more money, I'd _____ .

2 I wouldn't _____ even if you paid me!

3 If I had to choose between _____ and _____ , I'd _____ .

4 If I could only _____ , I'd _____ .

5 If I wasn't _____ , I'd _____ .

13 Work in pairs. Look at these situations. Discuss how would you react and what you would do. Explain why.

1 You're a receptionist and a customer is refusing to pay for the drinks he has taken from the minibar in his room. He says he didn't take any and is getting quite angry.

2 You're in a hotel and you can't get to sleep because of noise next door.

3 You're camping. It's raining and water is coming in through your tent.

4 You're sharing a kitchen in a hostel and you see someone leave their dirty dishes.

5 You've rented an apartment and the air conditioning is broken. It's boiling and the owner of the apartment isn't answering their phone.

6 You're a cleaner, and you find $100 left on the bed when you are cleaning the room after a guest has left.

G For further practice see Exercise 2 on page 87.

BEST HOLIDAY EVER!

SPEAKING

1 **Look at the different kinds of holidays for primary school children. Rank them from 1 (best holiday for kids) to 6 (worst holiday).**

- going to Disneyland with the family
- going to stay with relatives in the countryside
- going with other kids to a summer camp
- going camping with parents
- renting a place near the beach with the whole family
- two weeks with parents in a hotel in a foreign city

2 **Work in groups. Explain your choices. Discuss what's good / bad about each kind of holiday.**

READING

3 **Read the series of messages from a social media site on page 21. Find out:**

1 why Mark started the thread about holidays.

2 two ways Zinaida's holidays were different to kids' holidays today.

3 which three people often stayed near water.

4 who had a close encounter with danger.

5 who has nice memories of cooking.

6 who sometimes stayed in a theme park.

7 who suffered a loss.

8 who spent two weeks with each set of relatives every year.

9 who last went somewhere over 20 years ago – and why they're going back.

4 **Match the verbs 1–8 with the words (a–h) they were used with on the social media page. Can you remember who used these words – and why?**

1	mess around	a	on the fence
2	sit	b	for long walks
3	rent	c	breakfast on the terrace
4	climb	d	a cottage
5	have	e	by the river
6	get	f	chickens
7	scare	g	a tree
8	go	h	bored

GRAMMAR

used to

We often use (*never*) *used to* + infinitive (without *to*) instead of the past simple to describe past habits or states – especially to talk about things that have changed since.

Used to does not have a present form. For habits in the present, use the present simple + *sometimes*, *never*, *two or three times a week*, etc.

5 **Look at these sentences from the social media page and answer the questions below.**

a *My parents **used to own** an apartment on the beach.*

b *We **went** swimming all the time.*

c *We **once made** cornflake cakes.*

d *My son **usually spends** his summers like this.*

e *It **was** so strict.*

f *They **used to take** us on day trips.*

1 Which sentences describe past habits?

2 Which sentences describe past states?

3 Which sentence describes a single event in the past?

4 Which sentence describes a present habit?

 Check your ideas on page 87 and do Exercise 1.

6 **Decide which of these sentences you can rewrite using (*never*) *used to* and rewrite them.**

1 I didn't like camping, but I love it now.

2 I did judo when I was younger, but then I stopped.

3 We usually camp, but we rented a flat this year.

4 He's quite fit and healthy now, but he smoked quite heavily when he was younger.

5 I had really long hair when I was at college, but I had it cut short a few years ago.

6 It's become very popular. It wasn't crowded before.

PRONUNCIATION

7 ▶ 62 **Listen and check your answers to Exercise 6. Notice that *used to* is pronounced /juːstə/.**

8 **Work in groups. Tell each other about:**

- something you never used to like, but do now.
- a place, activity or thing that used to be popular.
- three things you used to love doing and three things you used to hate doing when you were a kid.
- three things that have changed in your life.

G For further practice, see Exercise 2 on page 88.

SOUNDS AND VOCABULARY REVIEW

9 ▶ 63 **Listen and repeat the sounds with /ʌ/, /ɒ/, /ʊ/ and /uː/. Are any of them difficult to hear or say?**

10 ▶ 64 **Work in groups. Listen to eight sentences using the words below. Together, try to write them down. Then listen again and check.**

booking	holiday	money	room
deposit	look	pool	toothbrush

11 **Work in teams. You have three minutes to write collocations / phrases for the words in Exercise 10.**

 Mark Reed Am returning to the place I spent my childhood holidays this week. First time in more than two decades. Started me thinking. Where did you all spend your holidays when you were kids?
5 hours ago   Like

 Zinaida Vozgova I used to spend holidays with my grandparents out of town – that meant lots of fresh air, messing around by the river, fresh fruit and vegetables … and no TV or technology, which isn't typical for our kids now …
5 hours ago   Like

 Biggi Wimmer Went to Italy every year. Near Trieste. My parents used to own an apartment on the beach. We went swimming all the time. Can't remember what my parents did! By the way, **Mark**. Where did YOU use to go as a kid? And how come you're going back?
4 hours ago   Like

 Julia Tcvetkova Used to spend a fortnight in a tiny village out in the countryside in Siberia. Sounds dull, but I never used to get bored. Remember sitting on the fence before sunset, watching the cows being brought back to the village. And running around the fields after my dog … before the neighbours took him away for scaring their chickens!
4 hours ago   Like

 Mark Reed Eastbourne on the south coast of England, **Biggi**. Used to be my favourite place in the world. Not sure I'll feel the same anymore!
3 hours ago   Like

 Christina Rebuffet-Broadus We either went to Disneyworld in Florida or the Smoky Mountains in Tennessee in the summer! At Disney, we stayed in the Polynesian Village. In the Smokies, we used to rent a cottage in the mountains. We woke up one morning to find a black bear climbing a tree near the terrace we used to have breakfast on!
1 hour ago   Like

 Mark Reed **Julia**: so sad to hear about your dog! **Christina**: Wow! Crazy! Oh, and **Biggi** – work trip. Meeting new clients.
55 minutes ago   Like

 Biggi Wimmer Got you **Mark**. Hi **Julia**. Mad story. Where are you from?
48 minutes ago   Like

 Zinaida Vozgova There was another option – summer camp, which I did a couple of times. I really hated it! It was so strict. Nowadays, though, everything's changed – camps have become more creative and child-friendly, with lots of activities and English classes and so on. My son usually spends his summers like this.
41 minutes ago   Like

 Julia Tcvetkova Siberia-Lithuania-St. Petersburg-Cape Town-London.
37 minutes ago   Like

 Biggi Wimmer Wow! Complicated life. :-)
26 minutes ago   Like

 Julia Tcvetkova But interesting!
10 minutes ago   Like

 Sandy Millin My brother and I always spent a fortnight with each set of grandparents – one in Gloucester, the other near Liverpool. They used to take us on day trips to places all over the south- and north-west – to places like Bristol and the castles of North Wales. We also spent time playing board and card games and going for long walks in the local area, among many other things. Food was also a big part of it: for example, I remember making homemade pizzas with one grandma and I think we once made cornflake cakes with the other. Really fond memories. Cool question **Mark**. Thanks for asking and reminding me.
3 minutes ago   Like

VIDEO 5

THE FUTURE OF A VILLAGE

1 Work in groups. Look at the photo of Essaouira, Morocco and discuss:

- what you think the main industry in Essaouira is.
- what difficulties a place like this might have and why.
- how the people there might solve these problems.

2 ▶️ **19** Watch the video and take notes on Essaouira, its economy and how it's changing.

3 ▶️ **19** Work in pairs. From your notes, try to complete the summary and the definitions below. Then listen again to check.

Local fishermen don't have regular work now because there are fewer [1]_____ , some work has moved [2]_____ and they can't [3]_____ with big ships. The town is trying to increase [4]_____ to replace employment in the fishing industry. Essaouira used to be well-known in the [5]_____ , and lots of rock stars and other people visited it because of the historic old town, which is on [6]_____'s World Heritage List. Since 1996 there has been a [7]_____ in the number of tourists. This has caused concern among local people about water, land use and [8]_____ .

Glossary

Trawlers are [9]_____ .

The *Medina* is [10]_____ .

4 Work in groups. Discuss these questions.

- Would you like to stay in Essaouira for a holiday? Why? / Why not?
- How has the economy changed in your country?
- What industries used to be stronger? Why did they decline? What's replaced them?
- Do you know any places where tourism has increased a lot? Has that been a good thing? Why? / Why not?

UNDERSTANDING FAST SPEECH

5 ▶️ **20** Read and listen to this extract from the video said at natural pace and then slowed down. To help you, groups of words are marked with / and pauses are marked //. Stressed sounds are in CAPITALS.

the FISHermen are prePARing / for aNOTHer year OUT on the WAter // all aROUND the PORT / you can hear the SOUNDS of BOAT building / and SMELL fresh PAINT in the air.

6 Now you have a go! Practise saying the extract at natural pace.

REVIEW 5

1 Complete the text with one word in each space. Contractions like *don't* count as one word.

¹_____ you're looking for interesting places to go this summer, ²_____ panic! There are plenty of options to choose from. If you want something cheap and adventurous, and dream of the kind of holidays you ³_____ to go on when you were young, ⁴_____ you should try camping in Croatia. However, if you're the kind of person who ⁵_____ never sleep under the stars, then why ⁶_____ try a new city instead? Perhaps you ⁷_____ to think about a break in a capital you've never visited before. ⁸_____ to Chisinau in Moldova or Reykjavik in Iceland. You never know. They might be amazing!

2 Put the words in the correct order to make questions.

1 did / that / use / where / you / do / to

2 it / see / about / why / you / go / doctor / don't / and / a

3 do / what / it / you / happened / you / would / if / to /

4 what / think / about / I / you / ought / do / to / do / it

5 ask / it / should / you / think / I / do / who / about /

6 please / you / give / the / me / password / the / for / could / wi-fi

7 anywhere / you / would / could / where / world / go / go / the / if / in / you

8 the / did / stay / went / when / use / you / to / where / islands / to / you

3 Write replies to the questions in Exercise 2 to create short dialogues.

4 Choose the correct option.

1 I'm quite fit. I *usually / used to* go running after work. It helps me relax.

2 I *went / used to go* swimming last Friday.

3 *Not / Don't / Shouldn't / Not to* go to work if you're feeling ill.

4 Where *are / will / would* you recommend going?

5 I *won't / wouldn't* stay there if I *am / were* you. It was horrible the last time we visited.

6 I *wouldn't / won't* work weekends if I *hadn't to / didn't have to*.

7 They might do better if they *wouldn't be / aren't / wasn't / weren't* so expensive.

8 I *didn't never used to / usen't to / didn't use to / wasn't used to* like cheese when I was a kid, but now I love it.

5 ▶ **65** Listen and write the six sentences you hear.

6 Match the verbs (1–8) with the nouns they collocate with (a–h).

1	get	a	your feet
2	brush	b	my lip
3	settle	c	out of breath
4	change	d	your hair
5	wipe	e	a deep breath
6	take	f	a room
7	share	g	my mind
8	bite	h	your stomach

7 Decide if these words and phrases are connected to health problems or places to stay.

ache	an inhaler	the shower block
aspirin	the low season	sneeze
get a rash	a reduced rate	a temperature
the heating	serve breakfast	a wake-up call

8 Complete the sentences with the best prepositions.

1 I'm afraid we don't have any record _____ your booking.

2 Can you send someone _____ to have a look at the AC in my room, please?

3 Sorry. I've just got a lot _____ my mind at the moment.

4 I hate missing breakfast. I can't work _____ an empty stomach.

5 It's boiling in here. Can you turn the heating _____ a bit?

6 I'm not looking forward to the spring because I suffer _____ really bad hay fever.

7 That's a matter _____ opinion. I don't see it like that, personally.

8 I didn't see his face. He had his back _____ me.

9 Complete the email with one word in each space. The first letters are given.

We went camping for a week and it rained the ¹wh_____ time we were there. The night we arrived, there was a huge storm that ²la_____ for hours, so it was really hard to put up the ³te_____ . The next day, we realised the site was much more ⁴ba_____ than we expected: no shop, only one shared shower, horrible toilets! Awful! Then, to make ⁵ma_____ worse, I got really ill. I guess it was probably the flu. I had a really sore ⁶th_____ and a terrible ⁷he_____ that didn't stop for ages! Then I got an awful cough before finally I lost my ⁸vo_____ completely! I don't usually ⁹mi_____ camping holidays, but this was too much! Next time, I want a nice hotel that ¹⁰pr_____ meals and has free ¹¹wi_____ so I can connect to the web, and maybe even has a ¹²ba_____ service so we can get away from the kids for a night!

11

SCIENCE AND NATURE

IN THIS UNIT YOU LEARN HOW TO:

- talk about the weather
- discuss and respond to news stories
- talk about animals
- tell better stories
- talk about scientists and research
- understand newspaper headlines

SPEAKING

1 **Work in pairs. Discuss these questions.**

- Which of the words in the box describe the weather in the photo?

| boiling | freezing | snow | sunny |
| a breeze | rain | a storm | windy |

- Do you get weather like this in your country? When?
- Do you generally prefer cold weather or hot weather?
- What's your favourite / least favourite kind of weather? Why?
- What's the weather forecast for the next few days?

2 **Work in groups. Tell each other about a memorable experience connected to the weather in Exercise 1. Think about at least two of the following.**

- how you felt about the weather
- what temperature it was
- how strong the wind was
- how long the weather lasted
- how much rain / snow fell
- what problems you had because of the weather

DID YOU SEE THE NEWS?

VOCABULARY
Science and nature in the news

1 Complete the sentences with the verbs in the box.

ban	build	find	hit	launch
become	conduct	fund	investigate	spread

1 The forecast said that a huge storm is going to _____ the coast any time now.

2 They're not going to allow some researchers to _____ experiments on animals.

3 They're going to _____ five new nuclear power plants.

4 They said that if we don't do more to protect bees, they could _____ extinct.

5 It said in the paper that they expect to _____ a cure for depression soon.

6 I read that we're going to _____ a rocket into space next year.

7 The government is going to _____ more research into ways of improving mental health.

8 I read that they're going to completely _____ smoking next year.

9 Apparently, scientists are trying to create mosquitoes that don't _____ diseases.

10 A university is getting £5 million to _____ the effect of colour on memory.

2 Work in groups. Discuss whether you think each piece of news in Exercise 1 is good or bad. Explain your ideas.

3 Work in pairs. Try to think of:

1 two things that might happen when **a huge storm hits** an area.

2 two other things the government might **fund research into**.

3 two other animals / birds that could **become extinct** sometime soon.

4 two things they're still trying to **find a cure for**.

5 two other things you can **launch** – apart from a rocket.

6 two other things that governments sometimes **ban**.

7 two other animals that **spread diseases**.

LISTENING

4 ▶ 66 Listen to four short conversations about science and nature in the news. Which conversation mentions:

1 a discovery that might prevent deaths?

2 a government project to help the environment?

3 a problem with very negative effects?

4 a change in the weather?

26

6   Look at the sentences below. Decide which are reporting news, which are opinions / comments and which are suggestions. Write a suitable response to each.

1   They've opened a new park near my house.

2   Really? That's awful.

3   We should have a party to celebrate.

4   That's fantastic news.

5   They should do something about it.

6   They're conducting an experiment to investigate how the Big Bang worked.

7   It's going to be freezing tonight.

8   They should ban it.

PRONUNCIATION

7   ▶ 67 Listen to twelve different responses. Notice the intonation. Then listen again and practise saying the responses.

8   Work in pairs. Take turns saying the sentences from Exercise 6 and giving your own responses. Pay attention to your intonation.

CONVERSATION PRACTICE

9   You are going to have conversations like the ones in Exercise 4.

Student A: look at the news in File 5 on page 95.

Student B: look at the news in File 14 on page 97.

10   Take turns starting conversations about your news. Use the guide below to help you.

Student A	Student B
Did you see / hear ...?	
	No.
It said / It's ...	
	Really? That's ...
I know. It's ...	
	(make a comment – or a suggestion)
(agree)	

🎥 21 To watch the video and do the activities, see the DVD-ROM.

5   ▶ 66 Work in pairs. Decide which conversations these sentences are from. Explain your decisions. Then listen again and check your ideas.

a   They're going to pull down a lot of the horrible houses they've built along the coast.

b   Yeah, it said it could save millions of lives.

c   It's been so wet and windy recently.

d   It makes a change to hear some good news.

e   They're all dying, for some unknown reason.

f   They should do something – fund research or something.

g   We need more green spaces.

h   We should go out, then – go to the beach or somewhere.

DEVELOPING CONVERSATIONS

Responding to news and comments

When people tell us news that we haven't heard before, we often respond by saying *Really?* We then usually add a comment. Speakers can agree with comments by saying *Yeah* or *I know* and then adding their own comments.

A: *Really? That's bad news / awful / nice / great / interesting,* etc.

B: (*Yeah*) *I know. It's terrible / really good news / fantastic,* etc.

ANIMAL MAGIC

VOCABULARY Animals

1   Match six words in the box to the photos.

cow	fly	parrot	rabbit	shark
dog	lion	pigeon	rat	sheep

2   Decide if each animal in Exercise 1 could be described as a wild animal, a farm animal, an insect or a pet.

3   Work in pairs. Think of two more examples for each of the four categories in Exercise 2.

4   Work in groups. Discuss these questions.
   • What pets do people you know have?
   • Which of the animals in Exercise 1 can help humans? How?

READING

5   Read the stories about animals helping humans. Match each story (1–6) to a headline below. There is one headline you will not need.

Barking witness	Jail bird
Wedding goes with a 'woof'	Dinner not well done
Milk of human kindness	From zero to hero
Tips for birds	

6   Work in pairs. Discuss the following.
   • What do you think each headline means?
   • Do you think each story is nice, interesting, silly, surprising or boring? Explain why.
   • One of the stories isn't true. Which one do you think is invented? Why?

7   Work in pairs. Discuss what you think the words in bold in the stories mean.

8   Work in groups. Discuss these questions.
   1   Which animals can you think of that have an amazing sense of smell / hearing / sight?
   2   Can you think of eight things that dogs are often trained to do?
   3   Which other animals are used to detect things?
   4   What advantages and disadvantages of having pets can you think of?

GRAMMAR

Past perfect simple
The past perfect simple is formed using *had / hadn't* + a past participle.

*These pets **had brought** the couple together.*

9 Look at these examples from the stories. Then choose the correct option to complete the rules below.

a *The World Wildlife Fund ... **had asked** the fishermen to let scientists have the body, but the fishermen **insisted** on using it.*

b *The parrots **had previously lived** in a cage ... . One day the owner ... **heard** the parrots copying his customers' requests and ... **trained** them to actually take orders.*

1 We use the past perfect to emphasise that something happened *before / after* another past action.

2 We *usually / don't usually* use the past perfect with other verbs in the past simple.

3 When we describe actions in the order that they happened in, we usually use the past *perfect / simple*.

G Check your ideas on page 88 and do Exercise 1.

10 Match the two parts of the sentences. Then work in pairs and compare your answers. Discuss why the past simple or past perfect is used in a–h.

1 The ground was wet
2 Someone had dropped a wallet
3 They took him to court
4 There was a huge traffic jam
5 I had to wait outside our house until my mum got back
6 I was very nervous
7 I was really shocked
8 My dog was going crazy when I got home

a because I'd forgotten my keys.
b because it had rained the night before.
c because I hadn't made a speech in public before.
d because there were roadworks.

e because he hadn't paid his bills.
f because I hadn't taken him for a walk all day.
g so I picked it up and sent it back to them by post.
h when I saw the rat in the kitchen!

11 Write endings to these sentence starters using the past perfect. Then work in pairs and compare your ideas.

1 I was hungry because _____ .
2 She was quite upset because _____ .
3 I was really tired because _____ .
4 I was quite nervous because _____ .
5 Before I was eighteen, I'd never _____ .

12 Work in groups. Discuss what you think happened before each of these events. Use the past perfect.

1 Guards caught and arrested a pigeon in a jail.
2 Fishermen found a pet dog on a desert island.
3 A pet rabbit saved his elderly owners.

13 Find out what actually happened by reading File 15 on page 97.

G For further practice, see Exercise 2 on page 88.

SPEAKING

14 Work in pairs. Choose one of the following.

a Have you heard any other animal stories in the news recently? Describe what happened.

b Do an internet search for animal stories in the news. Then tell your partner about the one you liked most. Who found the best story?

MAN'S BEST FRIENDS

1 When Andrew and Harriet Athay got married in the west of England, their dog Ed acted as the best man! Also present on the **big day** were their two female dogs, Humbug and Goulash. These pets had brought the couple together. Andrew and Harriet first met when they were walking their respective pets along a beach. They then started chatting while the dogs were playing with each other.

2 A megamouth shark, which is very rarely seen in the wild, was eaten by Filipino fishermen after they caught it in **a net** by mistake. The World Wildlife Fund, which wants to protect the sharks from extinction, had asked the fishermen to let scientists have the body, but the fishermen **insisted on** using it to prepare a traditional Filipino dish called *kinunot*.

3 A Japanese restaurant is employing two parrots as waiters. The parrots take drinks orders from customers and repeat them to a waiter at the bar, who then brings the drinks to the table. The parrots had previously lived in a **cage** in a corner of the restaurant. One day the owner, Mr Otusaka, heard the parrots copying his customers' requests and after that, he **trained** them to actually take orders.

4 Rats may have a bad reputation, but, says a spokesman for the charity HeroRats, they are saving hundreds of lives in Africa because of their incredible **sense of smell** and intelligence. The rats are trained to **detect** mines and bombs lying in the ground. Being so small, they don't cause the mines to explode when they stand on them. They can also **detect** some diseases in humans.

5 Researchers from Newcastle University have discovered that farmers can help to **boost** milk production by being friendly and talking to their cows. They found that when farmers gave their animals names, these cows produced over 300 litres more milk a year than those without names.

6 A dog called Scooby has appeared in court in a murder case. A neighbour had found the animal's owner dead in her flat and the family had asked for an **investigation**. Police brought Scooby, who had been in the flat at the time of death, into court to see how he would react to the **main suspect**. On seeing the man, Scooby barked very loudly. The police now need to decide if there is enough evidence to take the case further.

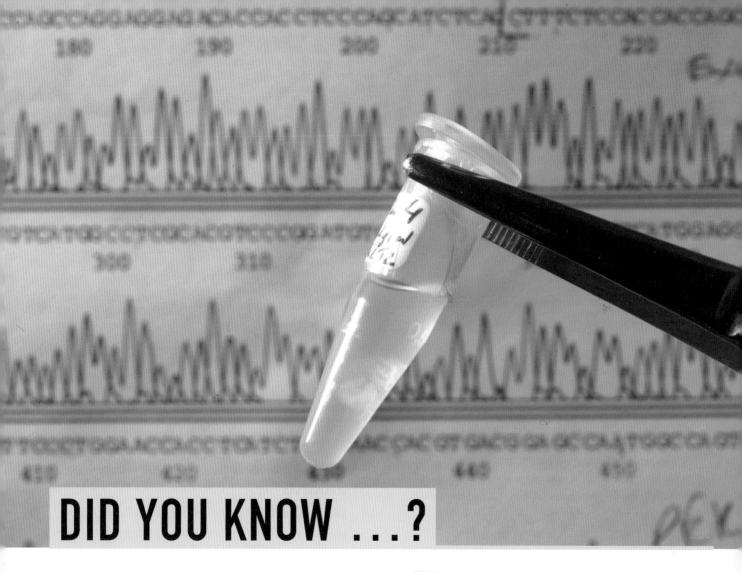

DID YOU KNOW ...?

SPEAKING

1 Work in pairs. Discuss these questions.

- Do you know much about science? Where did you learn what you know?
- Who are the most famous scientists in your country? What are they famous for?
- What TV or radio programmes about science do you know? Do you like them? What areas of science do they cover?

LISTENING

2 You are going to listen to a radio programme where a scientist answers questions from listeners. Work in pairs. Match each question (1–3) to a group of words (a–c). Explain your choices.

1 Are there 'crime genes'?
2 How do spiders walk on ceilings?
3 What is Graphene?

a hairs, atoms, electric charge, a balloon, attraction, weight
b a pencil, sticky tape, layer, to tear, be replaced, prize
c bananas, share, factors, violent, war, environment

3 ▶ 68 Listen to the radio programme and note down answers to the questions in Exercise 2.

4 Work in groups. Compare your ideas using the words in Exercise 2 and your notes.

5 ▶ 68 Listen again. Choose the correct option.

1 We share *15%* / *50%* of our genes with bananas.
2 Some violent criminals share *a particular* / *a part of a* gene.
3 Violence and crime can *learn* / *be learned*.
4 Each hair is also covered in hundreds of thousands of *tiny* / *tidy* hairs.
5 The hairs and ceiling atoms are attracted *by* / *to* each other.
6 It's the world's thinnest material – it's just one atom *thin* / *thick*.
7 If you *pull* / *peel* this tape away, some layers of graphite come off.
8 It's an incredible discovery and it was *ordered* / *awarded* a Nobel Prize.

6 Work in pairs. Discuss these questions.

- Did you know any of the answers to the three questions before you heard them? If yes, where did you learn about them?
- Which answer was most interesting for you? Why?
- How do you think the different factors mentioned in the first answer can cause violent behaviour?
- Have you heard about any new genes scientists have discovered?
- What other things could you use Graphene for?
- How many other Nobel Prize winners can you think of?

GRAMMAR

Passives

When we use a passive sentence, we use a different word order compared to an active sentence. We make the object of an active sentence the subject of a passive sentence.

7 Look at the pairs of sentences and answer the questions below.

1 a *Two Russian scientists **discovered** Graphene.*

   b *Graphene **was discovered** by two Russian scientists.*

2 a *If that process **is repeated** a few times, it eventually **leaves** a layer one atom thick.*

   b *If you **repeat** that process, you**'re** eventually **left** with a layer one atom thick.*

3 a *Could those things **be replaced** by Graphene?*

   b *Could Graphene **replace** those things?*

4 a *That stuff **is called** graphite.*

   b *We **call** that stuff graphite*

5 a *They **awarded** the discovery of Graphene a Nobel Prize.*

   b *It **was awarded** a Nobel Prize.*

1 Which verbs are active and which passive?

2 How are the passives formed?

3 Who does the action in each passive sentence? Do we know exactly?

G Check your ideas on page 88 and do Exercise 1.

8 Read the article below about a classic experiment. Choose the active or the passive form in 1–10.

In the 1950s Harry Harlow [1]*conducted / was conducted* a number of studies investigating the importance of love and contact between mothers and babies. In one experiment, young monkeys [2]*took away / were taken away* from their mothers and their mothers [3]*replaced / were replaced* by two models. The first model had a bottle of milk, but it [4]*made / was made* from wire and wood. The second model was like a soft toy. Even though the wire model provided food, the monkeys [5]*spent / were spent* much more time with the soft toy mother.

In another experiment, the monkeys [6]*put / were put* in a room with lots of strange things. If the soft mother was also in the room, the monkeys went straight to her. After they had been comforted by the mother, they [7]*explored / were explored* the whole room confidently. Where the monkey did not have the security of a mother or they had the wire mother, the monkeys were much slower to move round the room and some of the things [8]*didn't touch / weren't touched* at all.

These kinds of experiments [9]*don't allow / are not allowed* these days because removing baby monkeys from their mothers [10]*sees / is seen* as cruel.

In newspaper headlines, the verb *be* is often left out of the passive construction.

Rare shark eaten by fishermen

We do not leave out the verb *be* in normal sentences.

*A shark that **is** very rarely **seen** in the wild **was eaten** by Filipino fisherman after they caught it by mistake.*

9 Work in pairs. Look at the headlines. Discuss what you think each story is probably about.

1 **DOG AWARDED MEDAL BY THE QUEEN**

2 **Man arrested after stealing 10 kilos of bananas**

3 **ROCKET LAUNCHED ON 100-YEAR JOURNEY**

4 **Cure for rare disease accidentally discovered**

5 **SCIENCE COMPANY OFFICES DAMAGED IN FIRE INVESTIGATED BY POLICE**

10 Choose one of the headlines in Exercise 9 and write a short news report of 60–80 words.

G For further practice, see Exercises 2 and 3 on page 89.

SOUNDS AND VOCABULARY REVIEW

11 ▶ **69** Listen and repeat the sounds with /aʊ/, /ɔː/ and /ɒ/. Are any of them difficult to hear or say?

12 ▶ **70** Work in groups. Listen to eight sentences using the words below. Together, try to write them down. Then listen again and check.

allow	court	launch	power
bomb	dog	policy	storm

13 Work in teams. You have three minutes to write collocations / phrases for the words in Exercise 12.

*not **allow** smoking,*
*be **allowed** to keep pets,*
***allow** the cat out at night*

12

ON THE PHONE

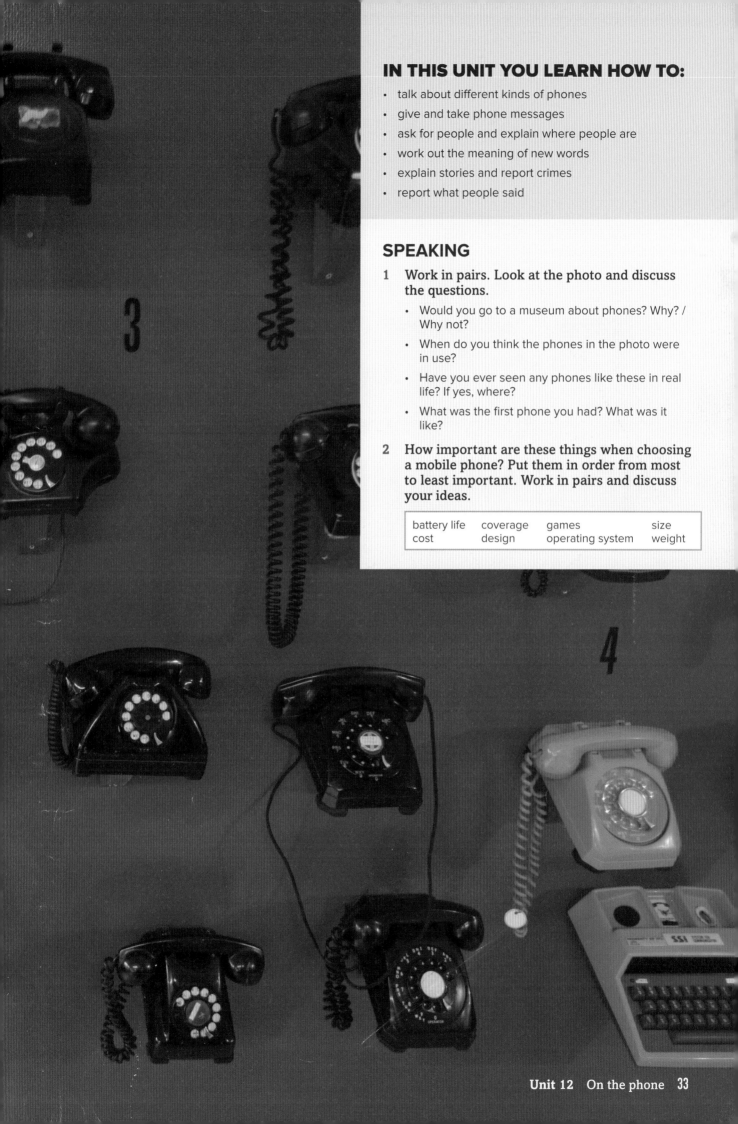

IN THIS UNIT YOU LEARN HOW TO:

- talk about different kinds of phones
- give and take phone messages
- ask for people and explain where people are
- work out the meaning of new words
- explain stories and report crimes
- report what people said

SPEAKING

1 **Work in pairs. Look at the photo and discuss the questions.**

- Would you go to a museum about phones? Why? / Why not?
- When do you think the phones in the photo were in use?
- Have you ever seen any phones like these in real life? If yes, where?
- What was the first phone you had? What was it like?

2 **How important are these things when choosing a mobile phone? Put them in order from most to least important. Work in pairs and discuss your ideas.**

battery life	coverage	games	size
cost	design	operating system	weight

CAN I LEAVE A MESSAGE?

VOCABULARY Using phones

1 Match the words in bold in these sentences to the meanings a–h below.

1 My son never answers his mobile when I call him. I always have to **text**.

2 When I called, I **was put on hold** for about 20 minutes with this terrible music playing.

3 I tried calling six times, but **the line was always busy**.

4 We couldn't finish our conversation because we **got cut off**.

5 Matt! Can I **call you back**? I'm having dinner.

6 The **coverage** isn't very good here. You might have to go outside to make a call with your mobile.

7 Sorry, I can't hear you very well. **It's a very poor signal**.

8 It was the wrong number, but she was very helpful and **put me through** to the right department.

9 We started to argue and I didn't want to hear any more, so I just **hung up**.

a put down the phone before the other person finished speaking

b send a written message ·

c pressed a button to connect me

d return your call later

e had to wait

f the person I wanted to speak to was on the phone to someone else

g lost the connection while we were on the phone

h the number of places it's possible to make phone calls from

i the connection on my phone isn't very good

2 Work in groups. Discuss these questions.

• Do you know anyone who never answers their phone?

• Do you usually text or phone more? Why? Does it depend who you're contacting?

• Do you know anywhere that often puts you on hold?

• Why might you get cut off during a phone call?

• Do you know anywhere with bad coverage?

• Have you ever hung up on anyone? Why?

LISTENING

3 ▶ 71 Listen to two short phone conversations. Complete the messages written after each conversation.

---

person
1_____ called.
time
Meet him at 2_____ – not 3_____ .

Diane 4_____ called. 5_____ is fine.

Phone her to sort out 6_____ .

Mobile: 7_____ .

Phone today – she's 8_____ tomorrow.

PRONUNCIATION

4 ▶ **72** Listen to these sentences from the conversation. Notice how only the key words are stressed.

No, he's <u>not</u> <u>up</u> yet. Is it <u>urgent</u>?

Just <u>tell</u> him we're meeting <u>earlier</u> – at <u>seven</u>, not <u>eight</u>.

5 Work in pairs. Look at the first conversation in audio script 71 on page 102 and underline the words you think are stressed. Then practise reading the whole conversation.

DEVELOPING CONVERSATIONS

Explaining where people are

We often explain where people are if they are not there when someone phones.

*Diane's **out** visiting a client.* (= she will return today)

*He's **away** on business.* (= he won't return for a day or more)

*It's her **day off**.* (= she doesn't work on this day of the week)

*He's **off sick**.* (= he's not at work because he's ill)

6 Complete the conversations with these words.

away	from	in	off	out	up

1 A: Hello. Is that Mary Williams?
   B: No, it's Jane. Mary's _____ . She's just gone to the shops. Is it urgent?

2 A: Hello, could I speak to Mr Haskell?
   B: I'm afraid he's _____ . He won't be back for a few days. Can I take a message?

3 A: Could I speak to Paul Philips? I phoned earlier.
   B: Of course. Hold the line. I'm afraid there's still no answer. He must still be _____ his meeting.

4 A: Hi. Frazer?
   B: No, it's actually Sylvia. I'm covering for Frazer. He's _____ sick today. How can I help?

5 A: Hi, is Jay there?
   B: Yes, but he's not _____ yet. Shall I wake him?

6 A: Hi, is Greg there, please?
   B: No, sorry. He's working _____ home today.

7 Work in pairs and practise reading the conversations in Exercise 6. Take turns to start. Continue each conversation with one or two lines each.

GRAMMAR

yet, already, still and just

These adverbs are often used with the present perfect or with other present tenses to emphasise the time something happened or when we expect something to happen.

8 Look at these sentences from the listening and match the adverbs in bold to the meanings (1–4) below. Which tense is used with each adverb?

a *He's not got up **yet**. Shall I wake him?*

b *I've **already** spoken to my boss and he's fine with the price.*

c *You've **just** missed him. He's **just** walked out of the door.*

d *I'm afraid there's **still** no answer. He must still be in his meeting.*

1 It shows the action is very recent.

2 It shows something happened before – often sooner than expected.

3 It shows something hasn't happened, but we expect it to happen. We also use it in questions.

4 It shows an action or situation continues unchanged.

G Check your ideas on page 89 and do Exercise 1

9 Choose the correct ending to each sentence.

1 Could you tell him I've already spoken to Brittany ...
   a so he doesn't have to email her now?
   b and we can't do anything until I have?

2 Tell him I'm still waiting for confirmation of the price ...
   a and it's better than we expected.
   b but I'll ring as soon as I get it.

3 Just tell him I don't have the money yet ...
   a and I'll send it to him right away.
   b but I'll definitely have it by Friday.

4 We've only just left the house ...
   a so could you tell her we're going to be late?
   b so tell her we'll be there earlier than expected.

5 Could you tell her we've already sorted out the problem ...
   a so there's no need for her to come over?
   b because I was out, but I'm dealing with it now?

6 I still haven't received the package ...
   a so can you ring and find out what's happened to it?
   b but I'm afraid it doesn't contain the parts I need.

10 Choose four of the sentence endings that were not correct in Exercise 9. Write a possible beginning for each sentence using *just, already, yet* or *still*.

CONVERSATION PRACTICE

11 You are going to have conversations like the ones you heard in Exercise 3. First write two messages you want to leave for different people. One should be more formal / a business situation, the other one should be for a friend.

12 Work in pairs. Roleplay four phone conversations. Take turns to start. Follow the guide in File 8 on page 96.

 22 To watch the video and do the activities, see the DVD-ROM.

PHONE FOR HELP!

READING

1 In newspaper stories, the first sentence usually summarises what happened. Work in pairs. Read the first sentences (1–3) taken from three stories, then read the questions and discuss what you think the answers are.

   1 *A police force has launched a campaign against misuse of the emergency phone number.*
      a What's the emergency number?
      b How are people misusing the number?
      c What things are the police doing in their campaign?

   2 *A doctor in Australia has saved the life of a young boy using a domestic drill and a mobile phone.*
      a What happened to the boy?
      b What did the doctor use the drill for – and why a 'domestic' one?
      c Why did he need the mobile phone?

   3 *A chef has saved his own life, thanks to the photo of a rare spider that he took with his mobile phone.*
      a Where was the man?
      b What happened to him?
      c What was the spider like?
      d How did the photo save his life?

2 Now read the news stories on page 37 and answer the questions in Exercise 1. Work in pairs and compare your answers.

3 Work in pairs. Discuss what the words in bold in the stories mean. Then complete these sentences with the words.

   1 He had to pay a 100-euro _____ for speeding.
   2 He _____ because of the heat, but he was OK in the end.
   3 After my wallet was stolen, I _____ it to the police, but they said they couldn't do anything about it.
   4 He keeps phoning, _____ me telling him to stop.
   5 There are hundreds of _____ of animals that are becoming extinct each year.
   6 I phoned the main number and then I was _____ to the correct department.
   7 It was urgent, so we _____ him to the hospital.
   8 My hand was almost twice its normal size and I had to keep ice on it to reduce the _____ .

4 Work in pairs. Discuss the questions.

   • Which story did you find most interesting or surprising? Why?
   • Why do you think people make inappropriate calls to the emergency number?
   • Have you heard of any other true stories of emergency operations?
   • How do you feel about insects and spiders? Are there any poisonous creatures in your country? Do you know what you should do if they bite / sting you?

UNDERSTANDING VOCABULARY

Forming negatives

In the first article, you saw these words: *totally unnecessary; inappropriate calls*

We often form negatives of adjectives and adverbs by adding a prefix. The most common prefix is *un-*, but you will also see *in-, il-, im-* and *ir-*.

5 Write the opposites by adding or removing a prefix.

   1 a wise decision
   2 it's illegal
   3 a fortunate result
   4 very impolite
   5 a happy marriage
   6 totally expected
   7 a practical solution
   8 very fair
   9 a comfortable bed
   10 an uncommon name
   11 a patient customer
   12 an inconvenient time
   13 completely possible
   14 a natural product
   15 an irrational fear
   16 a very unpleasant man

6 Work in pairs. Discuss the questions.

   1 What happens if someone does something **illegal**?
   2 What does a person do if they are **polite**? And **impolite**?
   3 What else can be **uncomfortable**? What's the result in each case?
   4 What makes a **happy** or **unhappy** marriage?
   5 What's the most **common** surname in your country? Do you know anyone with a very **uncommon** one?
   6 What would you say on the phone to someone if it was an **inconvenient time** to talk?

7 Work in pairs. Take turns to explain an adjective or its opposite from Exercise 5. Your partner should try and guess the word.

SPEAKING

8 Choose one of the situations below. Spend a few minutes preparing to tell a story. It can be true or invented. Think about when it was, where you were, what you were doing at the time, the main events and how you felt.

   • a time you were really glad you had a mobile phone
   • an unusual phone call you made or received
   • a time you rang the police, fire brigade or ambulance service
   • a time you helped someone in a difficult situation

9 Work in groups. Tell your stories. Ask questions about the stories you hear.

IT'S AN
EMERGENCY

A police force has launched a campaign against misuse of the emergency phone number. Every day, the police in northern England have to answer three hundred 999 calls, but a third of them are totally unnecessary. Last year, the calls that police received included someone wanting a ride home, a man complaining about his TV not working and two people who **reported** lost cats. A number were also from young children who had accidentally dialled 999.

The police are sending leaflets to houses to explain the problem and have introduced £80 **fines** for those making inappropriate calls.

A doctor in Australia has saved the life of a young boy using a domestic drill and a mobile phone. Nicolas Rossi, a thirteen-year-old boy from a remote town in Australia, fell off his bicycle and hit his head. Although Nicolas initially seemed fine, his mother, a nurse, noticed a **swelling** on his head. She **rushed** him to the nearest hospital, where the doctor realised the boy was in danger of dying if he didn't have an operation to reduce the pressure on his brain.

Unfortunately, Doctor Carson had never done the operation, which required him to make a hole in the boy's head, and he only had a normal household drill. After cleaning the drill, he phoned a colleague in Melbourne, who explained where and how to make the hole.

The one-minute operation was successful and the boy was **transferred** by plane to a Melbourne hospital, where he has made a complete recovery. Carson described his actions as 'just part of the job'.

A chef has saved his own life, thanks to the photo of a rare spider that he took with his mobile phone. Matthew Stevens, 23, was bitten by one of the world's most poisonous spiders, the Brazilian wandering spider, in a pub in south-west England, while he was cleaning the kitchen. The spider probably came into Britain in a box of bananas.

After the incident, Mr Stevens took a photo of the twelve-centimetre spider with his mobile phone, but then went home, **despite** his hand **swelling** 'like a balloon'. At home, he **collapsed** with breathing difficulties and had to be **rushed** to hospital. Fortunately, he was able to show the picture on his phone. The photo was sent to a university, where they identified the **species** of spider and found a cure for the poison.

WHAT A NIGHTMARE!

SPEAKING

1 Work in groups. Discuss these questions.

- Can you think of three different ways people often lose their phone or bag?
- What would be the first thing you'd do if this happened to you?
- Have you ever lost – or has anyone ever stolen – your phone, your bag or another important piece of property? If yes, what happened? What did you do to sort things out?

LISTENING

2 ▶ **73** Listen to three phone calls connected to a crime. Answer the questions.

1 What happened to Bettina?

2 What kind of company / organisation is each call to?

3 Why is she making each call?

3 ▶ **73** Listen again. Are these sentences true (T) or false (F)?

1 a Bettina has to answer some questions before her request can be dealt with.

  b Bettina's cards will be cancelled tomorrow.

2 a Bettina was walking home when her bag was taken.

  b She doesn't give a good description of the person that took her bag.

  c The police promise to try to find the bag.

3 a Bettina is calling from her apartment.

  b She has no way of proving who she is.

  c Bettina owns her apartment.

4 Work in pairs. Discuss:

- what you would do if you were Bettina.
- what you'd do if you were the guy from Abbey Locks.
- if you would report this kind of incident to the police in your country and what they'd do.
- what you could do to avoid a similar situation to Bettina's.

5 ▶ **74** Listen to another phone call one week later. Find out:

1 who Bettina is calling, and why.

2 what problem she now has. How do you think this happened?

GRAMMAR

Reporting speech

When we report things people said to us, we often use *said* / *told me* (*that*) + a clause. Reported speech usually moves one tense back from direct speech.

6 Look at these two sentences from the conversations. The first is direct speech from Bettina's first conversation with the bank. The second is how she reported it. Answer the questions below.

a *I've cancelled your cards and ordered new ones, and they'll be with you within three or four days.*

b *The guy I spoke to **told me he'd cancelled them and that the new cards would be with me** within three or four days ... but I still haven't received them.*

1 What tenses / structures are used in the direct speech in a?

2 What tenses / structures are used to report the speech in b?

3 How would you report someone saying '*I'm very sorry*'?

G Check your ideas on page 90 and do Exercise 1.

7 Look at this extract from an email that Bettina sent to a friend. The reported speech is in italics. Decide what you think the direct speech was.

I just couldn't believe someone could be using my card. I ¹*asked the guy how that had happened* and ²*he just said he had to speak to the manager*. I was then waiting for another ten minutes. Anyway, eventually I was put through to the manager ³*and she told me they had sent the cards to the wrong address*. ⁴*She said that there had been some security issues* and someone had probably hacked into my account and changed all my information before the cards were actually sent. Apparently, similar things have happened at other banks too! ⁵*She told me to change all my passwords* and ⁶*she promised the bank would repay any money I'd lost*.

8 Choose two of the following ideas. Spend a few minutes thinking about how you are going to report what was said. Then work in groups and tell your stories.

a A problem you had with a bank.

b A time you reported something to the police.

c The most surprising thing you can remember anyone telling you.

d Some promises someone in power made, and whether they kept them or not.

e A lie that someone told you, and how you found out it was a lie.

f An argument you had, and how it ended.

G For further practice, see Exercise 2 on page 90.

VOCABULARY Reporting crimes

9 Complete the sentences below with these pairs of words.

bought + got `	hacked + stole
came + kicked ₊	having + making ´
followed + threatening ·	hitting + kicking ♪
grabbed + ran ₍	texting + crashed ·

1 Two guys just walked up to me, _____ my bag and _____ off.

2 Someone _____ into my account and _____ most of my money!

3 I _____ home from work and found that someone had _____ my front door down.

4 I _____ something from a website that wasn't secure. I guess they _____ my bank details from there.

5 He just suddenly started _____ and _____ me for no reason.

6 This woman was _____ while she was driving, and _____ into the side of me.

7 It was really scary. This guy _____ me home and started _____ me.

8 Our neighbours are _____ a party and they're _____ a terrible noise!

10 You are going to roleplay a conversation between someone reporting a crime and a police officer. First, invent some details about the crime. Think about the following.

• what kind of crime it was

• if it affected you or if it was just something you saw

• where and when it happened

• what exactly happened and who was involved

• what you want the police to do now

11 Work in pairs. Roleplay the conversation. Use as much new language from the unit as possible. Then change roles and have another conversation. Start like this:

Police officer: *Yes Sir / Madam. How can I help you?*

Student: *Hi, I 'd like to report a crime ...*

SOUNDS AND VOCABULARY REVIEW

12 ▶ 75 Listen and repeat the sounds with /ʊə/ and /əʊ/. Are any of them difficult to hear or say?

13 ▶ 76 Work in groups. Listen to eight sentences using the words below. Together, try to write them down. Then listen again and check.

euro	hour	mobile	secure
home	insurance	photo	stolen

14 Work in teams. You have three minutes to write collocations / phrases for the words in Exercise 13.

cost 30 euros, pay 100 euros a week, spent 50 euros

VIDEO 6

MEMORY MAN

1 **Work in pairs. Discuss the questions.**

- What's happening in the photo?
- Are you good at remembering these things?

appointments	English words	numbers
books and films	jokes	your childhood

- Why do you think you are good / bad at remembering these different kinds of things?
- Do you know anyone who has a really good memory? How do they do it?

2 ▶ **23** **Watch the first part of the video (0.00–1.59) about an Italian man, Gianni Golfera. Complete the notes.**

> *Examples of Gianni's good memory:*
> - *can remember and repeat [1]_____ in order and then backwards*
> - *has memorised over [2]_____ books*
> - *can also remember [3]_____*
>
> *Memory research*
>
> *Malgaroli's memory research: wants to compare the genes of [4]_____ and _____*
>
> *We know memory is coded in the hippocampus, but need research on:*
> - *how it's coded*
> - *where [5]_____ and why there.*
> - *why some people [6]_____*
> - *why only a few people are like Gianni*

3 ▶ **23** **Is a good memory mainly genetic or mainly a matter of learning and environment? Watch the second part of the video (2.00–end) to find out.**

4 ▶ **23** **Put the adverbs in bold in the correct places in the sentences. Then watch the whole video again to check your answers.**

1 He practises to improve the power of his memory. **continuously**

2 He's memorised a series of historical books. **even**

3 Improving his memory has become like a full-time job. **almost**

4 He has a normal life. **relatively**

5 In other words, he's like other people. **just**

6 His genes are responsible for his great memory. **partly**

7 Researchers think it's because of his very hard work. **mainly**

8 Learning how to remember to remember. **basically**

5 **Work in groups. Could you learn anything from Gianni? Make a list of ways to remember English vocabulary. Then put them in order from the most effective method to the least effective.**

UNDERSTANDING FAST SPEECH

6 ▶ **24** **Read and listen to this extract from the video said at natural pace and then slowed down. To help you, groups of words are marked with / and pauses are marked //. Stressed sounds are in CAPITALS.**

if you really NEED // to USE your BRAIN caPAcity / to STORE / some kind of inforMAtion / you HAVE this / this abiLity / AND you know // it's just a MAtter of EXercise

7 **Now you have a go! Practise saying the extract at natural pace.**

REVIEW 6

1 Complete the text with one word in each space. Contractions like *don't* count as one word.

I got my daughter her first pet for Christmas. She
[1]_____ wanted one for ages, so I decided to get
her one. I went to the dogs' home and was surprised
by how many questions they asked. They asked me
[2]_____ the dog would sleep, [3]_____ we'd had
a dog before, how old my daughter [4]_____ , all
kinds of things! In the end, I got a lovely Dalmatian for
her. The guy there [5]_____ me that the dog needs
to [6]_____ walked at least twice a day. My daughter
is [7]_____ finding that quite hard! In fact, I've
[8]_____ reminded her about it – again! It'll take time,
I can see!

2 Complete the second sentence so that it has a similar meaning to the first sentence, using the word given. Do not change the word given. You must use between two and four words including the word given.

1 In Canada, I saw snow for the first time in my life.

I _____ snow before I went to Canada. **NEVER**

2 I still haven't finished writing that report for work.

I need to get on with that report. I _____ . **YET**

3 They should ban smoking in all public spaces, if you ask me.

If you ask me, smoking in all public places
_____ . **BE**

4 I got home and then remembered my laptop was still in the office.

I got home and then I realised _____ my laptop at work. **LEFT**

5 Someone stole my car while I was away on a business trip.

While I was away on a business trip, _____ . **WAS**

3 Choose the correct option.

1 She *told / said* me that she'd be late.

2 They asked me if I *did want / wanted* the job.

3 When *did that happen / was that happened*?

4 *You've / You'd* just missed him, I'm afraid. He left for lunch two minutes ago.

5 I still *haven't received / don't receive* your email.

6 We wanted to find out *what / what did* our customers thought of us.

7 *I still wait / I'm still waiting* to hear back from my bank.

8 Most of what we sell *is imported / imports* from China.

4 ▶ **77** Listen and write the six sentences you hear.

5 Match the verbs (1–8) with the nouns they collocate with (a–h).

1	ban	a	an experiment
2	grab	b	the environment
3	conduct	c	the coast
4	spread	d	my bag
5	hit	e	the swelling
6	protect	f	smoking
7	reduce	g	a terrible noise
8	make	h	disease

6 Decide if these words and phrases are connected to science and nature in the news, phones or crimes.

become extinct	fund research	a poor signal
a busy line	get cut off	put on hold
crash	investigate the effect	run off
find a cure	pay a fine	threaten

7 Complete the sentences with the best prepositions.

1 Someone hacked _____ my bank account and stole all my money!

2 A strange guy just walked _____ to me and started screaming _____ me.

3 I bought something _____ a website that I guess wasn't very secure.

4 They kicked my door _____ and stole my TV and my computer!

5 This is the wrong number. I'll put you _____ to the right department now.

6 They launched a rocket _____ space a few years ago.

7 I'm afraid she's _____ a meeting at the moment.

8 I'm quite lucky because I can work _____ home one day a week.

8 Complete the text with one word in each space. The first letters are given.

I tried to call him at least ten times, but he never
[1]an_____ his phone! I then [2]te_____ him a
few times and eventually, he [3]ca_____ me back,
but at a really [4]in_____ time. I was driving through
the woods and the [5]co_____ there is terrible. To
make matters worse, there was a huge [6]st_____
and the [7]wi_____ was really strong. It was raining
too, so I couldn't hear him very well. To be honest, I just
find him quite an [8]unp_____ man – very rude and
aggressive. I think it'll be [9]im_____ to do business
with him. I really don't trust him. It's an [10]un_____
decision to work with him, if you ask me.

- describe different kinds of films
- say what you have heard about things
- talk about how things make you feel
- talk about the film industry and culture
- discuss your favourite music, books or films
- ask how long people have been doing things

SPEAKING

1 **Work in pairs. Look at the photo and discuss the questions.**

- What do you think is happening in this photo?
- How do you think this photo is connected to film production? Why?
- What kind of films might the bears feature in?
- Would you go and see films like that? Why? / Why not?

2 **Work in groups. Discuss the questions.**

- What was the last film you saw?
- What kind of film was it?
- Who was in it?
- What was it like?

CULTURE

IT'S SUPPOSED TO BE AMAZING

VOCABULARY Films

1 Work in pairs. Think of an example for each kind of film below. Can you think of any other kinds of film?

an action movie	a musical
a comedy	a romantic comedy
a historical drama	a science-fiction film
a horror movie	a thriller
a martial arts movie	a war movie

2 Discuss which kinds of films might:

- have amazing special effects.
- have a happy ending.
- have complicated plots.
- be really scary.
- be quite violent.
- have amazing costumes.
- be set in space.
- have car chases and explosions.
- be quite predictable.
- be really boring.

LISTENING

3 ▶ 78 Listen to two friends discussing which film to go and see. Answer the questions.

1 What do you hear about these three films?

In the Heat of the Moment

The Cottage

It's a Love-Hate Thing

2 Which film do they decide to go and see in the end?

3 Where's it on?

4 What time does it start?

4 ▶ 78 Listen again and complete the sentences with three words in each space. Contractions like *don't* count as one word.

1 I was starting to fall asleep _____ .

2 Yeah, I'm thinking of _____ a movie.

3 Yeah, I've seen it already, actually. I saw it _____ .

4 Not bad, but not as good as _____ .

5 I got _____ with it after a while – and the ending _____ .

6 OK. _____ , I don't really like horror movies.

7 That sounds _____ ! Where's it on?

8 We could _____ a coffee or something first.

DEVELOPING CONVERSATIONS

supposed to

To report what we have heard or read about a film, a person, etc. we often use *be supposed to* + infinitive (without *to*).

*It's a new horror movie. It's **supposed to be** really scary.*

*It's **supposed to have** great special effects.*

44

UNDERSTANDING VOCABULARY

-ed / -ing adjectives

A small group of adjectives can end in either -ed or -ing. When they end in -ed, they describe people's feelings. When they end in -ing, they describe the thing or person that causes the feeling.

*I got a bit **bored** with it after a while.*

*What a **boring** lecture!*

8 Choose the correct option.

1 I got really *bored / boring* about halfway through.

2 The ending was really *surprised / surprising*.

3 I'm quite *excited / exciting* about the new Collocini film.

4 I just wasn't really *interested / interesting* in any of the characters.

5 The film was in English – with no subtitles – so I found it quite *tired / tiring* to watch.

6 It wasn't a bad film. I just found it quite *depressed / depressing*.

7 I must admit, I was quite *confused / confusing* by the ending.

8 The guy behind me was eating all through the film. It was really *annoyed / annoying*.

9 Write a sentence for each adjective that was not correct in Exercise 8.

CONVERSATION PRACTICE

10 Think of three films you would like to see. They can be new films or old films. Note down what you know about each film. Think about:

• what it's called.

• who directed it.

• who's in it.

• what kind of film it is.

• what it's supposed to be like.

11 Work in pairs. Roleplay conversations like the one you heard in Exercise 3. Student A starts, and Student B makes suggestions using the notes from Exercise 10. Discuss which film you want to go and see, where it's on and what time to meet. Then change roles and have another conversation. Begin like this:

A: *So what are you doing this afternoon? Have you got any plans?*

B: *I'm thinking of going to see a film. Would you like to come?*

A: *Maybe. What's on?*

B: *Well, there's a film called ...*

25 To watch the video and do the activities, see the DVD-ROM.

5 Match the two parts of the sentences.

1 I haven't seen *Hell Blood 3*,

2 I've never heard The Boredoms,

3 I've never tried Indonesian food,

4 I haven't been to the new shopping centre yet,

5 I've never seen him play tennis,

6 I've never been to Hawaii,

a but he's supposed to be really good at it.

b but it's supposed to be a violent film.

c but they're supposed to be quite strange.

d but it's supposed to be a beautiful place.

e but it's supposed to have a great selection of stuff.

f but it's supposed to be quite spicy.

6 Think of one example of each of the following things and say what each one is supposed to be like.

• a very famous film that you've never seen

• a new film that you haven't seen yet

• a famous book you've never read

• a group, singer or album you haven't heard

• a country you've never been to

• a kind of food you've never tried

7 Work in groups. Share your ideas.

MAKING MOVIES

SPEAKING

1 Work in groups. Discuss the questions.

1 Does your country have a film industry? How big is it?

2 How is the industry doing? Why?

3 Do most local films show at the cinema or do they go straight to DVD? Why?

4 What kind of films are most popular in your country?

5 What are the most important local films from recent years?

6 Who is the most famous director from your country?

7 Do you know how many films he / she has made?

8 Do you like his / her work? Why? / Why not?

READING

2 Read the article on page 47. Work in pairs and discuss how the writer of the article might answer the questions in Exercise 1.

3 Match the verbs (1–8) with the words (a–h) they are used with in the article.

1 reach	a more ambitious
2 follow	b Benin culture
3 give	c a bad image
4 make	d a middle-class cinema audience
5 be	e a crossroads
6 steal	f no money
7 promote	g very similar plots
8 be aimed at	h valuable works of art

4 Compare your ideas with a partner. Can you remember who or what does each of the things in Exercise 3? Read the article again and check your ideas.

5 Work in pairs. Discuss the questions.

• What similarities and differences are there between the Nigerian film industry and the film industry in your country?

• Would you like to watch any of the Nollywood films? Why? / Why not?

• Do you think people get a good image of your country from films? Why? / Why not?

• Have you heard of any similar stories to *Invasion 1897*?

• What films have made people more aware of an issue? What was the issue? Did it make a difference in real life?

• How do you feel about Hollywood movies? Are they popular in your country? Do you think they have more of a positive or a negative impact? Why?

GRAMMAR

Noun phrases

In the text you read: *you're likely to be offered* **the latest DVDs from the Nigerian film industry**.

The latest DVDs from the Nigerian film industry is an example of a **noun phrase**: a group of several words around a main noun. The main noun in this phrase is *DVDs*. All the other words add information about the DVDs.

6 Look at these extracts from the article. Answer the questions below.

a **Nollywood films** *are made for £20,000*

b *the* **film cameramen** *have to work in the streets*

c *stole many valuable* **works of art**

d *make people aware of* **the issue of stolen art**

1 Which is the main noun in each extract?

2 What is the singular and plural form of the main noun in each example?

 Check your ideas on page 90 and do Exercise 1.

7 Make a noun phrase using the words.

1 industry / the / fashion

2 a / director / famous / film

3 the / country / from / our / films

4 a / of / my / parents / photo

8 Write a sentence using each noun phrase.

PRONUNCIATION

9 ▶ 79 Listen to how these compound nouns are pronounced and mark where the main stress is.

cash machine

cash machine	film industry	success story
city centre	football boots	sunglasses
crossroads	heart disease	tennis court
flatmate	security system	traffic lights

10 Spend two minutes memorising the compound nouns in Exercise 9. Then work in pairs.

Student A: close your book.

Student B: act, draw or explain the compound nouns. See how many your partner can guess.

11 Work in groups. Change one word in each compound noun in Exercise 9 to make a new compound noun. The first group to think of twelve new compound nouns wins.

the film industry: *the* **fashion** *industry, a film* **star**

G For further practice, see Exercise 2 on page 91.

NOLLYWOOD DREAMS

Sarah Walters reports on an African success story looking to the future

In many cities of the world, if you're stuck in a traffic jam, you'll find people trying to sell you drinks and food, but in Nigeria you're also likely to be offered the latest DVDs from the Nigerian film industry, known as Nollywood. Nollywood produces around 1,500 films a year, and is second only to India as the most productive film industry in the world. In just 25 years, and with no government support, it has grown from nothing to be worth around $7 billion a year. Nollywood now employs thousands and is one of Africa's great success stories, but it has also reached a crossroads, as profits have fallen recently and it's unclear what its future direction will be.

The majority of Nollywood films are made for around $30,000 and take ten days to complete. In comparison, making a top Hollywood movie can take a year and cost $200 million. Nollywood directors use very basic special effects, the actors sometimes write their own lines and the film cameramen have to work in the streets while real life continues around them. This low-budget approach has allowed Nollywood to grow very quickly, as almost anyone with talent can make films. However, it's also the source of several problems.

Low budgets often mean films are poor quality and there's no money to develop new talent. Films often follow similar plots and star the same actors, so have become too predictable. Typical Nollywood films are voodoo horror or gangster films; even stories about poor people becoming successful, or domestic dramas, contain elements of magic and violence. Some complain that this focus on black magic and crime gives a bad image of modern Nigeria.

Another problem is illegal copying. Films aren't usually shown in cinemas (there are currently less than 30 cinemas in a country of 150 million people), but are distributed as DVDs through market stalls and street sellers, so it's difficult to control copying. After two weeks, most films have been illegally copied and the producers make no more money.

However, Nollywood is changing, as seen in the work of its leading director, Lancelot Oduwa Imasuen. Imasuen has already directed around 200 feature films (Steven Spielberg at the same age had directed just fourteen!). His early films followed the Nollywood pattern – fast production and voodoo horror – but Imasuen's recent films are more ambitious. *Invasion 1897* had a budget of $1 million and tells the story of how the British invaded the kingdom of Benin, sent the king to prison and stole many valuable works of art, which are now in the British Museum in London. The film was first shown at several international festivals and many universities in Nigeria. As well as making a profit, it aims to promote Benin culture and make people aware of the issue of stolen art. Some think that films like this show a possible future direction for the Nigerian film industry because they are aimed at a more profitable middle-class cinema audience.

I'M A BIG FAN

VOCABULARY Music, art and books

1 Put each word in the box under the correct heading in the table.

album	crime fiction	painting
author	exhibition	poetry
comedy	instrument	portrait
composer	landscape	sculpture
concert	novel	singer

Music	Art	Books

2 Write six questions about music, art and books, using words from Exercise 1.

Do you like listening to music? *Who's your favourite* singer? *Why? What's your favourite* album? *Why?*

3 Now work in groups. Ask each other your six questions. Try to use these phrases in your answers.

I'm a big fan of ... .

It changes. I've been reading / listening to ... a lot recently.

She's got an amazing voice / style / technique.

I think my all-time favourite is a song / painting / novel by ... .

I don't know why I like it so much. I just do.

It's just really exciting / sad / beautiful, etc.

LISTENING

4 ▶ **80** Listen to four people talking about music, art and books. Match each speaker to one photo. Then work in pairs and explain your ideas.

5 ▶ **80** Listen again. Decide which speaker:

a has been a bit disappointed with something.

b escaped problems when they were a kid.

c has been studying a language.

d has changed their tastes recently.

e decided what kind of work they wanted to do a long time ago.

f is going to perform live.

g has travelled to see someone they're a fan of.

h is interested in politics and society.

6 Choose one of the following topics to talk about. Spend a few minutes thinking about what you want to say. Then work in groups and share your ideas.

- singing competitions
- art and music in education
- a film / TV series based on a book
- modern art

GRAMMAR
Present perfect continuous

7 Look at these sentences from the listening. Complete the rules in the Grammar box below.

a *For the last few weeks,* **they've been showing** *a series on TV based on the books.*

b **I've been learning** *Turkish since 2012.*

c **We've been rehearsing** *The Rite of Spring recently for a concert.*

d **I've liked** *her ever since then.*

e **I've known** *I wanted to be an artist since I was three.*

The present perfect continuous is formed using
¹_____ / has + ²_____ + the *-ing* form of the verb.
It is used to talk about activities that started in the past and are unfinished.

To show the amount or period of time something lasted, use a time expression starting with ³_____ .

To show when something started, use a time expression starting with ⁴_____ .

Some verbs are generally not used in the present perfect continuous. We use them in the present perfect simple form. For example: *be, believe, hate,* ⁵_____ and ⁶_____ .

G Check your ideas on page 91 and do Exercise 1.

8 Respond to these comments by writing a *How long ...?* question. Use the verb in brackets in the present perfect continuous or simple.

How long have you been going there?

1 I'm a member of a gym. (go there)

2 They have their dance class on Tuesdays. (do)

3 She speaks English well. (learn)

4 I'm a drummer in a band. (play)

5 He's running in a marathon next week. (train)

6 Peter's my oldest friend. (know)

7 Franco is Violetta's boyfriend. (go out)

8 It's our wedding anniversary today. (be married)

PRONUNCIATION

9 ▶ **81** Listen and check your answers to Exercise 8. Notice that in normal speech *have* is usually pronounced /əv/ and *has* is pronounced /əz/. Then listen again and practise saying the sentences.

10 Work in pairs. Take turns asking and answering your questions from Exercise 8.

Student A: reply using *for.*

Student B: reply using *since.*

11 Change partners. Ask each other the questions below. If your partner answers positively, ask a follow-up *How long ...?* question and continue the conversation.

A: *Do you belong to any clubs?*

B: *Yeah. I'm a member of a cycling club.*

A: *Really? How long have you been doing that?*

B: *For quite a while. Since I was about 20 or 21, I guess.*

A: *And how often do you all meet?*

- Do you belong to any clubs?
- Do you go to any classes outside school / work?
- What hobbies or interests do you have outside school / work?
- What languages do you know?
- Do you play any musical instruments?
- Who's your oldest friend?

G  For further practice, see Exercise 2 on page 91.

SOUNDS AND VOCABULARY REVIEW

12 ▶ **82** Listen and repeat the sounds with /h/. Are any of them difficult to hear or say?

13 ▶ **83** Work in groups. Listen to eight sentences using the words below. Together, try to write them down. Then listen again and check.

behind	halfway	historical	horror
habit	happy	hobby	rehearse

14 Work in teams. You have three minutes to write collocations / phrases for the words in Exercise 13.

the guy **behind** *me,*

get stuck **behind** *a big truck,*

stand **behind** *me*

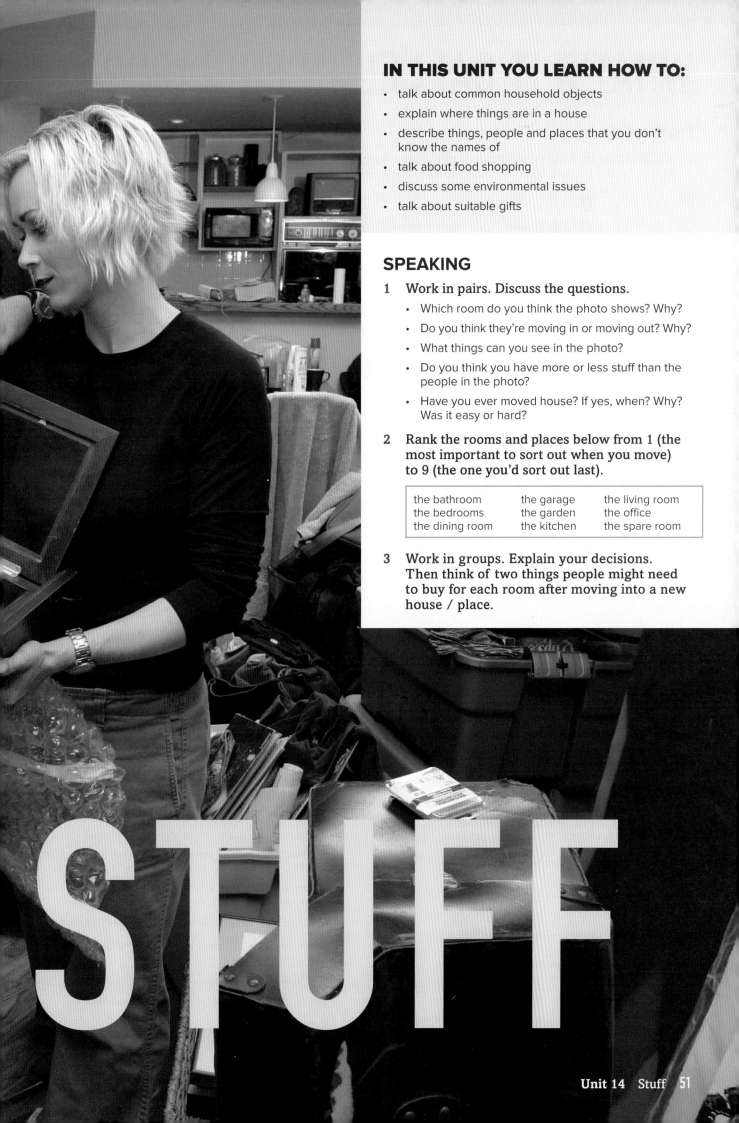

IN THIS UNIT YOU LEARN HOW TO:

- talk about common household objects
- explain where things are in a house
- describe things, people and places that you don't know the names of
- talk about food shopping
- discuss some environmental issues
- talk about suitable gifts

SPEAKING

1 Work in pairs. Discuss the questions.

- Which room do you think the photo shows? Why?
- Do you think they're moving in or moving out? Why?
- What things can you see in the photo?
- Do you think you have more or less stuff than the people in the photo?
- Have you ever moved house? If yes, when? Why? Was it easy or hard?

2 Rank the rooms and places below from 1 (the most important to sort out when you move) to 9 (the one you'd sort out last).

the bathroom	the garage	the living room
the bedrooms	the garden	the office
the dining room	the kitchen	the spare room

3 Work in groups. Explain your decisions. Then think of two things people might need to buy for each room after moving into a new house / place.

STUFF

WHAT'S IT CALLED IN ENGLISH?

LISTENING

1 ▶ 84 Listen to three new flatmates planning a shopping trip. Decide which of the things in the picture they are going to buy – and what each of these things is called.

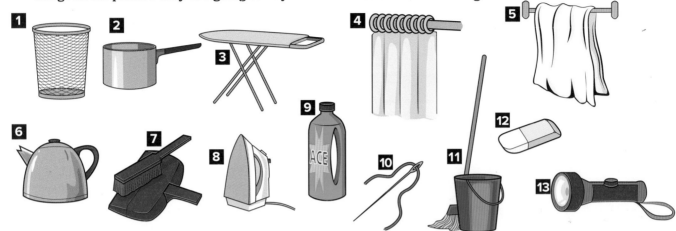

2 ▶ 84 Listen again and complete the sentences with three words in each space. Contractions like *don't* count as one word.

1 We'll have to give everything _____ and sort the place out.

2 Maybe we should go into town and _____ .

3 One minute. I'll get a pen and we can _____ .

4 When you use the brush, what _____ the thing that you use to get rubbish from the floor?

5 It's a kind of liquid that's really good _____ .

6 It's in the kitchen. In the cupboard _____ .

7 We should _____ for these things.

8 Oh yes, of course. A kettle! I _____ a kettle!

VOCABULARY Things in the house

3 Which of these things can you see in the pictures?

a bin	a hammer and nails	a pan	a stapler
a cloth	a mop and bucket	a plaster	a torch
a desk	a needle and thread	a rubber	a towel

4 Complete the sentences with words from Exercise 3.

1 Have you got _____ I could borrow? I'd like to have a shower.

2 Have you got _____ ? I'd like to clean the table.

3 Have you got _____ ? I've just cut myself.

4 Have you got _____ ? I'll make us some soup.

5 Have you got _____ ? I need to go out into the garden and it's really dark out there.

6 Have you got _____ ? I need to put a button back on my shirt.

7 Have you got _____ ? I've spilt water everywhere.

8 Have you got _____ ? I need to join these bits of paper together.

5 Work in pairs. Look again at the things in Exercise 3. Tell each other:

• if there are any things you don't have.

• which things you use the most.

• if there are any things you never use.

• where exactly each of the things in the box are in your house.

DEVELOPING CONVERSATIONS

Explaining where things are

We often give two descriptions of where things are: one general, one more specific. Notice the prepositions used. For example:

*It's **in** the kitchen – **in** the cupboard **under** the sink.*

6 Choose the correct prepositions.

1 There's one *at / in* the bathroom *on / at* the shelf.

2 There's one *above / down* the sink in the kitchen.

3 There's one *on / at* the desk in my study.

4 There's one *at / on* the side – next to the sink.

5 There's one *at / in* the corner of the garage.

6 There's one *in / at* the cupboard *down / under* the stairs.

7 There's one *in / at* a drawer in the kitchen, the one *up / next to* the fridge.

8 There's one in the garage, in a box *at / by* the door.

7 Work in pairs. Which things might be in the places in Exercise 6?

A: *There could be a towel in the bathroom on the shelf.*

B: *Yes, or maybe different kinds of medicine.*

GRAMMAR Relative clauses

8 Work in pairs. How many of these things can you name? What do you call …

1 the thing in the kitchen that you can pull open and keep things like knives and forks in?

2 something fixed to a wall which you put books and things like that on?

3 the money which you borrow from a bank to buy a house or apartment?

4 a person that lives next door to you, or upstairs or downstairs from you?

5 a man who owns the house or apartment that you rent?

6 the place in the house where guests can stay or where you can store things?

7 the place near – or connected to – your house where you can keep your car?

8 the place just outside an upstairs window where you can stand?

9 Match the words in the box to the descriptions in Exercise 8.

balcony	garage	mortgage	shelf
drawer	landlord	neighbour	spare room

10 Work in pairs. Identify the relative clauses and pronouns in Exercise 8. Then complete the rules in the Grammar box.

We use relative clauses to add information about what a thing, person or place is / does. Relative clauses usually begin with a relative pronoun.

For things, we use _____ or _____ .

For people, we use _____ or _____ .

For places, we use _____ .

G Check your ideas on page 91 and do Exercise 1.

11 Complete the sentences with a relative pronoun.

1 An oven is a large piece of equipment _____ you use to heat and cook food in the kitchen.

2 A builder is a person _____ builds or repairs houses.

3 A building site is the place _____ a new building is constructed.

4 A deposit is the money _____ you pay when you start renting a place. You get it back when you leave.

5 A babysitter is a person _____ you pay to come to your house and look after your kids.

6 A shed is a wooden building in the garden _____ you can store things.

7 A handle is the part of a door or a window _____ you use for opening it.

8 A lawn is an area of cut grass in the garden _____ kids can play.

9 A plumber is a person _____ installs or repairs pipes and things like showers, sinks and toilets.

12 Think of a thing, a job and a place that you don't know the words for in English, and write three *What do you call …?* questions. Then work in groups to ask and answer your questions.

G For further practice, see Exercise 2 on page 92.

CONVERSATION PRACTICE

13 Work in pairs. Imagine you are going on a picnic. You need to plan what to take.

Student A: look at File 9 on page 96.

Student B: look at File 16 on page 97.

Spend a few minutes thinking about how to describe each thing, using relative clauses.

14 Now roleplay a conversation with your partner. Take turns describing your objects.

26 To watch the video and do the activities, see the DVD-ROM.

WHAT A LOAD OF RUBBISH!

VOCABULARY Containers

1 Label the pictures of three families' shopping with the words in the box.

a bar of chocolate	a packet of biscuits
a box of cereal	a pot of yoghurt
a can of cola	a sack of rice
a carton of milk	a tin of tomatoes
a jar of honey	a tray of meat

2 Work in pairs. Decide if each container is usually made of metal, glass, plastic, cardboard or cloth.

3 Work in pairs. Discuss the questions.
- Which family do you think spends the most?
- Which family has the healthiest diet?
- Which family do you think causes the most damage to the environment? Why?
- How does your family's food shopping compare to these families'?

READING

4 Work in groups. Discuss the questions.
- Does your family shop at a supermarket? Which one? Why?
- What environmental issues are connected to shopping?

5 Read the article on page 55 about supermarket shopping and the environment. Find out four things you shouldn't buy. Explain why.

6 Discuss in pairs whether you think these sentences are true (T) or false (F).
1 100% efficiency is impossible.
2 The writer lives in New Zealand.
3 The writer doesn't recycle anything.
4 Producing aluminium is very inefficient.
5 Plastic bottles reduce transport costs.
6 Tap water is better for the environment than bottled.
7 The author eats a lot of meat.
8 Eating a lot of cheese is bad for the environment.
9 The sausages which were found were 30 years old.

7 Work in groups. Discuss the questions.
- Based on what you read, what do you think the professor in the article would say to each of the families in Exercise 1?
- Do you do any of the things the professor suggests? Which ones?
- Is there anything in the article you don't believe? Why?
- Do you recycle any of the containers in Exercise 1?

8 Work in pairs. Read the fact file and discuss:
- if you find any of the facts surprising.
- what your country does to encourage recycling.

FACT FILE

- It's estimated it costs around $100 per tonne to dispose of rubbish and $1,000 a tonne to get rid of chemicals such as paint.
- Switzerland charges people for throwing away rubbish. People mustn't leave rubbish outside without a sticker on the bag to show they have paid.
- It recycles 50% of its waste and burns all the rest.
- Sweden heats 20% of its homes by burning rubbish.
- Estonia has the best record on rubbish in the EU. It wastes only 0.5kg per person per day.
- The airports in New York are built on top of rubbish.

RUBBISH FOOD

There are laws of nature that we can't ignore, like gravity and waste. We know what goes up must come down and, similarly, we can't avoid the fact that everything we produce and consume leads to waste. In the case of my supermarket shopping, there's loads of waste. Professor Liam Taylor, an expert on the environment, is trying to convince me I could waste less.

From my shopping basket, he picks up a polystyrene tray of six New Zealand kiwi fruits covered in clear plastic. 'These probably caused three tons of carbon dioxide by being flown twelve thousand miles. To make things worse, this kind of plastic is almost impossible to recycle. What's wrong with local apples?'

'Nothing', I weakly reply, 'I just prefer kiwis.'

'Hmm. Well, if you must have them, eat Italian ones – and buy them with no packaging.'

He looks at the bottles of water and cans of cola. Before he can say anything, I say, 'I'm always careful to recycle those.'

'Well, that's good, but the aluminium in those cans is bad. They have to mine four tonnes of rock to get one tonne of aluminium, and the transport costs of the cans and glass bottles are higher as they are heavier than plastic. Anyway, what's wrong with having tap water? It's much more efficient.'

'I … er … prefer … .' The professor's look stops me from finishing the sentence!

'If you must have soft drinks, buy them in recyclable plastic bottles and get the largest size, because they use less plastic than lots of small bottles. The same is true of those small boxes of cereal.'

The next problem is the amount of meat I've bought. He tells me the chicken is OK, but generally meat is bad for the environment. 'Firstly, cows and sheep produce a lot of natural gas which causes global warming. Secondly, they're an inefficient way to get food energy. Better to be vegetarian, especially if the vegetables are locally grown and you don't eat too many dairy products.'

I am becoming depressed as all my favourite things get crossed off my shopping list. 'What about those cakes?' I say. 'They were made in the supermarket bakery and the packaging is biodegradable, so they must be OK.'

He laughs. 'Well, I guess the cake is, but forget about biodegradable!' Apparently, a team of archaeologists recently investigated sites where rubbish had been buried. They found newspapers that were thirty years old, and which you could still read, next to perfectly preserved sausages!

I feel slightly sick and very, very guilty.

GLOSSARY

biodegradable: if something is biodegradable it means that it can be naturally changed by bacteria and can safely become part of earth or water.

GRAMMAR

must / mustn't

We use *must* to show something's essential, either because of a law or rule, or because we feel it's essential. *Mustn't* means it's essential not to do something. *Must* can also be used when we are guessing something is true. *Must* is often replaced by *have to*, but it's not always possible.

9 Look at the extracts and decide if *must / mustn't* can be replaced by *have to / don't have to*.

   a *What goes up **must** come down.*

   b *If you **must** have soft drinks, buy them in recyclable plastic bottles.*

   c *The packaging is biodegradable, so they **must** be OK.*

   d *People **mustn't** leave rubbish outside without a sticker on the bag.*

Ⓖ Check your ideas on page 92 and do Exercise 1.

PRONUNCIATION

10 ▶85 Listen to the examples of *must / mustn't* and notice how you often don't hear the final *t*. Then practise saying the sentences.

11 Complete the sentences with a form of *must* or *have to* and the verb in brackets. Sometimes both *must* and *have to* are possible.

   1 The new law means companies _____ waste by 10% in the next two years. (reduce)

   2 You _____ chemicals down the sink. (pour)

   3 You _____ annoyed you can't park your car at work now. How are you going to get here? (be)

   4 We _____ to work or we won't finish everything. (get back)

   5 I _____ to call Frank and tell him the meeting's cancelled. (remember)

   6 You _____ to give me the key back. (forget)

   7 Luckily, we _____ tax on rubbish, as I don't have much money. (pay)

   8 If you _____ that stuff, can you go somewhere else. It smells disgusting. (eat)

12 Write four laws to help improve the environment or reduce waste. Use *must / mustn't*. Work in groups to choose the best ideas.

Ⓖ For further practice, see Exercise 2 on page 92.

THANK YOU SO MUCH

SPEAKING

1   **Work in groups. Discuss these questions.**

- Can you think of a time you got a lot of presents? What did you get?

- Do you think people ever get too many presents? Why? / Why not?

- What was the last present you received? What was the occasion? Were you happy with it?

- What's the best present you've ever received / given? What was so good about it?

- Have you ever received any strange or bad presents? Who from? What was wrong with them?

LISTENING

2   ▶ 86 **Listen to four people talking about presents they have received. Answer the questions for each speaker.**

1   What presents did they get?

2   What was the occasion?

3   Were they happy with the presents when they got them?

3   **Work in pairs. Take turns re-telling the whole stories using the words below.**

1   loved the way / gave me clues / click the link

2   lived close / save loads / lose weight

3   kind of message / from then on / broke up

4   suddenly said / to be polite / blowing away

4   ▶ 86 **Listen again. Did you miss anything from the stories?**

5   **Work in pairs. Discuss the questions.**

- Which of the presents mentioned do you think is the best / worst? Why?

- What message do you think the third speaker's ex-boyfriend was sending her? Do you think she was right to break up? What would you do if something similar happened to you?

UNDERSTANDING VOCABULARY

Verbs with two objects

In the listening you heard *My big sister bought me my own website.* Some verbs, such as *buy*, can be followed by one or two objects.

*My big sister bought **a website.***

*My big sister bought **me a website.***

When there are two objects we usually say the person first and the thing second, but if we want to put the thing first, then the person is added in a phrase that begins with *for* or *to*.

*My big sister bought a website **for me.***

*She sent an email **to me** with the link in it.*

6 Complete the sentences with these pairs of words.

ask + a personal question	make + some tea
buy + a car	read + a story
cook + dinner	send + a card
lend + some money	tell + a secret

1 My parents don't give me presents any more – they just _____ me _____ for my birthday.

2 Sorry about that. I couldn't talk earlier. I had to _____ my kids _____ before they went to sleep.

3 I can't believe it! My dad has promised to _____ my brother _____ when he graduates! He doesn't even have a licence yet!

4 I'm going to _____ my flatmates _____ tonight. I'm making a traditional dish from my country.

5 I've left my wallet at home. Can you _____ me _____ ? I'll pay you back tomorrow, I promise.

6 You must be exhausted. Come and sit down and I'll _____ you _____ – unless you'd prefer a coffee.

7 If I _____ you _____ , do you promise not to tell anyone else?

8 Do you mind if I _____ you _____ ? How much did you pay for it?

7 Work in pairs. Discuss the questions.

- Do you ever send cards / e-cards to people? Why?
- Do you ever cook dinner for people? When was the last time? What did you cook? What was it like?
- When was the last time someone cooked you dinner? What was it like?
- Have you ever lent someone some money? Did they pay you back?
- Who do you usually tell your secrets to? Why?

8 Complete the sentences. Add the words in brackets in the correct place.

1 We paid them so I expected something better. (a lot of money)

2 I sent presents for Christmas, but they haven't called. I wonder if they received them. (to all the family)

3 My husband made breakfast in bed on Valentine's Day. It's a shame he burnt the toast! (me)

4 My grandparents have been married for 40 years so we want to give them for their anniversary. (something special)

5 She cooked this amazing meal. Honestly, she should start her own restaurant. (for us)

6 It was a bit embarrassing because they brought some wine, but we don't drink! (us)

SPEAKING

9 Work in groups. Decide what is the best present to get in each of the situations below. Explain your ideas. Some of the expressions in the box may help.

It depends *what they do / where they live / what kind of things they like*, etc. If … then …

It's a safe choice.

It's not very original.

You want to get them something unusual like a … .

It's (not) the kind of thing a *teenager / elderly person*, etc. would *like / use / wear*.

What would they do with it? Where would they put it?

I think … would be more appropriate.

They can always take it back and change it.

1 It's your grandparents' golden wedding anniversary. They've been married for 50 years.

2 Your cousin turns thirteen next week and you want to buy her something special.

3 Some friends of yours – or of your family – have just had their first baby.

4 It's Valentine's Day next week and you want to get your boyfriend / girlfriend something romantic.

5 You've been invited to someone's house for dinner and you want to take something for them.

6 Someone where you work is retiring next month.

7 Some friends have moved into a new house and have invited you to a party there.

SOUNDS AND VOCABULARY REVIEW

10 ▶ 87 Listen and repeat the sounds with /e/, /ə/, /ɔː/ and /ɜː/. Are any of them difficult to hear or say?

11 ▶ 88 Work in groups. Listen to eight sentences using the words below. Together, try to write them down. Then listen again and check.

burn	chemical	environment	preserve
bury	drawer	present	store

12 Work in teams. You have three minutes to write collocations / phrases for the words in Exercise 11.

burn *my hand*,
burn *some rubbish*,
the dinner's ***burnt***

VIDEO 7

OXFORD

1 Look at the photo of Oxford. What do you know about this place? Think about:

- its location.
- its history.
- what it's famous for.
- any literature / art / music that is connected to the city.

2 📹 27 Watch the first part of the video (0.00–1.14). Decide if the sentences are true (T) or false (F).

1 Oxford is to the east of London.

2 It was originally a place where farmers took their cows across the river.

3 Oxford University is the oldest university in the English-speaking world.

4 The university was founded in 1096.

5 The university is made up of different colleges.

6 The Harry Potter novels were written in Oxford.

3 📹 27 Watch the second part of the video (1.15– end) and find out:

- how the author of *Alice In Wonderland* knew the girl that Alice was based on.
- when the author used to tell kids the stories that became *Alice In Wonderland*.
- two examples of how the *Alice* stories were possibly based on real people and places.
- why The Eagle and Child pub was important.

4 Choose the correct option. Then watch the whole video again and check your ideas.

1 Historians *know / have known* people *were teaching and studying / had taught and studied* here as far back as 1096.

2 In recent years, the college building *has become / became* famous as a filming location.

3 He *took / was taking* them out on boat rides along the river and *told / had told* them many stories.

4 Dodgson *based / was based* the stories on situations, places and people that were familiar to the children.

5 The city *has also influenced / also influences* the writing of other great fantasy writers.

6 They *often met / were often meeting* at The Eagle and Child.

5 Work in groups. Tell each other about:

a other places you know that people visit because they're connected to books / films.

b any other famous universities you know about.

c what your home town / city is most famous for.

d any famous people from your home town / city.

e any films / TV series set in places you know well.

UNDERSTANDING FAST SPEECH

6 📹 28 Read and listen to this extract from the video said at natural pace and then slowed down. To help you, groups of words are marked with / and pauses are marked //. Stressed sounds are in CAPITALS.

MANy beLIEVE the SHOP in the STOry / REPresents a SMALL SHOP / JUST aCROSS the ROAD from CHRISTchurch // In DODGson's TIME / the SHOPkeeper was an OLD WOman / with a SHEEP-like VOICE

7 Now you have a go! Practise saying the extract at natural pace.

REVIEW 7

GRAMMAR

1 Complete the text with one word in each space. Contractions like *don't* count as one word.

For the ¹_____ few weeks, they have ²_____ showing a series on TV ³_____ is all about the history ⁴_____ Africa. It ⁵_____ be good, because my son, ⁶_____ is never normally interested in that kind of thing, ⁷_____ watched every single episode. It's amazing! I've ⁸_____ known him to watch something so keenly. He keeps telling us we ⁹_____ watch anything else when it's on! We're not even ¹⁰_____ to suggest other things to watch! It's not open for discussion. This week, the show was about one of the cities ¹¹_____ white Europeans first landed – and what's happened to it ¹²_____ their arrival.

2 Complete the second sentence so that it has a similar meaning to the first sentence, using the word given. Do not change the word given. You must use between two and four words including the word given.

1 Things have become much more expensive over the last few months.

_____ has risen a lot over the last few months. **LIVING**

2 We got married ten years ago.

We _____ ten years now. **FOR**

3 The use of phones during the test is not permitted.

Remember: you _____ use your phones during the test. **TO**

4 I must remember to write and say thank you.

I _____ write and say thank you. **FORGET**

5 My brother has been reading lots of books about history recently.

My brother has started to develop _____ recently. **INTEREST**

6 I imagine you're quite hungry after all that travelling.

_____ quite hungry after all that travelling. **BE**

3 Choose the correct option.

1 I bought some amazing *leathers boots / boots leather / leather boots* in Mexico.

2 I've been going to Spanish classes *for / since / during* the start of the year.

3 We've *been knowing / known* each other for years. We went to school together.

4 That's the place *where / that* my dad used to work in.

5 *That / You / It* must be tired after such a long journey!

6 Be ambitious. You *don't have to / mustn't* be scared to dream big!

7 What do you call the place *where / that / which* you eat at school or in an office?

8 How many times have you *been seeing / seen / been seen* that movie now?

4 ▶ 89 Listen and write the six sentences you hear.

5 Write a sentence before or after the sentences you heard in Exercise 4 to create short dialogues.

VOCABULARY

6 Match the verbs (1–8) with the nouns they collocate with (a–h).

1 lend		a	the table
2 spill		b	a traditional dish
3 reach		c	a novel
4 promote		d	a personal question
5 read		e	the local culture
6 clean		f	money
7 ask		g	a crossroads
8 make		h	water all over the floor

7 Decide if these words and phrases are connected to films, things in the house, or music and art.

a carton	an exhibition	sculpture
a comedy	an explosion	special effects
a composer	a landscape	a stapler
costumes	a pan	a torch

8 Complete the sentences. Use the word in brackets to form a word that fits in the space.

1 It's a _____ drama set in England in the 12th century. (history)

2 I can't watch most horror movies. I find them too _____ . (scared)

3 It wasn't a bad film, but the ending was very _____ . (predict)

4 It's just a really _____ habit he's got. (annoy).

5 I don't read much _____ . I prefer novels and short stories. (poet)

6 Some really _____ works of art were stolen from the museum last night. (value)

9 Complete the text with one word in each space. The first letters are given.

We've recently moved house. To be honest, I found the whole process really ¹ti_____ . There was so much to do – and we had to buy a lot of new things as well. We needed a mop and ²b_____ so we could give the place a clean. The ³d_____ room was particularly dirty! Then my husband wanted to put up a big ⁴po_____ of his parents in the ⁵l_____ room, so we had to go and get a ⁶h_____ and nails to do that. Next, my son cut himself while he was playing, and we didn't have any ⁷pl_____ , so it was another visit to the shops! Tonight I just want to stay in, watch a nice ⁸ro_____ comedy, eat my way through a ⁹p_____ of biscuits and relax!

IN THIS UNIT YOU LEARN HOW TO:

- talk about the economy
- use time phrases to say when things happen
- compare prices
- talk about money issues and problems
- say different kinds of numbers

SPEAKING

1 **Look at the photo. Discuss the questions:**

- Why do you think the illustration on this twenty-dollar bill was chosen?
- Do you know any other places or people that appear on American banknotes? If so, why do you think they were chosen?
- What illustrations are there on the banknotes in your country? Do you think they are a good choice? Why / Why not?
- Do you know of any other illustrations of different foreign notes?

2 **Work in groups. Imagine you are designing new banknotes. For each of the categories below, choose three illustrations. Explain your choices.**

- famous people
- buildings
- cultural images

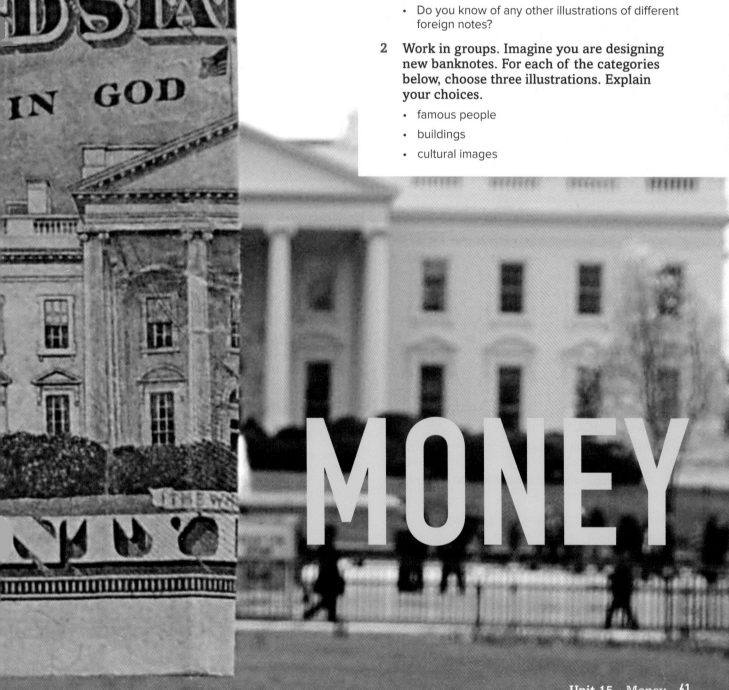

MONEY

COST OF LIVING

VOCABULARY

The economy and quality of life

1 Work in pairs. Check you understand the situation in bold. Then think of one more consequence (good or bad) of each situation.

1 Our **currency is very strong**, so it's cheap for us to travel abroad. *exampley*

2 Our **currency is really weak** at the moment. It's very expensive to import things from abroad.

3 A lot of people can't afford basic things because **the cost of living is very high**.

4 **Inflation is currently quite low.** Prices haven't changed much since last year.

5 **There's a lot of unemployment.** Around 25% of the working population don't have a job.

6 **Unemployment has fallen** a lot over the past year, so more people have work.

7 The **average salary is about $35,000 a year** there, so I can earn more than here.

2 Work in groups. Discuss the questions.

a How do the following things affect your quality of life?

- job security
- cost of living
- time off
- climate
- pace of life
- transport
- crime
- family

b Are there any other factors that you think are important for a good quality of life?

c Which things do you think are most important? Why?

LISTENING

3 ▶ 90 Listen to Aidan and Laima talking about life in Freedonia. Laima is on holiday there and Aidan works in a school. Find out:

1 what the quality of Aidan's life in Freedonia is like.

2 how well the economy is doing.

3 why he wants to leave.

4 ▶ 90 Listen again and choose the words you hear.

1 The economy's doing quite badly *at the / in this* moment.

2 I'm actually going back to Canada *in / for* a few months.

3 Unemployment has gone up quite a lot over the *last few months / rest of the month*.

4 I could get paid a lot more *back home / in Canada*.

5 Eating out is *twice / half* the price in my country.

6 That's true, but it used to be cheaper *in / at* the past.

7 Anyway, *in / at* the end, I miss my family and friends.

8 I don't mind the cold weather so much. You get used to it after a *time / while*.

5 Work in pairs. Discuss the questions.

- From what you heard, do you think Aidan is making the right decision? Why? / Why not?

- Apart from family and friends, what would you miss if you lived abroad – or, if you are living abroad at the moment, what do you miss?

GRAMMAR

Time phrases and tense

Some adverbs and time phrases are generally used with particular tenses. For example, *currently* usually goes with a present tense, especially the present continuous, whereas phrases starting with *since* more often go with the present perfect.

*Inflation **is currently** quite low. Prices **haven't changed** much **since last year**.*

*The economy **is currently doing** quite well.*

6 Look at the audio script for Track 90 on page 105 and find a sentence using each of the time phrases 1–6. Which tense or structure (a–d) is used with each time phrase?

  1 in a few months

  2 at the moment

  3 over the last few months

  4 in a years' time

  5 in the past

  6 over the last two years

  a the present continuous

  b the present perfect simple

  c used to

  d be going to / will

Ⓖ Check your ideas on page 93 and do Exercise 1.

7 Complete the sentences with the correct form of the verbs (present continuous, present perfect, *be going to* or *used to*).

  1 At the moment, the economy _____ quite well. (do)

  2 Unemployment _____ over the last few months. (fall)

  3 The cost of living _____ a lot in the last five years. (go up)

  4 Eating out _____ a lot cheaper when I was a kid. (be)

  5 There _____ an election in four months' time. (be)

  6 The government _____ currently _____ popularity. (lose)

  7 According to the government, inflation _____ over the next few months. (fall)

  8 Crime _____ less of a problem when I was younger. (be)

  9 Our currency _____ stronger at the moment. (get)

  10 We _____ more job security in the past. (have)

8 Work in groups. Discuss which of the sentences in Exercise 7 are true for your country. Explain your ideas.

Ⓖ For further practice, see Exercise 2 on page 93.

DEVELOPING CONVERSATIONS

Comparing prices

We often compare prices in different places and times:

*Eating out is **twice the price** in my country.*

*Milk is **much more expensive (now) than** it used to be.*

We often then give an example:

You can get a three-course meal for about $6 here. A meal back home costs $20.

You can't get a litre for less than a euro now. It used to be only 70 cents.

9 Complete sentences 1–4 with a word from the box and a price. Then write a similar follow-up sentence for 5–8.

can	laptop	packet	smartphone
kilo	litre	pair	suit

  1 Clothes are much cheaper there than elsewhere. A designer _____ only costs _____ .

  2 The crisps in here are four times more expensive than they are in the shops. A _____ here costs _____ .

  3 Soft drinks there are twice the price they are here. You can't get a _____ for less than _____ .

  4 Computers are much cheaper than they used to be. You can get a _____ now for _____ .

  5 Petrol is a lot cheaper there. _____

  6 Shoes are much more expensive there. _____

  7 Electronic goods are much cheaper there. _____

  8 Rice is much more expensive than it used to be. _____

10 Work in pairs. Take turns starting conversations and responding using the ideas from Exercise 9.

A: *Clothes are much cheaper there than elsewhere.*

B: *I know. A designer suit only costs about 1,200.*

11 Work in groups. Tell each other about very expensive / cheap places you know and give examples. Are there any things that have risen or fallen in price over the last few years?

CONVERSATION PRACTICE

12 You are going to roleplay conversations about life in different countries.

Student A: talk about the economy and quality of life in your own country.

Student B: read the role card in File 11 on page 97. Talk about the economy and quality of life in that country.

13 Now change roles.

Student A: read the role card in File 7 on page 96.

Student B: talk about your own country.

 29 To watch the video and do the activities, see the DVD-ROM.

MY INHERITANCE

READING

1 Work in groups. You are going to read about a woman attending the reading of her father's will. A *will* is a legal document that says what should happen to a person's possessions after they die. Before you read, discuss these questions.

- Why do you think it important to have a will?

- What age do you think most people write their will?

- What are the most special or valuable things you have? Would you leave them to anyone in particular? Why? / Why not?

- Have you heard of any stories about wills in the news?

2 Read the story. Find out why the author was surprised.

3 Work in pairs. Discuss the questions.

1 Find the different sayings the author's parents had. What do you think they meant?

2 Based on what you read, what do you think the daughters enjoyed when they were growing up, and what do you think they complained about? Why?

3 How do you think the parents became rich?

4 Why do you think they didn't tell their daughters?

5 How do you think the daughters felt about it when they found out?

WILL POWER

None of us had any idea what was going to happen when we arrived at the lawyer's office. Dad had died two months earlier in his bed in the same two-bedroom house where we'd grown up. Apart from the house, we didn't expect Dad to leave anything of value. I mean, for years after my mum died, he'd gone to a neighbour's house to watch TV. I offered to buy him a TV once, but he just said, 'Never buy what you can borrow!' That was typical of him. I guess he liked his neighbour's company as well.

My mum had never worked and Dad was an insurance salesman. We assumed he wasn't successful because we were never bought toys and we wore second-hand clothes. We just thought he couldn't afford these things.

Dad used to find bits of wood and turn them into toy boats and dolls. Mum taught us to make and repair clothes, which we used to do together at night. They had funny little sayings that they'd repeat whenever we complained about things: 'Money's silver, but a needle and thread is gold!' 'Early to bed, early to rise, makes a man healthy, wealthy and wise'; 'Never buy what you can borrow, never throw away what you can repair.' We used to laugh at them, and sometimes invented our own silly sayings: 'A fool spends what the wise man saves'; 'A glass of water is worth all the tea in China.' We laughed, but having so little money was often annoying. I think we were the only family in our school without a TV; we never drank soft drinks, and sharing a room with two big sisters for sixteen years was difficult.

So we walked into the lawyer's office and sat down. We were serious, but not sad any more. Dad had had a good life. The lawyer started reading; I was hardly paying attention, really, but then the numbers seemed to continue without end. 'Wait, I'm sorry,' I said. 'How much did you say he had?' The lawyer smiled, 'Yes, I imagine it does need repeating. Two million, seven hundred and eighty-one thousand, six hundred and fifty three pounds and eighteen pence.'

❝ We didn't know what to say! Nearly three million pounds! How? Why? We had so many questions, so many feelings. ❞

LISTENING

4 ▶ **91** Check you understand these sentences. Then listen to the rest of the story and decide if the sentences are true (T) or false (F).

1 Her father had won the money.

2 He bought shares in a company that doubled in value.

3 The daughters didn't receive all of the money.

4 She's still angry about the situation.

5 The money will help other people.

6 She's planning to spend the money on a holiday.

5 Work in pairs. Discuss the questions.

- How would you feel if you were in this situation?

- Do you agree that the parents did a fantastic thing? Would you do it? Why? / Why not?

- What would you do if you had a quarter of a million pounds now?

VOCABULARY Money verbs

6 Look at the story again and at the audio script for Track 91 on page 105. Find as many words as you can that are connected to money. Compare your ideas with a partner.

7 Complete the conversations with the correct form of the verbs in the box.

borrow	earn	invest	owe	win
buy	give	leave	save	worth

1 A: Sorry, can I _____ two euros? I don't have enough.

  B: Of course. Just take it. I _____ you three euros, anyway.

2 A: Why have you stopped going out so much?

  B: Well, I'm working more and I'm _____ for my university fees.

3 A: Hey, I've _____ ten euros on the lottery!

  B: Wow! Ten euros. What are you going to do with it? _____ it in shares? Buy a boat?

  A: There's no need to be sarcastic. I was going to _____ you a coffee actually, but maybe I won't now.

4 A: Would you like to _____ money to a children's charity each month?

  B: I'm sorry. I can't afford to. I don't _____ much in my job.

  A: It doesn't have to be much. Every little helps.

  B: I'm sorry. Not today. I'm in a hurry.

5 A: That's a nice painting. It looks quite old. Is it _____ much?

  B: I don't know. My granddad _____ it to me when he died. I don't know how valuable it is, but I'd never sell it.

8 Work in pairs. Answer the questions about the word *pay*.

1 What different ways can you **pay for** something?

2 What kinds of **bills** do people have to **pay**?

3 When do you have to **pay** a bank / someone **back**?

4 How and when do people **get paid**?

5 When do you have to **pay interest**?

6 Who do you **pay to do** something?

7 Where do people have to **pay attention**?

8 Say three things you might offer to **pay for**.

PRONUNCIATION

9 Work in pairs. How do you say these numbers from the story?

1 £2,000,000   5 £4.12

2 781,000   6 2.7

3 653   7 ¼

4 1965

10 ▶ **92** Listen and check your ideas.

11 ▶ **93** Listen and complete the sentences with the numbers you hear.

1 The minimum wage at that time was _____ an hour.

2 Inflation fell to _____ last month.

3 The government is going to invest _____ in schools.

4 _____ of the population own a car.

5 The new factory will create _____ jobs.

6 The house cost _____ .

7 We borrowed _____ from the bank.

8 We'll finally pay back the mortgage in _____ .

SPEAKING

12 Work in groups. Discuss the questions.

- What do you spend most of your money on? Are you any good at saving money?

- What are good things to invest money in? Have you ever invested in shares? Were they successful?

- In which jobs do you think people earn too much money? In which jobs do they earn too little? Why?

- Do you know anyone who's won any money? How?

- Have you ever lost money? How?

- Have you ever been left anything (e.g. in a will)? What?

- What charities have you given money to? What do they do?

- Does anyone owe you anything (money / a meal / a favour, etc.)? Why?

MONEY, MONEY, MONEY!

LISTENING

1 Work in groups. Discuss what money problems the people in these situations might have – and the best way of dealing with each problem.

   a a teenager living at home with parents

   b customers in a restaurant

   c young adults travelling cheaply round the world

   d a couple with two small kids

   e someone shopping in a second-hand / vintage store

   f someone unable to take money out of their bank account

2 ▶ 94 Listen to four conversations. Match each one to a situation in Exercise 1. Then work in pairs. Compare your ideas and discuss:

- what problems were mentioned in each conversation.
- how the problems were dealt with.

3 ▶ 94 Work in pairs. Complete the sentences with one word in each space. Then listen again and check.

Conversation 1

1 I'll get this. It's my _____ .

2 What's _____ ?

3 I've just realised I _____ my wallet in my other jacket.

Conversation 2

4 It's hard to find things like that in this _____ .

5 Look – there's a _____ here.

6 The best price I can _____ is 150.

Conversation 3

7 _____ have just gone up.

8 I haven't _____ to save much yet.

9 Maybe we can _____ some money from the bank.

Conversation 4

10 Your card was cancelled because of some _____ activity.

11 We _____ that your card was copied sometime last month.

12 Everything is covered by your _____ .

4 Work in groups. Discuss the questions.

- Have you ever had any similar problems to the ones you heard about? If yes, when? What happened?
- Which problem do you think was the most serious?
- Who do you think should pay on dates: the man, the woman or both? Why?
- Do you like vintage clothes? Why? / Why not?
- Are you good at negotiating good prices in markets?
- How much money do you think parents should give their children? Until what age?
- Have you heard any stories about credit cards being copied – or about any similar crimes?

GRAMMAR

Time clauses

We start time clauses with words like *when, as soon as, before, after* and *until*.

5 Look at these sentences from the listening. Then work in pairs. Discuss the questions below.

   a *I'll pay you back **as soon as** I get paid.*

   b *You can pay half back **when** you have the money, OK?*

   c *You'll receive your new PIN number **after** you get the card.*

   1 What's the whole time clause in each sentence?

   2 Do the time clauses refer to the past, the present or the future?

   3 In what tense is the verb in each time clause?

   4 What tenses / structures are used in the main clause of each sentence?

G Check your ideas on page 93 and do Exercise 1.

6 Choose the correct option.

   1 I'm going to try and find a part-time job when *I'm / I'll be* at university.

   2 What *do you do / are you going to do* after you graduate?

   3 Call me as soon as you *arrive / will arrive*, OK?

   4 *I'm going to move / I move* back home before the recession here gets worse.

   5 You'll just have to save until *you have / you'll have* enough money!

   6 The software is really good. It'll really speed things up, but it might take some time before *you get / you'll get* used to using it.

   7 *I'll pay / I pay* you back when I get paid, OK?

   8 Can you two please finish arguing about the bill after *I leave / I'll leave*?

   9 *We'll support / We support* you until you graduate. After that, though, you'll have to start looking after yourself!

  10 I'm waiting for confirmation of the dates, but *I call / I'll call* you as soon as I hear anything.

7 Complete the sentences below using your own ideas. Then work with a partner and compare what you have written. Explain your ideas.

   1 When I get home today, I'm going to ...

   2 As soon as I have enough money, I'm going to ...

   3 After this course ends, I'll probably ...

   4 Before I get too old, I'd really like to ...

   5 I'm going to carry on studying English until ...

G For further practice, see Exercise 2 on page 93.

VOCABULARY Dealing with banks

8 Complete each pair of collocations with one verb from the box.

cancel	charge	open	take out
change	make	pay	transfer

1 ~ a savings account / ~ a joint account with my partner

2 ~ a mortgage / ~ a loan

3 ~ a complaint / ~ a payment

4 ~ some money / ~ my PIN number

5 ~ £1,000 from my current account to my savings account / ~ money to my son in Thailand

6 ~ money into my account / ~ bills by direct debit

7 ~ my credit card / ~ a cheque

8 ~ 5% interest / ~ me 30 euros

9 Spend two minutes memorising the collocations in Exercise 8. Then work in pairs and take turns to test each other.

Student A: read out each verb in the box.

Student B: close your book. Try to say the pair of collocations for each verb.

Then change roles.

10 Work in pairs. Discuss the questions.

1 When might you want to open a joint account?

2 Can you think of three reasons why people might take out a loan?

3 Can you think of three reasons why people might make a complaint to a bank manager?

4 Why might someone decide to change their PIN number?

5 Why might someone need to cancel their credit card?

6 Why might someone need to cancel a cheque?

SPEAKING

11 Work in pairs. Choose two of the following situations to roleplay. Decide which roles you are going to play. Spend a few minutes planning what to say. Use the audio script on page 105 to help you. Then roleplay the conversations.

1 Two friends are having lunch in a café. They try to decide how they are going to pay. One person realises he doesn't have any money. They work out what to do about it.

2 One person wants to buy a second-hand car. The seller asks a very high price. The buyer tries to negotiate a better price. The buyer points out problems with the car. They try to reach a deal.

3 A teenager wants her dad to buy her a new laptop. The father is worried about how much it will cost and how he will pay for it. He suggests alternative ideas. They try to reach a deal.

4 A customer is phoning a bank to find out why their credit card was rejected in a shop. The bank employee explains the situation and tells the customer what will happen next.

SOUNDS AND VOCABULARY REVIEW

12 ▶ 95 Listen and repeat the sounds with /ɪ/, /ɔɪ/, /ə/ and /əʊ/. Are any of them difficult to hear or say?

13 ▶ 96 Work in groups. Listen to eight sentences using the words below. Together, try to write them down. Then listen again and check.

average	currency	joint	owe
borrow	election	mortgage	unemployment

14 Work in teams. You have three minutes to write collocations / phrases for the words in Exercise 13.

*the **average** salary, the **average** age, increase the **average***

16

EVENTS

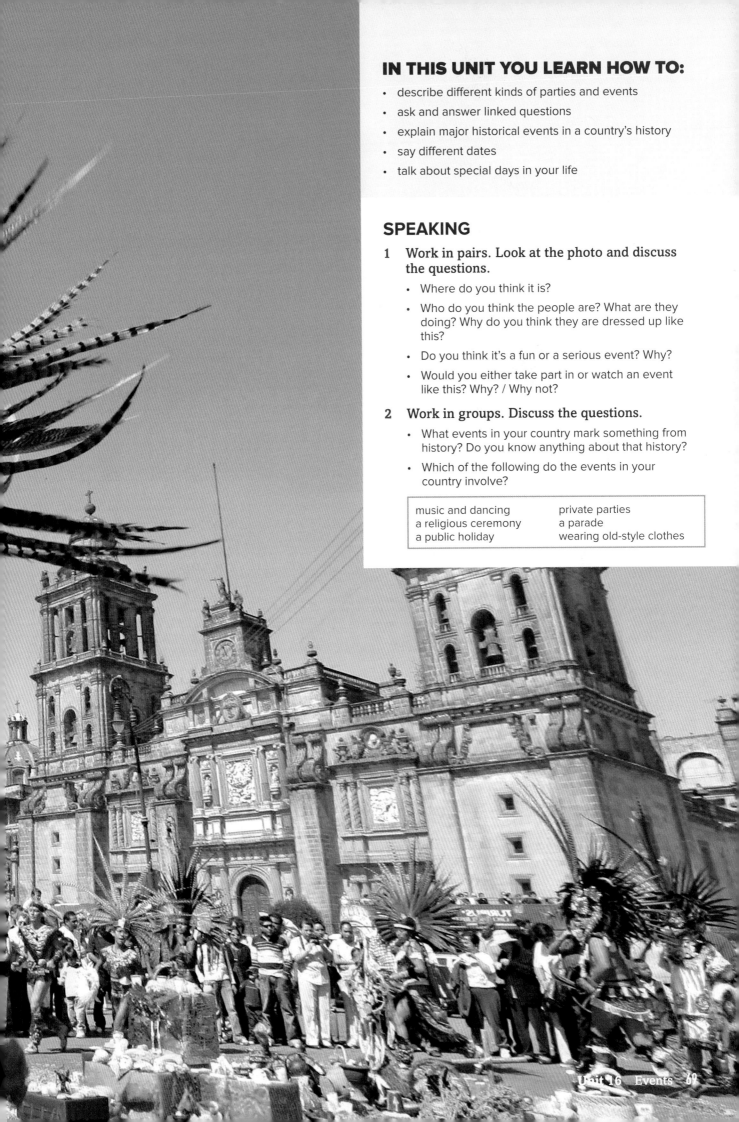

IN THIS UNIT YOU LEARN HOW TO:

- describe different kinds of parties and events
- ask and answer linked questions
- explain major historical events in a country's history
- say different dates
- talk about special days in your life

SPEAKING

1 **Work in pairs. Look at the photo and discuss the questions.**

- Where do you think it is?
- Who do you think the people are? What are they doing? Why do you think they are dressed up like this?
- Do you think it's a fun or a serious event? Why?
- Would you either take part in or watch an event like this? Why? / Why not?

2 **Work in groups. Discuss the questions.**

- What events in your country mark something from history? Do you know anything about that history?
- Which of the following do the events in your country involve?

music and dancing	private parties
a religious ceremony	a parade
a public holiday	wearing old-style clothes

HAVE A FEW FRIENDS ROUND!

VOCABULARY
Describing parties and events

1 **Complete the sentences about different kinds of parties with these words.**

friends round	launch	surprise
housewarming	leaving party	wedding reception

1 We've just moved to a new flat and we're having a _____ next week.

2 It's my last day in the office tomorrow and my colleagues have organised a _____ after work.

3 My brother's getting married in the summer and they've decided to have the _____ on a boat.

4 We've set up a new website and we've organised a big party to _____ it.

5 It was my birthday and I had a few _____ for dinner.

6 We're having a party for Keira on Friday, but don't tell her. It's supposed to be a _____ .

2 **Work in pairs. Tell each other as much as you can about the different kinds of parties:**

• you have held.

• you have been invited to.

3 **Match each question (1–5) to two answers (a–j). Check you understand the words in bold.**

1 What was the party like?

2 What was the place like?

3 What was the food like?

4 What was the music like?

5 What were the people like?

a Everyone was great – really **warm and friendly**.

b It was nice – not too loud. Just good **background music**.

c It was fantastic. It's an amazing **venue** for a party.

d A bit **cold** and **distant**, to be honest. No-one was really **mixing**.

e It was nice. They had a **buffet** and everyone **helped themselves**.

f Well, the first DJ was great, but the second guy completely **cleared the dance floor**.

g It was great. I thought the organisation of the whole **event** was very **impressive**. They did a brilliant job.

h It was great to begin with, but then there was a big argument and that **ruined** the rest of the evening.

i Oh, it was OK. They just put a few **bowls of olives** and crisps and things on the tables for people **to pick at**.

j It used to be a factory, but they **converted** it **into** an events venue a few years ago.

4 **Work in pairs. Think of one more way of answering each of the questions in Exercise 3.**

LISTENING

5 ▶ 97 **Listen to three conversations about parties. Answer the questions for each conversation.**

1 What kind of party was it?

2 Whose party was it?

3 Where was it?

4 What was it like?

8 Match the general questions (1–8) with the connected questions (a–h).

1 How was Michelle?
2 What was the weather like?
3 What time did the party go on till?
4 How did you feel when you found out?
5 Where did you have the party?
6 Who was there?
7 What's their new house like?
8 How was the launch party?

a Was it a bit of a shock? 4
b Anywhere nice? 5
c Was it late? 3
d Did everything go according to plan? 8
e Was she OK? 1
f Was it nice and hot? 2
g Is it big? 7
h Anyone I know? 6

9 Work in pairs. Take turns asking the questions in Exercise 8.

Student A: give positive answers.

Student B: give negative answers.

Continue each dialogue for one or two lines.

A: *How was Michelle? Was she OK?*

B: *Yeah, she was great. It was really good to see her again.*

A: *What's she doing at the moment?*

B: *What was the weather like? Was it nice and hot?*

A: *No, unfortunately. It was quite cold.*

B: *Oh dear. What a shame.*

CONVERSATION PRACTICE

10 You are going to have conversations about parties you have been to. First, think of three parties or celebrations you have been to in the last five years – or invent three. Think about the following questions:

- What kind of parties were they?
- What was the occasion for each?
- Where were they?
- What was the place like?
- Was there any food / music? If yes, what was it like?
- What were the other guests like?
- What time did the party go on till?

11 Imagine the parties / celebrations happened last night. Have conversations with other students. Start like this:

A: *So what did you do last night? Anything interesting?*

B: *Yeah, I did, actually. I went to …*

🎥 30 To watch the video and do the activities, see the DVD-ROM.

6 ▶ 97 In which conversations did you hear each of the adjectives below? Can you remember what each adjective described? Work in pairs and compare your ideas. Then listen again and check your answers.

easy to talk to	grilled	modern
full	impressive	spicy
gorgeous	lovely	typical

7 Work in pairs. Discuss the questions.

- What's the best kind of wedding reception to have? Why? How much do you think it's right to spend?
- Are there are any converted buildings in your area / town? Would they be good places to live / have a party?
- What different things might ruin a party?
- Do you prefer having friends round for dinner or eating out? Why?

DEVELOPING CONVERSATIONS

Linked questions

People often ask two questions together. A general *Wh-*question followed by a more specific *yes / no* question.

A: *So **what did you do last night**? **Anything interesting**?*

B: *Yeah, I had a little dinner party at my place.*

A: *So **how did it go**? **Was it good**?*

B: *Yeah, it was lovely. It was really nice to see everyone.*

A BRIEF HISTORY

VOCABULARY Historical events

1 Complete the fact file about Britain with the words in the box.

became	join	ruled	was killed
invaded	lasted	was established	won

FACT FILE: BRITAIN

London ¹_____ **by** the Romans around 2,000 years ago when they occupied Britain.

The Viking people from northern Europe first ²_____ Britain in 786. They eventually **occupied** half the country.

There was **a civil war** from 1642 to 1648 between Royalists (who supported the king, Charles I) and Parliament. Supporters of Parliament ³_____ **the war**, so in January 1649 **the king** ⁴_____ and England became a republic. **The republic** ⁵_____ **for** eleven years, until Charles II was made king.

Between the 16th and 20th centuries, Britain **established a huge empire** and at one stage **it** ⁶_____ **in** over a hundred countries, covering a quarter of the world. The United States **was once ruled by** Britain, but it ⁷_____ **independent in** 1776.

Britain was one of the countries that established the United Nations in 1945, but it didn't ⁸_____ **the European Union** (or EEC as it was then called) until 1973.

2 Work in pairs. How many of the words and phrases in bold in the fact file can you use to talk about cities and countries you know?

READING

3 You are going to read an article from a series called *Around the world in 300 words*. Read the introduction and discuss the questions in pairs.

1 Do you know anything about the country? What?

2 Why do you think people in the UK don't know much about it?

4 Read the rest of the article and answer the questions.

1 How long have people lived in Kazakhstan?

2 How has the Kazakh lifestyle changed?

3 When did the country finally become independent?

4 What's the main industry?

5 What's the most interesting information for you?

6 If you know about the country, is there anything important that isn't mentioned? Would you change anything in the text?

5 Work in pairs. Look at the prepositions in bold in the article. Underline the words that go with the prepositions. Then change the words before or after the preposition and write a new sentence.

People <u>have lived</u> **in** the region **since** the Stone Age.

Inequality has existed since the Stone Age. / People have lived in the region since **the 5th Century**.

GRAMMAR

Articles

There is no single clear rule for using articles (*a / an* and *the*). As a guide, we use *the* to show we think it's obvious which thing(s) we mean – there's nothing else it / they can be. We use *a / an* to show a thing could be one of several examples, and it's not important at this stage exactly which it is.

6 Work in pairs. Look at the sentences from the article. Explain why each article in bold is used.

1 *It's **the** ninth largest country in the world.*

2 *It's **an** exporter of many other natural resources.*

3 *They share **a** border.*

4 *Islam was introduced by **the** Arabs in **the** eighth century.*

5 *Kazakhstan became part of **the** Soviet Union.*

6 ***The** only thing they can say is we played them at football.*

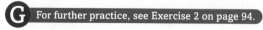 Check your ideas on page 93 and do Exercise 1.

7 Choose the correct option.

1 ***The / A** best day of my life was **the / a** day* I got married.

2 ***The / A** day I will never forget is* when I met President Putin.

3 **I've never seen** *a / the* whale in the wild, but I'd love to.

4 **I'd love to go to** *a / the* United Sates and see *a / the* Grand Canyon one day.

5 **I'm glad to say, I've never** broken *a / the* bone.

6 *The / A* left-wing party **won the / a last election** here. *The / A* party's leader is quite young.

8 Work in pairs. Take turns to say true sentences using the chunks in bold in Exercise 7.

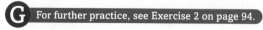 For further practice, see Exercise 2 on page 94.

SPEAKING

9 Work in groups. Discuss what should go in *Around the world in 300 words* for your country. Think about the following.

• What are the most important events?

• What places would you mention? Why?

• What would go under the headings *Place to visit, Big building, Special day* and *Firsts*?

KAZAKHSTAN

Ask most people on the streets of the UK what they know about Kazakhstan and the only thing they can say is 'We played them at football.' Ask where it is, and they may mention it's near Russia, but that's all. Yet Kazakhstan is huge – the ninth largest country in the world and the size of Western Europe. We think it's time people got to know it better. Oh, and yes, it is near Russia – they share a border and it's 6,846 kilometres long!

People have lived in the region **since** the Stone Age. The society was nomadic – different groups moved across the land to find grass and water for their animals, and places to grow food for the season. The name of Kazakhstan comes **from** a word meaning 'free spirit'.

However, some cities such as Talaz were established 2,000 years ago as part of the Silk Road trade route that went through the region.

Two key events had an important influence on the region: Islam was introduced **by** the Arabs in the eighth century, and Genghis Khan's Mongol army invaded in 1219. **Over** the next 200 years, the unique Kazakh language, culture and economy developed, based on nomadic life.

However, this traditional lifestyle changed **during** the 1800s, when the country was occupied by Russia. The population grew rapidly and there were political and economic problems. This resulted in food shortages and eventually led **to** fighting and a civil war in 1916.

In 1920, Kazakhstan became part **of** the Soviet Union. Over the following decade, the last Kazakh nomads were forced to live on farms or work in industry. Other people within the Soviet Union, including Germans, Ukrainians and Koreans, were sent to work there.

After Kazakhstan became independent on 16 December 1991, its economy grew rapidly. It's now the 11th largest producer of oil and gas in the world, as well as an exporter of many other natural resources.

A Kazakh family in their traditional yurt, a type of tent

The Pyramid of Peace cultural centre in Astana

POPULATION: 16.4 million

CAPITAL: Astana (changed from Almaty in 1997)

PLACE TO VISIT: The Charyn Canyon

BIG BUILDING: The Pyramid of Peace, Astana. The cultural centre aims to bring together all the great religions.

SPECIAL DAY: 22nd March. *Nauriz* celebrates Spring, friendship and unity. It was banned when the Soviets ruled.

FIRSTS: Humans here were the first to ride and use horses. The oldest rocket launch site in the world is Baikonur Cosmodrome. Russia rents the site for its space programme.

Next week KENYA

A DAY I'LL NEVER FORGET

SPEAKING

1   **Work in groups. Discuss the questions.**

1   When is your birthday? How do you usually celebrate?

2   When is the last day of term / of your English course?

3   When is the next public holiday? Do you have any plans for it?

4   Can you think of a date you always remember for personal reasons?

5   Can you think of a date with national or global significance?

LISTENING

2   ▶ 98 Listen and take notes on what day each person mentions – and why each day is special.

3   ▶ 98 Work in pairs. There are three words missing in each sentence. Can you remember what they are? Listen again and check your ideas.

1   a   She fought for women's rights and _____ .

    b   There's still some _____ , sure, but it's important to remember her life.

2   a   My great-grandmother on _____ was Ukrainian.

    b   I felt _____ with the place.

3   a   It's ~~a anniversary of~~ _____ the day Michael Jackson died.

    b   His death in 2009 was *a real* . *tragedy*

4   a   I climbed Mount Kinabalu in Malaysia, one of the highest mountains *in the region* .

    b   We ~~reached the near~~ _____ just as the sun was coming up.

5   a   It's the anniversary of the day that my *sight was restored* .

    b   Amazingly, it worked, and *thanks to my* surgeon, I can now see my two kids.

4   **Work in pairs. Discuss the questions.**

- Which of the five days mentioned do you think is the most / least special? Why?

- Who do you think are the most important women from your country? Why?

- Do you know where your mother's and father's sides of the family come from originally?

- Can you remember where you were when you heard about the death of someone famous?

GRAMMAR

Verb patterns (*-ing* or infinitive with *to*)

When two verbs are used together, the second verb often takes the *-ing* form or the infinitive with *to*. The choice of form depends on the first verb. There are no rules for this. You just have to learn the patterns.

5   **Work in pairs. Look at these verbs from this book. Which can be followed by the *-ing* form? Which can be followed by the infinitive with *to*?**

agree	consider	finish	offer	promise
arrange	decide	hope	plan	recommend
avoid	enjoy	mind	practise	refuse
can't stand	fail	miss		

G   Check your ideas on page 94 and do Exercise 1.

6   **Complete these sentences with the correct form of the verbs from the box. Then look at the audio script for Track 98 on page 107 to check your answers.**

be	buy	change	go	have	travel

1   She set up the country's first all-girls school and really helped *to change* the country for the better.

2   My mum and I decided _____ on a trip to the village that she came from.

3   I really wanted _____ there, but I just couldn't afford _____ a ticket.

4   When I was 23 or 24, I spent six months _____ round South East Asia.

5   I agreed *to have* this special new operation.

Some verbs can be followed by either the *-ing* form or the infinitive (with *to*) without any real change in meaning. There is also a small number of verbs that can be followed by both forms, but with these verbs there is a change in meaning when the *-ing* form or the infinitive (with *to*) is used after them.

7 For each pair of sentences, decide if the meaning of the words in italics is basically the same or different. If it's different, say why.

1   a   I *love* **going** for long walks in the countryside. I find it really relaxing.

    b   I *love* **to go** for long walks in the countryside. It helps me deal with stress.

2   a   I still *remember* **phoning** my dad and telling him I didn't want to go to university.

    b   It's her birthday today. I must *remember* **to phone** her later.

3   a   It *started* **raining** about halfway through the match.

    b   As we drove south along the motorway, it *started* **to rain** more.

4   a   I *stopped* **buying** their products when I found out how they're made.

    b   Sorry I'm late. I *stopped* **to buy** some food on the way.

5   a   I *hate* **exercising**, but I really need to lose some weight and get fit again!

    b   I really *hate* **to exercise**, but I love how it makes me feel afterwards.

8 Choose one of the following to talk about. Spend a few minutes preparing what you want to say. Then share your thoughts and feelings in groups.

- something you'll always remember seeing or doing
- something important you decided to do
- something you're hoping to do in the future
- something you really enjoy doing
- something important that you failed to do
- something you usually avoid doing if you can.

For further practice, see Exercise 2 on on page 94.

SPEAKING

9 Think of a special day that you have good memories of. Think about these questions.

- Where were you?
- Who were you with?
- What happened?
- How did you feel?
- Why was the day so special?

10 Work in groups. Tell each other about your special day. Who do you think had the most special experience? Why?

SOUNDS AND VOCABULARY REVIEW

11 ▶ 99 Lots of words contain consonant clusters (two or three consonants with no vowel sound between them). Listen and repeat the sounds you hear. Are any of them difficult to hear or say?

12 ▶ 100 Work in groups. Listen to eight sentences using the words below. Together, try to write them down. Then listen again and check.

background	discrimination	friend	spicy
clear	establish	impressive	traditional

13 Work in teams. You have three minutes to write collocations / phrases for the words in Exercise 12.

background music, from a poor *background*, from a rich *background*

VIDEO 8

COLUMBUS AND THE NEW WORLD

1 **Work in groups. Look at the monuments to Christopher Columbus. Discuss these questions.**

- Which of the monuments do you like best / least? Why?
- Why do you think there are so many monuments round the world to Columbus?
- Do you know any other places that have a Columbus monument? Which people are there lots of monuments to in your country? Why?
- How much do you know about the life of Christopher Columbus?
- How do you think each of the words below might be connected to his life?

spices	a new continent	parrots
a new route	Indians	the high point
three ships	Native Americans	disappointed
a month	gold	the Vikings

2 **[▶31] Watch the video. Find out how the words in the box in Exercise 1 are connected to Columbus. Then work in pairs. Compare what you understood.**

3 **[▶31] Watch the video again. Decide if the sentences are true (T) or false (F).**

1 By the 1400s, everyone had realised the world wasn't flat – it was round.

2 Columbus wasn't able to fund his voyage himself.

3 Columbus and his sailors almost gave up hope of finding land.

4 Columbus first landed in the country that is now known as El Salvador.

5 Columbus was confused about where exactly he was.

6 He never returned to the Americas.

7 Columbus didn't feel that his voyage had been a success.

8 Columbus died less than a decade after he set foot in the Americas.

4 **Choose the correct options to complete the sentences from the video.**

1 When he was a young man, he decided *studying / to study* geography.

2 Columbus wanted *finding / to find* a sea route from Europe to Asia.

3 He now knew that *the / an* earth was round.

4 Columbus persuaded King Ferdinand and Queen Isabella of Spain *giving / to give* him money.

5 After *the / a* month at sea, the sailors were very tired.

6 It was *the / a* small island in *the / a* Bahamas, probably *an / the* island known today as San Salvador.

7 People believed Columbus was *the / a* first European to reach America.

8 Columbus made 1492 one of *the / a* most important years in world history.

5 **Choose one of the following topics to talk about. Spend a few minutes preparing what you want to say. Then work in groups and share your ideas.**

- another famous journey – or famous explorer
- a historical figure who divides public opinion
- good and bad reasons why 1492 is so important
- a foreigner who's had a big impact on your country
- the advantages of studying geography or history

UNDERSTANDING FAST SPEECH

6 **[▶32] Read and listen to this extract from the video said at natural pace and then slowed down. To help you, groups of words are marked with / and pauses are marked //. Stressed sounds are in CAPITALS.**

HOWever / ONE THING is CERtain // on ocTOber TWELFTH / FOURteen NINEty-TWO / the NEW WORLD / AND the OLD / CHANged for ALL TIME

7 **Now you have a go! Practise saying the extract at natural pace.**

REVIEW 8

GRAMMAR

1 Complete the text with one word in each space.

I ¹_____ to really enjoy playing computer games ²_____ I was younger. Obviously, games ³_____ the past were quite basic compared to what's available now. I mean, I remember ⁴_____ excited by one of ⁵_____ early online multi-player games. It was ⁶_____ war game – you had to kill your enemies – but it was really simple! One year, I ⁷_____ it almost every day – hour after hour! It's strange to think about, because these days I can't ⁸_____ playing computer games – probably because I have to use computers so much at work. When I ⁹_____ home, I don't usually want to do much: have a bath, maybe; read ¹⁰_____ book – just nothing involving technology!

2 Complete the second sentence so that it has a similar meaning to the first sentence, using the word given. Do not change the word given. You must use between two and four words including the word given.

1 I went swimming every day after school when I was a kid.

I _____ every day after school when I was a kid. **GO**

2 I don't want to say anything yet because I want to discuss things with my partner.

I don't want to say anything _____ things with my partner. **UNTIL**

3 Remind me to call my daughter later.

I _____ my daughter later. **REMEMBER**

4 The cost of living is lower than it was last year.

The cost of living _____ last year. **HAS**

5 Unemployment is higher than it was a couple of months ago – and it's going to get worse.

Unemployment is _____ . **MOMENT**

3 Choose the correct option.

1 I considered *take / to take / taking* the job, but in the end, I decided *wait / to wait / waiting*.

2 Inflation *falls / is falling / has fallen* quite a lot over the last few months.

3 I *go / have been / 'm going* to Morocco in two weeks' time.

4 My daughter really wants *to get / getting / get* a pet. She loves *a cat / cats / the cats*.

5 *I'll phone / I phone* you as soon as I *will have / have* more information.

6 Can you two please just stop *talking / talk / to talk* and pay *attention / an attention*!

7 I used to go there all the time *when I was a kid / the other week / at the moment*.

8 I don't have much money. I'm *a student / student*. It's hard to pay *bills / the bills*!

4 ▶ 101 Listen and write the six sentences you hear.

5 Write a sentence before and after the sentences from Exercise 4 to create short dialogues.

VOCABULARY

6 Match the verbs (1–8) with the nouns they collocate with (a–h).

1	open	a	the European Union
2	occupy	b	the dance floor
3	borrow	c	the minimum wage
4	join	d	a leaving party
5	earn	e	a war
6	win	f	an account
7	organise	g	a country
8	clear	h	money

7 Decide if the language in the box is connected to banks, historical events or parties.

an amazing venue	cold and distant
become independent	an empire
a buffet	establish a city
cancel my card	a housewarming
charge interest	a mortgage
a civil war	a republic

8 Complete the sentences with the best prepositions.

1 It used to be a church, but it was converted _____ flats a few years ago.

2 He made a lot of money by investing _____ property.

3 It was lovely. They had the wedding reception _____ a boat.

4 I pay all my monthly bills _____ direct debit.

5 She's really pleased because she won 100 euros _____ the lottery.

6 I had a few friends _____ for dinner on Friday, which was nice.

7 Hi there. I'd like to pay this cheque _____ my account, please.

8 I need to transfer £500 _____ my current account _____ my son in Peru.

9 Complete the text with one word in each space. The first letters are given.

Along with two of my friends, I've recently ¹s_____ up a company and we're thinking of organising a big party to ²la_____ it. The problem is, though, the ³ec_____ isn't doing very well at the moment and there's a lot of ⁴un_____ , so lots of people can't ⁵a_____ even basic things like food and rent. Even if people are working, there's less job ⁶se_____ than there used to be – and ⁷av_____ salaries are lower too. Because of all that, we don't want to spend too much on a party. It would be wrong! Instead, we'll have something small and friendly: nice ⁸ba_____ music, maybe a buffet, you know.

5 WRITING Postcards

WRITING

1. Work in pairs. Check you understand the words in the box. What kind of holiday are all these words connected to? Do you think this is a good kind of holiday for a honeymoon? Why? / Why not?

captain	movies	port	seasick	sights
galleries	parties	ruins	ship	tour

2. Read the postcards from a couple on their honeymoon. Answer the questions.

   1. How do Sara and Bruce feel about their holiday? Why?

   2. What do they have the same opinion about?

SPEAKING

3. Work in groups. Discuss these questions.

   - What kind of holiday do you think Bruce prefers? Why?

   - Does everyone in your family like doing the same things on holiday? What usually happens when you go on holiday together?

   - Is it good for couples to have different tastes and interests?

   - Do you know any couples who are quite different to each other? In what ways?

VOCABULARY

Postcard expressions

We use lots of fixed phrases when writing postcards. There's often no subject for the verb – and sometimes no verb at all.

Greetings from paradise.

Weather's great.

Writing this from a ship somewhere near Italy.

4. Put the words in order to make postcard expressions.

   1. here / were / you / wish
   2. all / you're / hope / well
   3. to / wait / you / tell / can't / about / it
   4. are / here / we / in / Panama
   5. forward / soon / looking / to / you / seeing
   6. from / greetings / Greece
   7. in / this / writing / café / a
   8. in / a / having / London / time / great / here

Hi Mum,

Well, here we are on our cruise. We get to a new port every two days and go on guided tours and see all the sights – cathedrals, ancient ruins, galleries, museums. It's a very full schedule!

Life on the ship is great – discos, parties, dinner with the captain (the food's great), even movies and concerts!

Weather's great, although the evenings are quite cool. Wish you were here.

Looking forward to telling you all about everything. (Have about 300 photos to show you!).

Lots of love,

Sara xxx

Charlotte Jenkins,

The Manor House,

Briardene,

Oxfordshire,

England OX6 4PC

Hi Mike,

Greetings from paradise! Writing this from a ship somewhere near Italy, although it might be Greece – everywhere looks the same to me! Ruins, cathedrals, and crowded art galleries and museums – non-stop sightseeing tours!

Despite trying hard to enjoy myself, I can't say I'm having a good time. What's more, although it's our honeymoon, we're never alone – there's always a crowd of 'friends' with us. The best thing is the food – amazing! Unfortunately, I sometimes get seasick, despite the good weather!

Can't wait to get back!

Hope you're well.

All the best,

Bruce

Mike Beardsley,

9 Shearer Way,

Toonton,

County Durham,

England

KEY WORDS FOR WRITING

Examourary esguun

although and *despite*

Although and *despite* both introduce contrasts – often something that shows the main statement is surprising or unlikely. Notice the different grammar after each word.

Although *it's our honeymoon, we're never alone.*

Weather's great, **although the evenings are** *quite cool.*

Despite trying hard *to enjoy myself, I can't say I'm having a good time.*

I sometimes get seasick, **despite the good weather***!*

5 Complete the sentences with *although* or *despite*.

1 _____ the horrible weather, we had a great trip.

2 The beaches are fantastic, _____ you have to watch out for sharks.

3 I enjoyed the cruise, _____ I got seasick.

4 _____ getting very sunburnt, I enjoyed the holiday.

6 Complete the second sentence so that it has a similar meaning to the first sentence, using the word given. Do not change the word given. You must use between two and five words, including the word given.

1 We had a great time, although it rained a lot.

We had a great time, _____ . **RAIN**

2 Despite the crowds, we enjoyed the concert.

_____ , we enjoyed the concert. **CROWDED**

3 Despite being really tired, we stayed up all night and studied.

_____ , we stayed up all night and studied. **WERE**

4 Although it was really sunny, it was still quite cold.

It was quite cold, _____ . **BEING**

5 Although I had a headache, I still went skiing.

I went skiing, _____ . **HAVING**

7 Complete each sentence in three different ways. Then compare your ideas in groups. Decide who has the funniest / saddest sentence.

- The holiday was great, although … .
- We managed to catch our flight, despite … .

PRACTICE

8 You are going to write a postcard to a friend or relative. Before you write, think about these questions.

- Where are you on holiday?
- What type of holiday is it?
- What things have you done?
- What are you doing at the moment?
- Are you enjoying yourself?

9 Write your postcard. Use 100–120 words. Use as much language from this lesson as you can.

6 WRITING Plans and schedules

SPEAKING

1 All the pictures below are from the same meeting. Work in pairs. Discuss these questions.

- What do you think is happening in each picture?
- What do you think the people are talking about?
- What is their relationship with the others at the meeting?

a

b Figure 6

c

d

WRITING

2 Complete the email about a meeting with the words in the box.

begin	break	continue	is	feed back
gives	meet	move	present	starts

To: olga.williams@futuresforward.org
From: tom.petersen@futuresforward.org
Subject: Sales meeting in Oslo

Dear Olga,

I'm looking forward to seeing you at the Sales Managers' meeting in Oslo on Friday 13th July.

The meeting ¹ _is_ at the Clarion Royal Hotel.

Please find below the schedule for the day.

> **09.30–10.00**
> All managers ² _meet_ in the hotel lobby.
> The meeting ³ _starts_ with coffee and a short welcome from Liv Applund, International Sales Director.
>
> **10.00–12.30**
> We ⁴ _move_ to the conference room on the first floor.
> Each national manager then ⁵ _gives_ a presentation on this year's main challenges and results.
> Presentations ⁶ _conti_ until lunchtime.
>
> **12.30–13.30**
> Lunch in the hotel restaurant
>
> **13.30–15.00**
> We divide into small groups and ⁷ _begin_ our brainstorming session.
> Topic: sales strategy for the coming year.
>
> **15.00–16.30**
> Groups ⁸ _present_ their ideas.
> We then ⁹ _feed back_ on the presentations until 16.30, when we ¹⁰ _break_ for coffee.
>
> **17.00–17.30**
> The final session begins at 17.00, when Liv Applund answers any questions and concludes the meeting.

Hope this is all clear.

Let me know if you have any questions.

All the best,

Tom

GRAMMAR

The present simple for timetables

3 Read the sentence from the email. Choose the best option (a, b or c) to complete the sentence below.

*The final session **begins** at 17.00, when Liv Applund **answers** any questions and **concludes** the meeting.*

The present simple is used in the email

a to describe possible future events.

b to describe events that happen all the time or regularly.

c to describe definite future events.

4 Work in pairs. Compare your ideas. Then check by reading the Grammar box.

> We can use the present simple to talk about things in the future that are timetabled or scheduled.
>
> We **break** for coffee at 16.30.
>
> The train **leaves** at 4.45.
>
> What time **does** the meeting **finish**?

5 Complete the sentences with the present simple form of the verbs.

1 When _____ the next regional sales meeting? (be)

2 My flight _leaves_ at 13.30. (leave)

3 I _____ in Oslo until two o'clock in the morning. (not / land)

4 What time _does_ your train _arrive_ in Paris? (arrive)

5 We _brea_ for lunch at one. (break)

6 The lunch break _____ from 1.30 to 2.45. (last)

7 Remember – we _____ until eleven tomorrow. (not / start)

8 When _does_ the meeting _end_ ? (end)

KEY WORDS FOR WRITING

Time expressions

We use *then / after that* to show that one action follows another. They mean the same thing. However, *after that* usually begins a sentence or a clause.

At 10.00, we move to the conference room on the first floor.

*Each national manager **then** gives a presentation.*

***After that,** each national manager gives a presentation.*

To show the point in time when something will finish, we use *until*.

*Presentations continue **until** lunchtime.*

*She's in Britain **until** December.*

6 Complete the sentences with *then*, *after that* or *until.*

1 The hotel restaurant doesn't open _until_ six. ✓

2 The presentations finish at one. _after that_, there's an hour break for lunch.

3 We start at ten with a brainstorming session, which continues _until_ twelve. ✓

4 I have a meeting _until_ 12.45 but _then_ I'll call you back. ✓

5 I'm afraid you have to wait here _a that_ the room is ready.

6 The president gives her welcome speech at nine and _then_ we divide into groups.

7 We don't break for coffee _until_ 4.30, I'm afraid.

8 The restaurant is booked for one. We'll probably finish around 2.30 and maybe _after that_ we can find a quiet place to discuss Asia.

PRACTICE

7 You are going to write an email about a meeting at work, school or college. Work in pairs. Write a schedule for the meeting.

8 Now work on your own. Write an email to the people who are coming to the meeting. Use the present simple to talk about timetabled / scheduled events.

9 When you finish, check your work carefully and give it to your partner. Check each other's emails and make any changes or corrections you think are necessary.

7 WRITING Complaints

SPEAKING

1 **Work in groups. Discuss these questions.**

- Have you ever bought anything that didn't work?
- If yes, what did you do? Did you return it to where you bought it from? What was the result?
- If you have a problem with something you've bought, which of the things below do you usually do? Why?
  - go back to the shop
  - email
  - phone
  - search the internet

VOCABULARY Problems

2 **Label the photo below with the words in the box.**

| button | headphones | screen | volume control |

3 **Complete the sentences below with the words in the box.**

| battery | damaged | properly | recharge |
| crack | faulty | received | slow |

1 The screen has a _____ in it so you can't see the menu or video clearly.

2 The delivery service was very _____ . It took a long time to arrive.

3 The box that it was in was _____ .

4 The main button does not work _____ . It gets stuck and you cannot access the main menu.

5 I paid for it four weeks ago, but I still have not _____ it.

6 There is something wrong with the _____ . The player stops working an hour after you _____ it.

7 The headphones are _____ , so the sound is quite bad.

4 **Work in pairs. Discuss whether each problem in Exercise 3 is very serious, quite serious or not very serious. Give reasons.**

WRITING

5 **Read the letter of complaint. Choose the options that are best for formal writing.**

The Manager
Electronics Biz
Banbury
OX15 1LN

B Tarlon
45 Doone Street
Adderbury
OX17 3AZ

4th August 2016

Dear Sir / Madam,

[1]*Further to / After* my email of 26th July, I am writing to [2]*ask / enquire* where my replacement MP4 player is, and to make a formal complaint about the quality of service that your company provides.

On 15th June this year, I [3]*purchased / bought* an MP4 player from your store in Banbury. However, I soon realised it was faulty and returned it on 19th June. At this time, I [4]*asked for / requested* a replacement and a member of staff there promised to send one the following day, but it never arrived.

After [5]*numerous / loads of* phone calls to your call centre, I then sent an email last week, describing the problems I was having. In the reply I [6]*received / got*, I was told that a brand new player had already been sent. However, I still have not received it. I am [7]*really unhappy about / not at all satisfied with* the quality of the after-sales service you provide.

If I do not receive the MP4 player by next Monday, I shall take this matter to Consumer Affairs.

[8]*All the best / Yours faithfully,*

Brad Tarlon

Brad Tarlon

6 **Work in pairs. Discuss these questions.**

- Where do the two addresses and the date go in formal letters?
- Is this the same when you write formal letters in your language?
- Why do you think the letter starts with *Dear Sir / Madam*?
- What kind of information does each of the four paragraphs contain?
- Why does the letter end with *Yours faithfully*?

7 Cover the letter of complaint in Exercise 5. Try to complete these sentences with three words in each space. Then look at the letter again and check your answers.

1 I am writing to ... make a _____ the quality of service that your company provides.

2 On 15th June this year, I purchased an MP4 player _____ in Banbury.

3 A member of staff there promised to send one _____ , but it never arrived.

4 I then sent an email last week, describing the problems _____ .

5 In the reply I received, I was told that a _____ had already been sent.

6 I am not at all satisfied with the quality of the _____ you provide.

8 Work in groups. Discuss these questions.

- What would you do if you were in Mr Tarlon's situation?

- Which of these adjectives do you think describe Mr Tarlon? Why?

reasonable	impatient	stupid

- In your country, do you have a government office like Consumer Affairs that protects the rights of shoppers? What do you know about it? Is it effective?

KEY WORDS FOR WRITING

but and *however*

But and *however* both connect two opposing ideas, or introduce surprising information.

But connects two clauses in one sentence and starts the second clause.

*A member of staff there promised to send one the following day, **but** it never arrived.*

However connects two sentences and usually comes at the beginning of the second sentence, or sometimes after the subject.

*I was told that a brand new player had already been sent. **However**, I still have not received it.*

*We phoned to complain. The woman at the call centre, **however**, said we had to send our complaint in writing.*

9 Complete the sentences with *but* or *however*.

1 The camera was damaged when I bought it, _____ the company won't give me a new one.

2 I have asked for my money back. _____ , the company say that I caused the damage to the camera.

3 I have tried to speak to your sales manager three times. The line, _____ , is always busy.

4 The shop says I dropped the box, _____ I didn't.

10 Complete the sentences with your own ideas. Then compare your sentences with a partner.

1 I called your company to complain, but _____ .

2 I bought the book from your online store over three weeks ago, but _____ .

3 I received the camera yesterday, as promised. However, _____ .

4 You stated the total cost would be £15. However, _____ .

PRACTICE

11 Work in pairs. Think of a situation that requires you to write to complain about something. Your complaint could be about something you bought or something you are trying to organise. Discuss:

- the situation and why you are writing.

- the problem and what has caused it.

- what action you now want from the person / company.

- what you will do next if you don't receive a response that you're happy with.

12 Write an email or letter of complaint. Write 100–150 words. Use as much language from this lesson as you can.

'If she doesn't get well, do I get a refund?'

8 WRITING Invitations

SPEAKING

1 Make a list of events, receptions or parties in the last year that:

- you have been invited to.
- you have invited other people to.

2 Work in groups. Compare your lists. Explain:

- what the events were.
- who held each event and why.
- why you were invited – or who you invited.
- if the events were successful or not.

WRITING

3 Read the two emails. Decide if you would accept each invitation or not. Then explain your decisions to a partner.

To: Salma.Abad@ozmail.com
From: Carlos66@ozmail.com
Subject: Housewarming!

Hi Salma!

How're you? It's been so long since we last talked! What's new with you? I've just moved into a new flat in Bondi. It's really great to live so near the beach.

I'm having a housewarming party next Saturday. I hope you can come. Bring your brother if you like – he's really funny! Unless it rains, we'll have a barbecue in the garden! I'm going to make some salads, and there'll be drinks, but I'm asking people to bring something to cook on the barbecue, if that's OK.

Send me an email and let me know if you can come. It'd be great to see you.

Love,

Carlos

4 One email is more formal and the other is more informal. Decide if the following show formality or informality:

1 contractions (*I'm, he's,* etc.)
2 longer, more complex sentences
3 dashes (–) and exclamation marks (!)
4 direct questions
5 more passives

5 Work in groups. Discuss these questions.

- How do you show different levels of formality in your language?
- Do you think it's OK:
  - to ask guests to bring food to a party?
  - to ask people to give to charity instead of giving a present?

To: Marketing@BLTLtd.com
From: BMarchant@ BLTLtd.com
Subject: Reception for Simone Lacroix

Dear colleagues,

You are invited to a reception to mark the retirement of our business manager, Simone Lacroix.

The reception will take place in the main boardroom on the first floor at four o'clock on Friday afternoon. Drinks and snacks will be served.

Simone has been with us for the last fifteen years and has helped us through some difficult times. I am sure you would like to join us in giving her a proper goodbye as she returns to her native France.

If you are able to attend, I would be grateful if you would respond to this email so that we can confirm numbers.

Simone has asked if people could make a donation to the charity Southern Cat Rescue rather than give her a leaving present. If you wish to donate, please contact Ken in Sales.

Yours,

Ben Marchant

Communications Director

VOCABULARY

Formal and informal language

Some vocabulary such as *attend* or *Yours* (to end an email) sounds quite formal. A less formal way to say these things is *come* and *All the best*. Recognising and learning more and less formal ways of expressing ideas will improve your writing.

6 Mark each of the following MF (more formal) or LF (less formal).

1 if you are able to

2 Dear Mr Parker

3 Hiya

4 if you can

5 if you like

6 Dear Pete

7 Love

8 Give me a call

9 Respond by email

10 We look forward to seeing you

11 Cheers

12 If you wish

13 Kind regards

14 We're having some friends round

15 Yours sincerely

16 It'd be great to see you

17 Let us know

18 Please contact us on 020-7034-5019

19 We are delighted to announce

20 I would be most grateful if …

7 Work in pairs. Compare your ideas. Which five phrases might come very near the beginning of an invitation? Which phrases can you use already?

KEY WORDS FOR WRITING

if, *when* and *unless*

We can talk about the future using *if*, *when* and *unless* + the present simple.

If shows something will possibly or probably happen.

When shows we expect something to happen.

Unless means *if … not*.

*Bring your brother **if you like**.*

*Give me a call **when you have** time.*

***Unless it rains**, we'll have a barbecue in the garden!*

8 Match the two parts of the sentences.

1 If the train is late,

2 Unless there's a problem,

3 I'll give you a call

4 You can bring the kids

5 John says he'll come to the party,

6 Give me a call

a unless he has to work late.

b when you've got a minute.

c when I get to my hotel.

d we'll give you a call and let you know.

e there's no need to reply to this invitation.

f if you think they might enjoy it.

9 Complete the sentences with *if*, *when* or *unless*.

1 Give me a call _____ you arrive and I'll open the gate for you.

2 _____ you would like us to arrange collection from the station, please send us details of your train and arrival time.

3 You may bring a guest _____ you wish.

4 I am afraid I will be unable to attend, _____ I can change the date of my flight.

5 We're going to have a party _____ we finish our exams.

6 We'll go swimming in the river in afternoon, _____ it's too cold.

PRACTICE

10 You are going to write two email invitations to a reception or party. The first is an informal invitation to something you are organising. The second is an invitation to a formal event in a school or company. Work in pairs. For each invitation, think of:

• the reason for the reception / party.

• where it will be and when.

• if guests should bring anything.

• anything else special about it.

11 **Student A:** write the informal invitation.

Student B: write the formal invitation.

12 Check each other's invitations. Discuss anything you think should be written differently in each invitation.

GRAMMAR REFERENCE

9 MIND AND BODY

GIVING ADVICE

The most common way of giving advice – to say what you think is the best thing to do – is *should* + infinitive (without *to*). We often soften advice by adding *maybe* at the beginning of the sentence. It's also common to say *I think you should*.

Should is a modal verb. With modal verbs we use the same form for all persons, we do not add -*s* for the third person. We do not use *do / does* in questions, or *don't / doesn't* in negatives. The negative form is *shouldn't*.

Maybe you should go home and get some rest.
You shouldn't worry about it. It'll all be fine.
What should I do if the medicine doesn't work?
What do you think I should do?

Two other common ways of giving advice are *why don't you* + infinitive (without *to*) and *ought to* + infinitive (without *to*). They basically mean the same as *should*.

Why don't you get some sunglasses to protect your eyes a bit?
*(Maybe) you **ought to try** it.*

Exercise 1

Rewrite the sentences using the words in brackets.

1 You should go on a diet. (why)
2 You ought to put some cream on that rash. (should)
3 What do you think we should do? (ought)
4 You should phone and make an appointment. (don't)
5 Anyone taking drugs to improve their performance should be banned. (to)
6 Why don't you drink less coffee? (maybe)

Exercise 2

Complete the sentences with *should / shouldn't* and the verbs in the box.

do	eat	go	ignore	miss	watch

1 You _____ so much! You'll get fat if you're not careful!
2 I'm not surprised your eyes are sore. You _____ less TV!
3 If it hurts, you really _____ and see a doctor about it. You _____ just _____ it. It might get worse.
4 The government _____ more to sort the problem out.
5 I know you're busy, but it's an important appointment. You really _____ it if you can help it.

IMPERATIVES

We use imperatives to:
1 give instructions: **Take** *twice daily with food.*
2 give an order: **Be** *quiet.*
3 give advice: **Go** *and see your doctor if you're worried.*
4 encourage: **Come on!** *You can do it!*
5 make an offer: **Have** *a seat.*
6 warn: **Don't buy** *that one. It's bad quality.*
7 reassure: **Don't worry.** *It'll be fine.*

Structures with imperatives

We often use imperatives in conditional sentences, especially when giving advice.

Don't worry if you find it difficult. (= you shouldn't worry)
If you need anything, just **email** me.
If you can't sleep, **try** counting backwards from 100.

We often use *will* after imperatives.

Hurry up or we**'ll** miss the train.
Have a seat. I**'ll** stand.
Don't worry about cleaning up. I**'ll** do it.
Don't make so much noise. You**'ll** wake the baby!

We sometimes use imperatives as requests when talking to friends, but it's better to use *could you / can you* because imperatives can sometimes sound rude and too direct with people we're not close to. However, in all the examples above, imperatives sound fine.

Pass the salt. (with friends)
Could you pass the salt, please? (more polite, less direct)

DID YOU KNOW?

We often use *so* + adjective after negative imperatives.
Don't be so lazy!
Don't be so rude!

Exercise 1

Correct each pair / group of sentences by making one of the imperatives negative.

1 Panic. Stay calm.
2 Whisper. Speak up. We can't hear you.
3 Be careful. Slip.
4 Just sit there. Do something.
5 Take your time. Rush.
6 Be quiet. Make so much noise.
7 Get up. Be so lazy.
8 Wait for me. Go ahead. I'll catch you up.

DID YOU KNOW?

We can use imperatives to give advice to friends – instead of using *maybe you should / ought to ...*
Phone *them and* **make** *an appointment.* (with friends)
Maybe you should / ought to phone *them and* **make** *an appointment.* (more polite, less direct)

Exercise 2

Rewrite the sentences using *could* for requests and *should* for advice.

1 Pour me some water, please.
2 Try talking to someone about it.
3 Bring me the bill.
4 Help me carry these bags to the car.
5 Don't drive if you're taking that medication.
6 Don't call him now. It's too late.

10 PLACES TO STAY

SECOND CONDITIONALS

Second conditionals are sentences of two parts. We use them to talk about imagined situations or things that are unlikely or impossible.

The *if*-clause

In the *if*-clause, use the past simple to talk about imagined situations. It refers to now or the future.

... **if she ate** a nut by mistake.

(She doesn't plan to eat one, but imagine her eating one.)

... *if I could*.

(I can't move anyone, but imagine the situation is possible.)

The result clause

Use *would* + infinitive (without *to*) to talk about imagined results or further actions.

She'd be ill if she ate a nut by mistake.

(She isn't ill now, only because she hasn't eaten a chocolate with nuts in.)

I would move them if I could. (I want to move them, but I can't.)

might

You can replace *would* with *might* to show less certainty about the imagined result.

They **might attract** more people if they weren't so expensive!
(= maybe they would attract more people)

Exercise 1

1 Match the two parts of the sentences.

1 The company wouldn't have these problems
2 I'd be more willing to try camping
3 It's a nice hotel, but it'd be better
4 I think that if they opened a branch in Brighton,
5 I suppose if I had a lot of money,
6 If something like that happened to me,

a if the rooms were a bit more child-friendly.
b I'd complain. I'd be really angry about it!
c if they employed staff who spoke better English!
d I might stay in a top hotel, but there are other things I'd prefer to buy.
e if the weather here was a bit better.
f it'd be a big success.

2 For each sentence above, say what the real situation is now.

The company has problems because the staff don't speak good English.

Advice

We often use a second conditional to give advice.

If I were you, I'd book online. *It'd be cheaper.* (I'm not you!)

If I was / were in your situation, **I'd complain.**

Note that we often only say the *would* part, because the situation is obvious.

A: *Do you think I should say something to the manager.*

B: **I would**. *He was quite rude to you. (= I would, if I were you.)*

Exercise 2

Choose the correct form.

1 I might think about staying there if it *was / would be* nearer the beach.
2 *I'd / I'll* pick you up from your hotel if it *was / wasn't* so far from the centre of town!
3 If I *am / were* you, I *wouldn't / don't* have the hotel breakfast. *I'll / I'd* eat somewhere else instead.
4 *It'd / It's* be better if the website *was / will* be more user-friendly.
5 I'm having a good time here, but it *was / would be* even better if it *wasn't / wouldn't be* raining all the time!
6 If we *was / were* earning more money, we *can / could* stay in nicer places.

USED TO

To talk about past habits, we can use either *used to* + infinitive (without *to*) or the past simple.

They **used to take** us on day trips.

We **went** swimming all the time.

We also use both *used to* + infinitive (without *to*) and the past simple to talk about past states.

My parents **used to own** an apartment on the beach.

It **was** so strict.

The most common way to form the negative of *used to* is with *never*.

It sounds dull, but **I never used to** get bored.

You can also form the negative of *used to* like this:

It sounds dull, but **I didn't use to** get bored.

Note that when we talk about actions that only happened once in the past, we use the past simple. We cannot use *used to*.

We once **made** cornflake cakes.

There is no present form of *used to*. It is only used to talk about the past. For habits in the present, use the present simple.

My son usually **spends** his summers like this.

Exercise 1

Complete the sentences using *used to*, *never used to* or *usually*.

1 We moved to Zagreb this year. We _____ live in quite a small place on the coast.
2 I _____ go to the beach every day, but now I'm working I can't.
3 We _____ go to the cinema because the nearest one was 60km away!
4 Now that I'm in Madrid, we _____ go out three or four nights a week.
5 Although there weren't many facilities, we _____ get bored, because we _____ make our own entertainment at home.

DID YOU KNOW?

When we use the past simple, we often add time phrases. However, when we use *used to* we often leave the time phrases out.

My parents **lived** in Holland **in the 80's**.

My parents **used to live** in Holland.

I **didn't like** vegetables **when I was younger.**

I **never used to like** vegetables, but I love them now.

Exercise 2

Decide which five sentences are incorrect, then correct them.

1 Last week, I used to have to study for my exams.
2 Before I started working here, I used work as a researcher for a drug company.
3 He's lost a lot of weight. He used to weigh 100 kilos.
4 I didn't never used to have lunch at school. I always had lunch at home.
5 I didn't use to like swimming, but I go quite a lot now.
6 Most Sundays, me and my kids use to watch a DVD at home together.
7 When I was a kid, we usually go to the mountains during the summer.
8 My grandparents usually come to stay with us at Christmas.

11 SCIENCE AND NATURE

PAST PERFECT SIMPLE

We use the past perfect simple to show that something happened before another past action. The past perfect is often used after the verbs *realise*, *find out*, *discover* and *remember* to refer to an earlier event. It is usually used with other verbs in the past simple.

*I realised **I'd made** a mistake and changed the answer.*

*I suddenly remembered I **hadn't bought** any food for my dog.*

When we describe actions in the order that they happened in, we usually just use the past simple.

*One day the owner **heard** the parrots copying his customers' requests and **trained** them to actually take orders.* (First he heard them, then he trained them.)

Exercise 1

Complete the sentences using the past perfect simple form of the verbs.

1 That's it! We met at Mina's party! I knew I _____ you somewhere before. (see)
2 I suddenly remembered I _____ to bring my homework. (forget)
3 When I got home, I realised I _____ my keys in the office. (leave)
4 We found out we _____ at university at the same time, but we _____ . (be / not meet)
5 When we arrived at the hospital, they were ready to operate, but there was a problem. Because they _____ me not to, I _____ breakfast that morning. (not tell / eat)
6 To begin with, they were surprised he _____ so well in his exams, but then they discovered he _____ ! (do / cheat)

Exercise 2

Decide which actions happened first and change the verb to the past perfect.

1 After they had one date, he asked her to marry him.
2 I rang you as soon as I heard the news.
3 I never went on a plane until I went to Japan.
4 They had an argument before I arrived, so there was a bad atmosphere. It was quite uncomfortable.
5 I was fed up after I found out I didn't get the job.

PASSIVES

To make passive sentences, use a form of the verb *be* + a past participle.

	Subject	*be*	Past participle	
Present simple	The process	is	repeated	several times.
	She	is	employed	by the government.
	You	are	left	with a very thin layer.
	Mice	are	used	in experiments.
	We	are	taught	French in school.
	I	am	paid	1,000 euros a month.
Past simple	Graphene	was	discovered	by two Russian scientists.
	He	was	arrested	for drink driving.
	I	was	born	in Berlin.
	We	were	asked	to leave.
	They	were	told	about it.

	Question word	*be*	Subject	Past participle
Present	Who	are	you	employed by?
Past	Where	were	you	born?
		Was	he	arrested?

Modals

Passives after *can / could / should* use *be* + past participle.

*Experiments on animals **should be banned**.*

***Could** those things **be replaced** by Graphene?*

Who or what does the action

The most common reasons for using passives are because we don't know exactly who does an action, or because it's unimportant who does it.

However, you can introduce who or what does the action in passive sentences using *by*.

*Graphene was discovered **by two Russian scientists**.*

*We were stopped **by the police** when we were walking home.*

Avoiding passives

Passives are used a lot in formal writing. In speech, we often use *you* or *they* as a general subject to avoid using passives.

*Experiments on animals **should be banned**.*

***They should ban** experiments on animals.*

Exercise 1

Rewrite the sentences using passives.

They told me I couldn't work in there.
I was told I couldn't work in there.

1 You repeat the test a number of times
2 They send me junk emails all the time.
3 You usually make it with lamb, but you can use beef.
4 You could use Graphene in mobile phones.
5 They introduced new stricter limits on pollution last year.
6 They arrested two men after they found a bomb in their car.

DID YOU KNOW?

In passive sentences adverbs usually go between *be* and the past participle.

*This dish **is usually served** with rice.*

*I **wasn't badly hurt** when I fell – just a few small cuts.*

Exercise 2

Complete each pair of sentences with the verb given. Use one passive form and one active.

1 fund
   a I think the government should _____ more research into Graphene.
   b The study _____ by the company who made the product, so I'm not sure you can trust the results.

2 catch
   a The government wants fishermen to _____ fewer fish.
   b Their head scientist _____ lying about the results of their research.

3 break
   a I _____ my arm when I was taking my dog for a walk.
   b To test its quality, the stone _____ into tiny pieces.

4 wake up
   a _____ you _____ by that storm last night?
   b I've been in a rush all morning because I _____ late.

5 allow
   a We _____ not _____ to use the internet at work.
   b You heat the metal to a very high temperature and then _____ it to cool.

6 give
   a My gran _____ me some socks for my birthday.
   b It _____ to me as a leaving present.

Intransitive verbs

You can only make passives with verbs that take an object. The verbs below don't take an object and can't be used in the passive form. Verbs like these are often marked with an [I] in dictionaries. This means they are intransitive.

appear	come	exist	happen	progress	seem
behave	disappear	go	last	rise	sleep

Exercise 3

Decide which four sentences are incorrect, then correct them.

1 How was the accident happened?
2 The internet didn't exist when I was at university.
3 A dog was suddenly appeared in front of me.
4 Fortunately, none of us badly was hurt.
5 Prices in the shops have risen a lot recently.
6 Those batteries weren't lasted very long.

12 ON THE PHONE

JUST, ALREADY, YET, STILL

Just, *already* and *yet* are often connected to the present perfect (although they can be used with other tenses). *Still* is sometimes used with a negative present perfect, but is more common with other present tenses.

just

Just + the present perfect simple shows an action is recent. It often goes with *only*.

A: *Is Gary here?*
B: *You've **just** missed him. He's **just** walked out of the door.*

A: *Sorry, I'm late*
B: *Don't worry. I've **only just** got here.*

already

Already + the present perfect shows something happened before, often sooner than expected. It's usually in positive sentences.

*I've **already** spoken to my boss and he's fine with the price.*
*I can't believe you've **already** finished those biscuits.*

yet

Yet + the present perfect in a negative sentence shows something hasn't happened, but we expect it to happen. We also use it in questions.

*He's not got up **yet**. Shall I wake him?*
*Have you seen the latest Almodóvar film **yet**? You'll love it.*

still

Still shows an action or situation continues unchanged.

*I'm afraid there's **still** no answer. He must **still** be in his meeting.*
*He's 45, but he **still** lives with his parents.*

DID YOU KNOW?

When *yet* and *still* are used with present perfect negatives, they both have a similar meaning but the position in the sentence is different.

*I **still** haven't got through to him. I'll ring him again.*
*I haven't got through to him **yet**. I'll ring him again.*

Exercise 1

Write sentences with *just*, *already*, *yet* and *still* using the prompts below.

1 you / speak / the bank yet?
2 I / have / time yet. I'll do it tomorrow.
3 she / only just / graduate.
4 she / still / try / to decide / what to do with her life.
5 I'm afraid he / be / back yet.
6 don't worry! I / already / sort out / everything.
7 she / just / hand / the work to me this second. I'll put it in the post now.
8 he / already / make $1 million / and he's only 26!

REPORTING SPEECH

When we report what people said, we often move 'one tense back'.

present simple → past simple
present perfect → past perfect
past simple → past perfect
will → *would*
can → *could*

Direct speech: *I've cancelled your cards.*
Reported speech: *The guy I spoke to told me **he'd cancelled** them.*

Direct Speech: *They'll be with you within three or four days.*
Reported speech: *He said the new cards **would be** with me within three or four days.*

Direct speech: *I'm very sorry.*
Reported speech: *He said **he was** very sorry.*

Note that the time phrase may also change.
'This week' → *Last week / That week*
'Today' → *Yesterday / That day*

Exercise 1

Complete the reported speech sentences.

1 'We're installing a new computer system.'
  → I phoned last month and the man I spoke to told me you _____ a new system. Why is it still so slow?

2 'We've tried to deliver the order twice this week.'
  → The man I spoke to on Friday said you _____ to deliver my order twice that week, but that's impossible! I was at home all last week.

3 'According to our records, the package arrived in the country on May 1st.'
  → The last time I called, I was told that the package _____ already _____ in the country – and now you're saying it hasn't!

4 'Your cards will be with you by Friday at the latest.'
  → I called two weeks ago and was told that my cards _____ with me within a couple of days, but I still haven't received them.

5 'We can offer you a full refund.'
  → Last time I called, the guy told me you _____ me a full refund, but now you're saying there's nothing you can do!

DID YOU KNOW?

When we report questions that start with a question word, we don't use *do / does / did*. The word order becomes subject + verb.
'Where do you live?' → *She asked me where **I lived.***
'How old are you?' → *He asked me how old **I was.***

For *yes / no* questions that start with *do, can, would*, etc. add *if*.
'Can you hear me?' → *He asked **if I could** hear him.*
'Have you seen it before?' → *She asked me **if I'd seen** it before.*

Exercise 2

Complete the reported questions.

1 'Why do you want to work for us?'
  → They asked me why _____ .

2 'What are your career goals?'
  → They asked me what _____ .

3 'Who did you speak to last time you called?'
  → They asked me who _____ the last time I called.

4 'Where did you go to school?'
  → They asked me where _____ .

5 'Have you had many other interviews?'
  → They asked me _____ .

6 'Is there anything you want to ask?'
  → They asked me _____ .

13 CULTURE

NOUN PHRASES

These are some common patterns for noun phrases. The main noun is in bold. Notice its position in the two patterns.

noun + noun (compound nouns)	*a Nollywood **film*** *a film camera**man*** *the film **industry*** *a traffic **jam***
noun + preposition + noun	*a **work** of art* *the **issue** of stolen art* *the latest **DVDs** of the Nigerian film industry* *an **interest** in modern art*

Plurals

We usually only make the main noun plural.
*You get a lot of **traffic jams** in the city.*
*The **cameramen** work very long hours.*
*We are dealing with the **issues** around illegal copying.*

DID YOU KNOW?

There are no clear rules about when you can make a compound noun and when you have to use a prepositional phrase.

a **gym member**   OR   a **member of a gym**
the film industry   ~~the industry of film~~
~~life quality~~   **quality of life**.

You just have to notice common patterns and follow the rules above.

Exercise 1

1 **Match the noun phrases in the box with the correct group of words below.**

bookshelf	life guard	university gym
cookery book	member of a gym	war film
friend from university	quality of life	world war

1 watch a / make a / a long _____
2 experience a / fight in the / end the _____
3 improve my / a good / reduce the _____
4 work as a / have a / call the _____
5 put up a / be on the / fall off the _____
6 write a / buy a / a useful _____
7 Join the / go to the / do exercise in the _____
8 become a / be a / a regular _____
9 meet a / an old / visit a _____

2 Make the noun phrases from the box above plural, if possible.

's / '

To show that something belongs to a person, animal or organisation, we generally use *'s* after a singular noun (*Andrew's*) or irregular plurals (*children's rights*) and *'* after a plural noun (*my daughters' school*). We use a noun with *'s* or *'* instead of *his, her, their*, etc.

*I met **Andrew's / his** parents yesterday.*
***Bigelow's / Her** best film is The Hurt Locker.*
*It's against **Google's / its** policies.*
*I need to tidy the **children's / their** room.*
***My daughters' / their** English is very good.*

Exercise 2

Look at the student's text and write the correct noun phrases (1–7). The first one is done for you.

I'm very interested in the ¹~~industry of fashion~~ because my oldest sister is ²~~a shoes designer~~. ³~~The shoes of my sister~~ are very beautiful. I often watch the ⁴~~channel fashion~~ on TV. I love the beautiful models. I have been to a few ⁵~~show of fashion~~ with my sister because she sometimes gets invitations. I also go shopping for clothes every week. Really, I spend too much money because the ⁶~~clothes cost~~ is quite high here and I always have a big ⁷~~bill of card of credit~~ at the end of the month.

1 fashion industry
2 _____
3 _____
4 _____
5 _____
6 _____
7 _____

PRESENT PERFECT CONTINUOUS

The present perfect continuous (*have / has* + *been* + *-ing*) is used to talk about activities that started in the past and are unfinished.

***We've been rehearsing** The Rite of Spring recently for a concert.*
*I think she's just tired because **she's been working** so hard.*

for and *since*

For is used to give an amount of time.
*I've been playing the trumpet **for ten years now**.*
***For the last few weeks**, they've been showing a series on TV based on the books.*

Since is used to say when the period of time started.
*I've been learning Turkish **since 2012**.*
*I've been playing the violin **since I was about twelve**.*
*We **met at school and** we've been good friends **since then**.*

Verbs not in present perfect continuous

Some verbs are generally used in the present perfect simple – not the present perfect continuous, e.g. *be, believe, hate, like* and *know*.

Exercise 1

Write sentences in the present perfect continuous or simple with *for* or *since*, using the prompts below.

1 I / learn Chinese / I was eight.
2 I / go to the gym every day / the last two months.
3 They / be together / quite a long time.

4 The Social Democrats / be in power / the last election.
5 He / live there / last year.
6 I / try to find / a job / months.
7 She / make amazing films / quite a while now.
8 I / not really like / much of her work / her first album.

DID YOU KNOW?

We use the present perfect continuous to talk about how long – and to focus on the activity. We use the present perfect simple to talk about how many – and to focus on finished achievements in the time up till now. Compare:

*I've **been phoning** him all morning, but he's not answering. (= how long)*
*I've **phoned ten** shops, but none of them had the book! (= how many)*
*They've **been meeting** since April to discuss the project. (= how long)*
*We've **met** several times before. (= how many)*

Exercise 2

Choose the correct option.

1 El Sistema is a social programme in Venezuela. It aims to help children from poor backgrounds avoid problems like crime and drug addiction by teaching classical music. It has been running ¹*for / since* over 30 years and it ²*has been producing / has produced* several international stars, including the conductor Gustavo Dudamel. He ³*is conducting / has been conducting* the National Youth Orchestra for the last ten years. Since 2007, Scotland ⁴*has been having / has had* a similar scheme and many other countries are also considering adopting the idea.

2 Henning Mankell ¹*has been writing / is writing* since the late 1960s. He ²*has started / started* by writing plays, but then became internationally famous through his crime novels. He ³*has been winning / has won* several awards for his books. In 1985, he founded a theatre in Mozambique and ⁴*for / since* then, he's been working there part-time.

3 I've always ¹*loved / been loving* the Eurovision Song Contest. It's great. I've been watching it ²*for / since* I was eight, when a rock band from Finland won. Apparently, they ³*have been showing / have been shown* it on TV every year since 1956 and it is one of the longest-running TV programmes in the world. Abba and Celine Dion were both past winners.

14 STUFF

RELATIVE CLAUSES

We use relative clauses to add information about nouns. The relative clause usually comes immediately after the thing / person / place it describes.

*I have a friend **who lives near there**. It's a book **that upset a lot of people when it came out**.*

Relative clauses begin with a relative pronoun.
For things, we use *that / which*.
For people, we use *that / who*.
For places, we use *where*.

Exercise 1

Choose the correct option.

1 That's the woman *which / who / where* lives upstairs from me.
2 It's one thing *that / who / where* just really annoys me.
3 That's the shop *which / that / where* I bought my shoes.
4 He's the guy *which / who / where* owns the whole factory.
5 English is the subject *which / who / where* I enjoy most.
6 That's the room *that / who / where* you get your lunch.

DID YOU KNOW?

The relative pronoun replaces the noun / pronoun it refers to in the relative clause. Don't write both!

The Boredoms are a group. The Boredoms are from Japan. They have released about ten albums.

The Boredoms are a group **that** ~~The Boredoms~~ *are from Japan and* **who** ~~they~~ *have released about ten albums.*

I spoke to a woman. The woman was the manager.

The woman **who** *I spoke to* ~~her~~ *was the manager.*

You see that place. I used to work there.

That's the place **where** *I used to work* ~~there~~.

Exercise 2

Rewrite each pair of sentences as one sentence, using a relative clause.

1 Sertab Erener is a Turkish singer. She won the Eurovision Song Contest in 2003.

   _____ .

2 Storaplan is a very trendy area. There are lots of nice shops and restaurants there.

   _____ .

3 Sue Briggs was an English teacher. She persuaded me to go to university.

   _____ .

4 A campsite is a place. You stay there when you go camping.

   _____ .

5 Shostakovich was a Russian composer. He wrote some amazing pieces of music.

   _____ .

6 Istanbul is a city. Europe and Asia meet there.

   _____ .

7 What do you call those machines? They do the washing-up for you.

   _____ .

8 I need to buy one of those things. You wear it round your waist and keep money in it.

   _____ .

MUST / MUSTN'T

must and have to

When *must* means something is essential, you can also use *have to*. *Must* often sounds stronger than *have to*.

What goes up, **has to / must come** *down.*

If you **have to / must have** *soft drinks, buy them in recyclable plastic bottles.*

I **have to / must go** *to the shops. I'll be back in a bit.*

You can't use *have to* when *must* means 'I imagine this is definitely true'.

The packaging is biodegradable, so they ~~have to~~ **must be** *OK.*
You **must be** *tired after your journey.*
It **must be** *a horrible job collecting rubbish, but I suppose someone* **has to / must do** *it.*

mustn't and don't have to

Mustn't and *don't have to* mean different things. *Mustn't* means it's essential not to do something. *Don't have to* means it doesn't matter if we do it or not – it's not necessary.

People ~~don't have to~~ **mustn't leave** *rubbish outside without a sticker on the bag.*

I **mustn't be** *late. My teacher's already unhappy with me.*

I'm going to get up late tomorrow as **I don't have** *to go to work.*

Exercise 1

Choose all the correct options.

1 I *must / have to* rush. I'm late for class.
2 Oh, I *must / mustn't* remember to go to the cash machine
3 We *don't have to / mustn't* forget to get your number before you go.
4 I *don't have / mustn't* to be back at any particular time.
5 He *must / has to* be very pleased that he's finally found a job.
6 I guess I'll do the shopping, if I really *must / have to*, but I'd rather not.
7 A: I've already been waiting for over an hour.
   B: You *must / have to* be really fed up.

DID YOU KNOW?

Mustn't can sound quite strong, so we often prefer *can't* or *be not allowed to*.

People **aren't allowed to / can't leave** *rubbish outside without a sticker on the bag.*

I'm afraid **you're not allowed to / you can't** *eat food in here.*

Exercise 2

Complete the second sentence so that it has a similar meaning to the first sentence, using the word given. Do not change the word given. You must use between three and five words, including the word given.

1 People must pay tax for throwing rubbish away.
   People _____ for throwing rubbish away. **HAVE**
2 You mustn't leave rubbish bags on the street.
   You _____ rubbish bags on the street. **ALLOWED**
3 I must remember to call him.
   I _____ call him. **FORGET**
4 I imagine you're very excited about going away.
   You _____ about going away. **MUST**
5 You aren't allowed to enter the building without showing your ID.
   You _____ the building without ID. **CAN'T**

15 MONEY

TIME PHRASES AND TENSE

Present continuous	*currently* *at the moment*
Present perfect simple **(and present perfect continuous)**	*over the last two years* *in the last few months* *since last month / year*
be going to and will	*in a few days* *in two weeks' time* *over the next few weeks*
used to or the past simple	*in the past* *when I was younger* *when I was at school*
Past tenses (not used to)	*last night / year* *the other day / week* *five days / years ago*

Exercise 1

Which time phrases from the box can be used to complete each sentence?

over the last five years	in three months' time
in two years	the other week
last month	when I was young
three months ago	since last year
at the moment	in the last six months

1 Prices have gone up a lot …
2 Unemployment is falling …
3 They opened a new factory here …
4 There's going to be a general election …

Exercise 2

Write sentences using the prompts below.

1 The prime minister / lose popularity / in the last year.
2 I / spend a lot more money / in the past.
3 I / get a loan from the bank / the other month.
4 The recession / get worse / at the moment.
5 They / invest more in schools / over the next five years.
6 He / lose his job / three years ago.

PRESENT TENSES IN FUTURE TIME CLAUSES

We can talk about the future using time clauses that start with words like *when, as soon as, before, once, after* and *until*. The future time clause can come first or second in a sentence. We generally use the present simple in these clauses.

*You can pay half back **when you have** the money, OK?*
*You'll receive your new PIN number **after you get** the card.*

In the main clause, we can use modals such as *will* and *can, be going to* or imperatives.

***I'll pay** you **back** as soon as I get paid.*
***We won't see** any improvement until the economy gets better.*
***I can help** you with your homework as soon as I finish this.*
*When I leave school, **I'm going to study** Law at university.*
*After you finish that, **make** me a cup of coffee.*

As soon as (and *once*) show that one thing will happen quickly after another thing.
When shows we are sure that something will happen.
Until shows something stops happening at this time.

Exercise 1

Choose the correct option.

1 I'll email you *when / until* I get home tonight.
2 I'm not going to lend you any more *until / after* you pay me the money you owe me!
3 *After / Until* this course ends, I'm going to visit my cousin in the States.
4 I'm not going to talk to him *until / as soon as* he apologises.
5 I'm staying late tonight. I have to finish this work *before / when* I leave the office.
6 We should book a hotel *before / after* we arrive in Paris. We arrive very late.
7 She's still in hospital. *As soon as / Until* I hear anything, I'll call you.
8 My neighbours are going to look after our cat *when / after* we're away on holiday.
9 I'll do it *as soon as / before* I have time, OK?

Exercise 2

Decide which five sentences are incorrect, then correct them.

1 We'll obviously discuss the deal with everyone before we'll make a final decision.
2 When you're ready, tell me, OK?
3 We will can have something to eat when we get home.
4 After you'll register, you'll be able to access your account online.
5 I'll be OK for money when this cheque clears.
6 I'll come and visit you as soon as I'm feeling better.
7 Inflation continues to rise until the government does something about it!
8 I will believe in UFOs until I see one with my own eyes!

16 EVENTS

ARTICLES

the

We use *the* to show we think it's obvious which thing(s) we mean, and that there's no other example.
*It's **the** ninth largest country in the world.*
(There's only one ninth largest.)
*Islam was introduced by **the** Arabs …*
(There's no other example of Arab people.)
*… in **the** eighth century.*
(It's obvious which one they mean.)
***the** Soviet Union*
(There was only one Soviet Union.)
***the** only thing*
(*Only* shows there's no other thing.)

a / an

We use *a / an* to show a thing could be one of several examples, and it's not important at this stage exactly which one.
*They share **a** border.*
(They have borders with several countries.)
*It's **an** exporter of natural resources.*
(There are many exporters in the world.)

Texts

Following the rules above, when we first introduce a noun in a text we often use *a / an*. After that we use *the* to show we are talking about the same thing.

*There was **a** war during the 19th century. After **the** war **a** new government was established, but **the** government wasn't very popular.*

Exercise 1

Complete the short text with *the*, *a* or *an*.

I go to ¹_____ school near my house. It was established in the 19th century by a wealthy doctor and is one of ²_____ oldest educational institutions in ³_____ city. It was ⁴_____ private school until ⁵_____ Second World War. After ⁶_____ war, ⁷_____ state education sytem was created and fees were ended.

⁸_____ school is going to celebrate its 200th anniversary next year. We're going to have several events over ⁹_____ year, starting with ¹⁰_____ amazing party on 20th September, which is ¹¹_____ exact date the school opened. ¹²_____ president of our region is going to attend.

Names

We use *the* with many kinds of names to show they are the only example:

The Soviet Union, The River Nile, The Hilton Hotel, The Bolshoi Theatre, etc.

But for other kinds of place names we don't use an article at all:

Kazakhstan, Cuba, Europe, Asia, Oxford Street, Mount Fuji, Lake Como

Generalities

We sometimes use *the* to talk about the whole of a group of people or things.

*Islam was introduced by **the** Arabs.*

However, normally we don't use any article when talking about things in a general way. We are talking about the whole / all examples of the thing.

*~~The~~ **Islam** was introduced by the Arabs.*
*~~The~~ **War** is stupid and ~~the~~ people are stupid.*
*I don't like ~~the~~ **coffee**.*

Exercise 2

Correct one mistake connected to articles in each sentence.

1 He died during Second World War.
2 I think it's very important to study the history .
3 Our friends have the lovely cottage in the Black Forest.
4 I'm meeting the friend of mine later.
5 One day I'd love to try and climb the Mount Everest.
6 My father is pilot, so he's away from home a lot.
7 The happiness is more important than money.
8 I don't like the eggs. I don't know why. I just don't.

VERB PATTERNS

-ing and infinitive with *to*

When two verbs are used together, the second verb can take the *-ing* form or the infinitive with *to*. The choice of form depends on the first verb. There are no rules for this. You just have to learn the patterns.

Verbs which are usually followed by the *-ing* form include:

avoid	enjoy	miss
can't stand	finish	practise
consider	mind	recommend

Verbs which are usually followed by the infinitive with *to* include:

agree	fail	plan
arrange	hope	promise
decide	offer	refuse

Exercise 1

Choose the correct option.

1 My sister offered *taking / to take* me shopping for my birthday last year.
2 I can still remember the day I decided *becoming / to become* an architect. That was a big day for me.
3 I've just finished *writing / to write* my second novel. I'm going out to celebrate!
4 I've got my Chinese exams next week, so I'm practising *speaking / to speak* as much as I can.
5 I've promised *taking / to take* my girlfriend out somewhere tonight. It's her birthday. Would you recommend *trying / to try* that place near the beach?
6 If you can't find anyone else to do it, I don't mind *working / to work* late tonight.
7 I've arranged *meeting / to meet* a few friends in town later on tonight.
8 I usually avoid *working / to work* weekends if I can help it. My boss sometimes asks me, but I usually just refuse *doing / to do* it. I need my time off!

Exercise 2

Decide which seven sentences are incorrect, then correct them.

1 I've decided not going to university.
2 I thought we agreed not to talk about politics!
3 Do you mind to wait here for a few minutes?
4 I don't really enjoy to shop for clothes.
5 I spent nine months to travel round Africa.
6 A friend of mine recommended coming here.
7 I can't stand going to office parties. I find them very stressful.
8 I'm considering to look for work overseas.
9 When I can afford to take some time off work, I'd really like to go to Peru.
10 Sorry we're so late. We stopped having lunch on the way.
11 Can you please stop to make so much noise?
12 I must remember to buy some stamps later today.

INFORMATION FILES

FILE 4

Unit 10 page 17 **CONVERSATION PRACTICE**

Student A

Your parents' friends are going to Canada on holiday. There will be two adults and two children – aged fourteen and nine. They have seen an advert for four-bed apartments connected to a hotel. They are interested in going skiing in a place nearby and the adults want to spend some free time on their own. Ring the hotel in Canada and ask for information.

FILE 5

Unit 11 page 27 **CONVERSATION PRACTICE**

Student A

1	The police caught some terrorists with nuclear material. The police don't know where it came from. It's not clear what they planned to do with it.	**Ask:** Did you see the news about those terrorists with the nuclear material?
2	They're going to build a new zoo in a city near you. It's going to cost around $3 billion.	**Ask:** Did you hear about the zoo that they're going to build in ... (say the place)?
3	It's going to snow at the beginning of the weekend and then it's going to be cold and sunny.	**Ask:** Did you see the forecast for the weekend?

FILE 7

Unit 15 page 63 **CONVERSATION PRACTICE**

Student A

You are from a country called Remonesia, which is somewhere in South East Asia.

- Invent exactly where it is.
- Decide what the quality of life is like there and give one or two reasons for this.
- Decide how the economy is doing and give one or two examples.
- Say you are thinking of moving. Explain why.

FILE 8

Unit 12 page 35 **CONVERSATION PRACTICE**

Student A	Student B
Act dialling a number.	
	Answer.
Ask for someone.	
	Explain they're not there.
Leave a message.	
	Check contact details.
Leave details. Check when they'll be back.	
	Answer.
End conversation.	

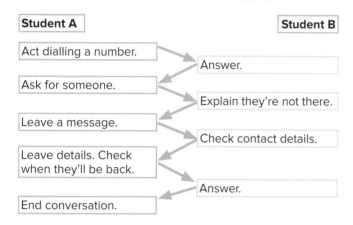

FILE 9

Unit 14 page 53 **CONVERSATION PRACTICE**

Student A

FILE 11

Unit 15 page 63 **CONVERSATION PRACTICE**

Student B

You are from a country called Lidland, which is somewhere in northern Europe.

- Invent exactly where it is.
- Decide what the quality of life is like there and give one or two reasons for this.
- Decide how the economy is doing and give one or two examples.
- Say you are thinking of moving. Explain why.

FILE 12

Unit 10 page 17 **CONVERSATION PRACTICE**

Student B

You have friends who have found a hostel 20km from Edinburgh in Scotland. They want to stay for four days and go to the arts festival in the city. They also want to go on a day trip round the Scottish countryside. They are students and don't want to spend too much money.

FILE 14

Unit 11 page 27 **CONVERSATION PRACTICE**

Student B

1 They have found a cure for the flu. It's a new drug that deals with 90% of all cases. It could save thousands of lives.

Ask:
Did you hear about the new cure for the flu?

2 There's going to be a storm this weekend. It's going to rain a lot and be very windy.

Ask:
Did you see the weather forecast for the weekend?

3 The right whale is almost extinct. There are only around 500 left in the wild. Scientists don't know if there are enough to survive.

Ask:
Did you see the article about the right whale?

FILE 15

Unit 11 page 29 **GRAMMAR**

1 Guards caught and arrested a pigeon in a jail. The pigeon had carried drugs to prisoners at the jail. Apparently, it had flown over 60 kilometres from one prisoner's home town.

2 Fishermen found a pet dog on a desert island. The dog had disappeared when its owner was travelling on a cruise. The dog had fallen into the sea and had swum to the island. Fishermen who sail near the island found the dog several weeks later. It had survived by eating small animals.

3 A pet rabbit saved his elderly owners. The couple hadn't turned off the gas on their cooker properly and the house was filling with gas. The rabbit detected the smell, ran up the stairs and woke his owners, who were sleeping.

FILE 16

Unit 14 page 53 **CONVERSATION PRACTICE**

Student B

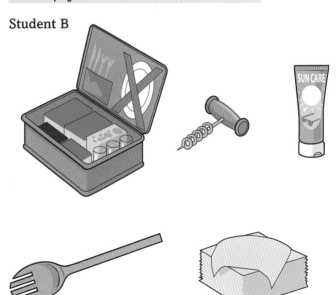

AUDIO SCRIPTS

UNIT 9

▶ TRACK 53

1

A: Hi, how are you?

B: Not very well, actually. I think I have the flu.

A: Oh no! You poor thing! Are you sure it's not just a cold?

B: It might be, I suppose, but it doesn't feel like it. I've had it for a few days now. I just feel really weak and tired all the time and my muscles ache a lot.

A: That sounds horrible. Maybe you should go home and get some rest.

B: Yes, maybe you're right.

A: No-one will thank you if you stay and spread it!

B: That's true. Could you tell Mr Einhoff I'm sick?

A: Yes, of course.

B: Oh, and could you give him my homework?

A: Yeah, of course.

B: Thanks.

A: No problem. Well, you take it easy and get well soon.

B: I'll try! Bye.

A: Bye. See you.

2

D: Atchoo!

C: Bless you!

D: Oh! I am sorry! That's the fifth time in as many minutes!

C: That's OK.

D: I always get like this at this time of year! It's awful, because I hate winter, but then as soon as the sun comes out, I can't stop sneezing! And my eyes get really sore as well. I really want to rub them, but that just makes them worse!

C: Oh, that sounds horrible. Are you taking anything for it?

D: Yes, I went to the chemist's last year and they recommended these pills so I take four of these every day, and they help, but they don't stop it completely.

C: Well, why don't you get some sunglasses to protect your eyes a bit?

D: That's not a bad idea, actually ... but I think I might feel a bit funny walking round in sunglasses all day!

C: Yeah, I know what you mean, but maybe you ought to try it. You never know. It might work for you.

D: Well, maybe if things get really bad.

▶ TRACK 54

1 It's just a question of mind over matter.

2 What's the matter?

3 I don't mind.

4 It doesn't matter.

5 Never mind.

6 To make matters worse ...

7 You don't mind?

8 I've got a lot on my mind.

9 That's a matter of opinion.

▶ TRACK 55

1

A: Are you OK?

B: Hic! Yeah, I've just got hiccups. Oh gosh! Hic! It's really annoying.

A: Here. I know a cure. It never fails.

B: Hic.

A: Take some water in your mouth, but don't drink it.

B: Mmm.

A: Now put your fingers in your ears. Bend down and put your head between your knees and swallow the water slowly.

B: Mmmm?

A: Swallow the water!

B: Mmm.

A: OK. You can breathe now. Have you still got them?

B: Um, no. No, I don't think so.

A: You see. It works every time.

B: Maybe, but I wouldn't want to do it in public! People would think I was mad!

2

C: Yes. Can I help you?

D: Yes, I would like something for a bad stomach, please.

C: Does it hurt or have you been sick?

D: Not sick. It's more gas. It's uncomfortable.

C: OK. It sounds like indigestion. It's after you eat, right?

D: Yes.

C: And you're going to the toilet normally? No diarrhoea?

D: Diarrhoea? No.

C: OK, so I think these are what you need. They're indigestion tablets. You mix them with water and drink them after your meals. They're the most effective, I think.

D: OK.

C: What flavour would you like? Orange or blackcurrant?

D: Oh, orange.

C: That'll be 4.25. Don't take more than four tablets a day – and if they don't deal with the problem, consult your doctor.

D: OK. Thanks. I will.

3

E: The burn's not too bad. We'll give you some cream for it, but you'll need some stitches in that cut. It's quite deep. What happened?

F: Well, I cut my head dancing with my son.

E: I'm sorry?

F: I was dancing with my five-year-old son and I stepped on one of his toys and I fell and hit my head on the side of the table.

E: Oh dear. What about the burn, then?

F: Well, my wife came in when she heard me shout and while she was helping me stand up, she knocked a cup of coffee off the table and it went all over my leg.

E: Oh dear. I am sorry. I shouldn't laugh!

F: Don't worry. It was very stupid!

E: Nurse, could you dress the burn after I've done these stitches?

G: Of course.

/bliː/, /fiː/, /niː/, /bre/, /swe/, /be/, /he/, /tʃe/, /peɪ/, /reɪ/, /eɪk/, /feɪ/

▶ **TRACK 57**

1 My eyes ache and I need to sleep!
2 I can't bend my knee very well.
3 She was bleeding from her head.
4 Can you take a deep breath for me, please?
5 These shoes really hurt my feet.
6 I had a terrible pain in my chest.
7 Raise your head and face me, please.
8 The bed was wet with sweat.

UNIT 10

▶ **TRACK 58**

R = receptionist, D = David

R: Hillborough Hotel.
D: Oh, hello. I'm ringing on behalf of a friend. He wants some information.
R: Sure. What would you like to know?
D: Um, well, do you have any triple rooms?
R: I'm afraid not. We only have doubles.
D: Oh, right. Is it possible to get a double with an extra bed? They have a small kid.
R: That should be possible.
D: And how much would that be per night?
R: For the room, that's 110 euros per night, with a supplement for a child's bed.
D: Sorry. Does that include the cost of the extra bed or not?
R: It does include it, yes.
D: And breakfast is included too?
R: I'm afraid not. It's 125 with breakfast. What dates are they thinking of coming?
D: Um, Tuesday the twelfth to the seventeenth of August.
R: OK. Let me just check our availability. Hmm, I'm afraid we're fully booked that weekend on the sixteenth and seventeenth.
D: And what if they came the previous weekend?
R: Saturday night no, but from Sunday through to Friday we currently have rooms available.
D: So that's the tenth till the fifteenth – including Friday night?
R: That's correct.
D: OK. I'll need to check with them about that. And just a couple of other things.
R: Sure.
D: They're thinking of hiring a car. Can they get any reduced rates if they book through the hotel?
R: They can, actually. We have a partnership with a local hire firm. The cost starts at 25 euros a day.
D: OK. Great. Do you have parking at the hotel?
R: There is a car park, which is 20 euros a day, and there is some street parking nearby.
D: Right. OK. Well, I think they're travelling around Ireland after Dublin, so maybe they could hire the car later in the week.
R: Of course, whatever suits them.
D: OK. Let me just talk to my friends. Could you tell me your name for when I call back?

R: Yes, it's Jackie, but any of my colleagues can deal with the booking.
D: Oh wait, sorry – one last thing. Will they need to make a payment when they make the booking?
R: Yes, we'll need to take a 10% deposit on a credit card.
D: So if for whatever reason they didn't come, they'd lose that money?
R: I'm afraid so. The complete payment is made on arrival.
D: OK. Thanks.

TRACK 59

R = receptionist, C = Customer

R: OK, so can I take your credit card details for the deposit?
C: Sure.
R: What kind of card is it?
C: Visa.
R: And the name on your card?
C: Mr D E Gwaizda. That's G – W – A – I – Z – D – A.
R: OK. That's an unusual name.
C: Yeah, it's Polish originally.
R: OK. And the card number on the card?
C: 1003 6566 9242 8307.
R: And the security number on the back of the card – the last three digits there?
C: 718.
R: And the expiry date?
C 06 17
R: And can I just take a contact number in case there are any problems?
C: Sure. 0044 796 883 412.

▶ **TRACK 60**

A, B, C, D, E, F, G, H, I, J, K, L, M, N, O, P, Q, R, S, T, U, V, W, X, Y, Z

▶ **TRACK 61**

R = receptionist, M = manager, L= Lady Zaza

R: Hello. Reception.
M: Hi. I'm calling on behalf of Lady Zaza, in the presidential suite.
R: Oh, yes. It's a real pleasure to have her in the hotel.
M: Yeah, well, there was no way we could stay in that last place. The service there was a joke!
R: Well, I hope everything's OK with our rooms. We really didn't have much time to prepare them.
M: Yeah, everything's fine, basically, but there are just a couple of things she's asked for.
R: OK.
M: Well, first, can you ask room service to send some fresh flowers to the room? Lady Zaza enjoys arranging them. She'd like a hundred bunches of red flowers and eighty bunches of white.
R: Certainly. I'll send someone up with them in a minute.
M: And tell them to bring more of her favourite chocolates too, please. And please remember to remove the ones with nuts. She'd be very ill if she ate one by mistake. And the hotel wouldn't want that.
R: Absolutely not. I'll make sure they're taken out.
M: She'd also like the light bulbs in her room changed. She said it's too dark.
R: Oh … of course.

M: And can you bring her a kitten?

R: Er, a kitten?!

M: Yeah. Stroking it helps her relax. She wants a white one.

R: I doubt I can find one …

M: What Lady Zaza wants, Lady Zaza gets.

R: Would it be OK if the cat was a different colour?

M: No. It needs to match the colour of the flowers. Oh, and one last thing. Can she get a wake-up call at four a.m., please? She'd like to use the gym.

R: Well, the gym doesn't usually open until six, but I'm sure we can organise something for her.

M: Great. That's it for now. Oh, wait. Just one second. She's saying something.

L: They did it again! You've got to do something!

M: Yeah, OK. OK. Hello?

R: Yes, hello.

M: Lady Zaza can hear the people downstairs. They're talking or watching TV or something and she wants them to be moved.

R: Moved? I'm afraid that's just not possible.

M: Sure it's possible. You've got hundreds of rooms in this place.

R: I know, but I'm afraid we're fully booked. We don't have any other rooms available.

M: So you're telling me you can't move them?

R: I really would move them, if I could, but I'm afraid it's absolutely impossible. I'm terribly sorry.

M: Well, that's just not good enough. I'd like to talk to the manager.

R: She's not here at the moment, I'm afraid, but I'm sure that if she was, she'd tell you exactly the same thing.

M: Is that right?

R: I'm afraid so, yes.

M: OK. Well, I'll tell her … but she's not going to like it.

▶ TRACK 62

1 I never used to like camping.

2 I used to do judo when I was younger.

4 He used to smoke quite heavily when he was younger.

5 I used to have really long hair when I was at college.

6 It never used to be crowded before.

▶ TRACK 63

/rʌʃ/, /hɒl/, /lʊk/, /puːl/, /mʌn/, /pɒ/, /bʊk/, /luːz/, /dʌb/, /hɒs/, /kʊd/, /ruːm/

▶ TRACK 64

1 Could I make a booking for Friday?

2 We don't want to lose our deposit.

3 I never used to like group holidays, but now I do.

4 Could I have a look at your book?

5 How much money did you spend?

6 I spent the whole week by the pool.

7 I'd like to book a double room.

8 I lost my toothbrush somewhere in the hostel.

▶ TRACK 65

1 Where would you go if you could go anywhere in the world?

2 I never used to enjoy camping, but I've grown to really love it.

3 Don't have any more of that coffee if you want to sleep tonight!

4 I don't think you should worry too much about it.

5 I used to get terrible nosebleeds, and then one day they just stopped!

6 I'd never go to work again if I didn't really have to.

UNIT 11

▶ TRACK 66

1

A: Did you read this article about bees?

B: No.

A: They're all dying, for some unknown reason.

B: Really? That's terrible!

A: I know. It's really bad news because we really depend on bees. If bees become extinct, we won't have any fruit or vegetables.

B: I hadn't thought about that. They should do something – fund research or something.

A Absolutely.

2

C: Did you see the forecast for tomorrow?

D: No.

C: It's going to be nice – really hot and sunny.

D: Really? That's great!

C: I know. It's good. It's been so wet and windy recently.

D: We should go out, then – go to the beach or somewhere.

C: Yeah, that's a good idea.

3

E: Did you hear what they want to do in Morovia?

F: No. What?

E: It said on the news that they're going to pull down a lot of the horrible houses they've built along the coast and create a national park instead.

F: Really? That's great.

E: I know. It's good news.

F: They should do more to protect the countryside here, too.

E: Definitely. We need more green spaces.

4

G: Did you see they've discovered a new way to kill the mosquitoes that spread malaria?

H: No.

G: Yeah, it said it could save millions of lives.

H: Really? That's great.

G: I know. It's really good.

H: It makes a change to hear some good news.

G: Absolutely.

▶ TRACK 67

1 Really? That's great!
2 Really? That's interesting.
3 Really? That's nice.
4 Really? That's bad news.
5 Really? That's awful.
6 I know. It's fantastic.
7 Yeah. It's good news.
8 Yeah, I know. It's really bad news.
9 I know. It's terrible.
10 That's a good idea.
11 Absolutely.
12 Definitely.

▶ TRACK 68

P = presenter, S = scientist

P: OK. So the first question from listener Mary Martin is based on a recent news story: Are there crime genes?

S: Well, yes and no. First, remember we share 50% of our genes with bananas, but you wouldn't say humans were half banana! There are studies that have found some violent criminals share a particular gene. But, BUT, this is one of many, many factors. Many people have the gene, but aren't violent. Violence and crime can be learned. Home life, culture, war, even the environment and pollution can be factors.

P: OK. Something rather different now. Yevgeny from Russia asks: How do spiders walk on ceilings?

S: OK, right, yes, well researchers have discovered that spiders' feet are covered in hairs. But then each hair is also covered in hundreds of thousands of tiny hairs, each about an atom wide. Basically, when these tiny hairs move next to the atoms of the ceiling material, it creates a small electric charge so the hairs and ceiling atoms are attracted to each other. It's a bit like how you can rub a balloon on your hair, then stick it to a wall. The spider has so many hairs, the attraction is quite strong – strong enough to hold 100 times the weight of the spider.

P: Right, well, from some very thin hairs to Graphene and Jamie Seguro's question: What is Graphene?

S: Graphene, OK. Well, this is probably the most important discovery of the last 20 years.

P: Really? So what is it and who discovered it?

S: It's the world's thinnest material. It's just one atom thick, and it was discovered by two Russian scientists working at the University of Manchester. The first amazing thing is, it's very easy to find, because it's basically a very, very thin layer of the stuff in a pencil.

P: What, a normal pencil?

S: Yep. That stuff is called graphite. Basically, you take some graphite and put it on some sticky tape – normal sellotape. Then you take some more tape, press it on the graphite. If you peel this tape away, some layers of graphite come off. And if that process is repeated a few times, it eventually leaves a layer one atom thick.

P: So can you see it?

S: Not without a microscope, no, but even though it's so thin Graphene is incredibly difficult to tear: it's the strongest material we know. But then because it's thin you can bend it easily. And it's really, really good at conducting electricity – much better than the wires that are used in our home or the chips in computers.

P: So could those things be replaced by Graphene?

S: Some day, hopefully, because it's so easy to get and so efficient. We could save a lot of money. It's an incredible discovery and it was awarded a Nobel Prize.

▶ TRACK 69

/laʊ/, /lɔː/, /rɒk/, /pɒ/, /paʊ/, /faʊ/, /stɔː/, /dɒ/, /kɔː/, /bɒ/, /mɔː/, /ɔːt/

▶ TRACK 70

1 You're not allowed to keep pets.
2 They found the bomb before it went off.
3 They took it to court and won.
4 You ought to feed your dog less.
5 The last version was launched in October.
6 They have a policy to fund more research.
7 The rocket lost power and crashed.
8 The storm caused a lot of damage.

UNIT 12

▶ TRACK 71

1
A: Hello.
B: Hi, it's Brendan. Is Neil there?
A: No, he's not got up yet. Is it urgent?
B: No, it's OK. Just tell him we're meeting earlier – at seven, not eight. And tell him he's very lazy! Twelve o'clock and still in bed!
A: Well, he was out late last night. Has he got your number, Brendan?
B: Yeah, he has. So what time will he be up?
A: I imagine in about an hour. He didn't get back home till four.
B: Oh right. Well, I'll see him later. Thanks.
A: That's OK. I'll give him your message. Meet at seven, not eight.
B: Yeah.
A: Bye now.

2
C: Good morning, DBB. How can I help you?
D: Yeah, hi. Could I speak to Jane Simpson, please?
C: Of course. I'll just put you through to her.
D: Thanks.
...
E: Hello.
D: Hi, Jane?
E: No, it's actually Poppy. I'm afraid Jane's out visiting a client. Would you like to leave a message?

D: Yeah, could you tell her Diane called? I've already spoken to my boss and he's fine with the price, so we can go ahead with the work. Can you ask her to phone me when she gets back so we can sort out the details?

E: Of course. Has she got your number?

D: I don't think she has my mobile. It's 07729 651 118

E: OK. 07729 651 118. And what was your name again? Sorry.

D: Diane Lincoln. L-I-N-C-O-L-N. So when will she be back?

E: Probably later this afternoon. I think she said she was going for lunch.

D: Oh, right. Well, hopefully I can speak to her today. I'm actually away on holiday from tomorrow.

E: Oh, right. Well, I'll let her know anyway.

D: OK. Thanks. Bye.

E: Bye.

▶ TRACK 72

A: No, he's not up yet. Is it urgent?

B: Just tell him we're meeting earlier – at seven, not eight.

▶ TRACK 73

1

A: Hello. Better Banking.

B: Oh, hello there. I need to cancel my cards, please. As soon as possible.

A: OK, no problem, but I'm afraid I have to take you through security first. Can I get your full name, please?

B: Um … oh, yes. Of course. It's Bettina Kraus. That's B-E-double T-I …

…

A: OK. That's fine. I'll just put you through to the right department. One moment, please.

…

C: That's fine. So I've cancelled your cards and ordered new ones, and they'll be with you in the next three or four days. We'll also send you a new PIN.

B: Oh, that's great. Thank you so much for your help.

C: You're welcome. Is there anything else I can do for you today?

B: No. That's all for now. Thanks again. Bye.

2

D: OK. So can you just tell me how it happened?

B: Yes. I was walking from the bus stop to my friend's house and I was talking on the phone so I wasn't really paying attention. Then someone came past me on a bicycle and just grabbed my bag and rode off. The strap on the bag broke because he pulled so hard.

D: And can you give me a description of the person on the bike?

B: Not really. Young. Maybe fifteen or sixteen. Wearing dark clothes. And a hood.

D: Anything else?

B: I'm afraid not. It all happened so quickly, you know.

D: OK. Well, I can give you a reference number so you can contact your insurance company, if you have one.

B: OK. And what about my bag?

D: Well, it's a big city out there and obviously we don't have the people to go and look for the person who did this, but if we do hear or find anything, we'll let you know.

3

E: Hello. Abbey Locks. How can I help you?

B: Yeah. Hello, er, basically, my bag's been stolen and it had my keys in it, so I need to get into my apartment.

E: OK. Do you want us to change the lock or just get you in? Was there anything with your address in the bag?

B: Oh gosh, yes. I had my driving licence in my purse.

E: OK. You'll want new locks then. Are you at the property?

B: No, I'm phoning from my friend's house.

E: Right, well I suggest you go back home. We can send someone within an hour. Can I just get the address, please?

B: Sure. It's Apartment 4, number 72 Montague Terrace, BR2 0SZ.

E: OK. Got it. Someone will be with you soon. Do you have proof of ID and proof of address?

B: No, I don't. No. Everything was in my bag. I mean normally I'd ask my landlady who lives next door, but she's away.

E: Wait, you rent the apartment?

B: Yes – is that a problem?

E: Well, we would normally talk to the owner of the property.

B: But she's abroad!

E: Don't you have a contact number?

B: I did – in my phone … oh what a nightmare!

▶ TRACK 74

F: Hello there. You're speaking to Alan. I understand you're calling about your cash and credit cards. Is that correct?

B: Yes, that's right. I called last week. Someone stole my bag and I phoned to cancel my cards.

F: OK.

B: And the guy I spoke to told me he'd cancelled them and that the new cards would be with me in three or four days … but I still haven't received them.

F: Right. Let me just check. OK. I can see that the cards were actually sent out as promised. Last Tuesday. And in fact, your credit card was used just yesterday.

B: No, that's not possible.

F: £1,845, spent in IKEA in Aberdeen.

B: But I've never even been to Aberdeen. How did that happen?

F: I'm not sure. I'm very sorry. I think I have to speak my manager.

▶ TRACK 75

/jʊə/, /stəʊl/, /həʊm/, /aʊə/, /fəʊ/, /ʃʊə/, /fəʊn/, /kjʊə/, /məʊ/

▶ TRACK 76

1 He had to pay a 200-euro fine.
2 I usually work from home.
3 She'll be back in about an hour.
4 Do you have insurance for your phone?
5 I've lost my mobile somewhere.
6 Take a photo with your phone.
7 I'm lucky my job's quite secure.
8 My car was stolen from outside my home.

▶ TRACK 77

1 We've only just left the house.
2 I suddenly realised I'd left my keys in my flat.
3 I was stopped by the police as I was driving home.
4 The lions are usually fed at about three in the afternoon.
5 I knew we'd met before, but I just couldn't remember where.
6 They said the new battery would be here within three or four days.

UNIT 13

▶ TRACK 78

A: What a boring lecture!
B: I know. It wasn't very good. I was starting to fall asleep near the end!
A: So what are you doing this afternoon? Have you got any plans?
B: Yeah, I'm thinking of going to see a movie and ... um ... listen, would you like to come with me?
A: Maybe. What's on?
B: Well, there's this film called *In the Heat of the Moment* – directed by Umberto Collocini. It's supposed to be really good.
A: Yeah, I've seen it already, actually. I saw it the other day.
B: Oh yes? What was it like?
A: Not bad, but not as good as everyone is saying. The costumes were great and it's set on an island in Thailand, so it looks amazing.
B: Yeah, that's what I'd heard. So what was wrong with it?
A: Oh, I don't know. I just found it a bit too slow. I got a bit bored with it after a while – and the ending was very predictable.
B: Oh, right.
A: And that Scottish actor's in it as well. You know. What's his name?
B: Bryan McFletcher?
A: Yeah, that's him. I just find him really, really annoying. He can't act! Anyway, what else is on?
B: Um ... let me see. Oh, there's *The Cottage*.
A: Yeah? What's that?
B: It's a new horror movie. It's supposed to be really scary.
A: OK. To be honest, I don't really like horror movies. I'd rather see something a bit lighter, if possible.
B: OK. Right. Well, how about this? *It's a Love–Hate Thing*. It's a romantic comedy set in Paris and New York and it stars Ellen McAdams and Ryan Rudd.
A: That sounds more like it! Where's it on?
B: The Galaxy in Cambridge Road.
A: OK. And what time does it start?
B: There's one showing at two thirty and then another one at quarter to five.
A: So shall we try the half past two one? We could go and have a coffee or something first.
B: OK. Great.

▶ TRACK 79

cash machine, city centre, crossroads, flatmate, film industry, football boots, heart disease, security system, success story, sunglasses, tennis court, traffic lights

▶ TRACK 80

1

I'm a big fan of a Turkish singer called Sertab Erener. I first heard her when she won the Eurovision Song Contest and I've liked her ever since then. I think she's got an amazing voice. She actually trained as an opera singer. I've got five or six of her albums and a couple of years ago I went to Istanbul to see her sing live. In fact, I've discovered Turkey through her music and want to spend more time there. I've been learning Turkish since 2012 and I'm now starting to understand her songs better too. My all-time favourite is *Life Doesn't Wait – Hayat Beklemez*. Excuse my bad pronunciation.

2

I've been playing the trumpet for ten years now with El Sistema, which is a programme that helps young people from poor backgrounds learn classical music. I really, really love playing, and without El Sistema I would probably be in a bad situation! When I joined, I was only eight, but I was already in trouble with the police. My favourite composers are Russian – Shostakovich and Stravinsky. We've been rehearsing The Rite of Spring recently for a concert. It's fantastic – the best.

3

My favourite author is the Swedish crime writer Henning Mankell, especially his stories with the detective Wallander. The stories are good thrillers. They're unpredictable, but they're also about social issues and are a bit political which makes them extra interesting. For the last few weeks, they've been showing a series on TV based on the books. It's OK, but the main character is different to the character in my imagination and, of course, there's less suspense because I've already read the books! I don't know if I'll keep watching.

4

I'm at art school, where I'm studying Fine Art. I've known I wanted to be an artist since I was three. I've always been more of a painter, especially people – portraits, but recently I've become much more interested in sculpture. I think my favourite artist at the moment is an English sculptor called Henry Moore. He did these beautiful, strange, abstract sculptures – often based on human figures. I saw an exhibition of his work last year. I don't know why I liked it so much, I just did – especially a sculpture called King and Queen.

▶ TRACK 81

1 How long have you been going there?
2 How long have they been doing that?
3 How long has she been learning?
4 How long have you been playing?
5 How long has he been training?
6 How long have you known him?
7 How long has she been going out with him?
8 How long have you been married?

/haɪnd/, /həd/, /hɒrə/, /hiːz/, /hæ/, /hɑːf/, /hɪs/, /hɒŋ/, /hɒb/, /hɜːs/, /hɔːl/, /hɪə/

▶ **TRACK 83**

1 The woman behind me had a horrible laugh.
2 He's got some really annoying habits.
3 I left about halfway through the film.
4 It's quite sad, but it has a happy ending.
5 It's a historical drama set in Hong Kong.
6 Everyone needs to have a hobby.
7 I really hate horror movies.
8 We rehearse every week in a hall near here.

UNIT 14

▶ **TRACK 84**

A: It's nice.
B: Yes, it is, but it's also very dirty!
C: I know. We'll have to give everything a good clean and sort the place out. Maybe we should go into town and buy some stuff.
A: Yeah, it's a good idea. One minute. I'll get a pen and we can write a list. OK. So … .
B: Well, we need those things for cleaning. A brush and a … I don't know the name. The thing that you put rubbish in. What's the name?
C: Do you mean a rubbish bin?
B: No, not that. When you use the brush, what do you call the thing that you use to get rubbish from the floor? The thing that you put the dirt into with the brush?
C: Oh, you mean a dustpan. A dustpan and brush.
B: A dustpan and brush. Yes, that's very useful.
C: And maybe we should get some cleaning stuff as well. Have we got any bleach?
A: What is bleach?
C: Oh, it's a kind of liquid that's really good for cleaning things, you know, like for cleaning the floor and the toilet. It's a kind of chemical. It's quite strong.
A: Oh, we have some. It's in the kitchen – in the cupboard under the sink.
C: Oh, OK. I didn't notice that, but that's good.
B: We need to buy that machine that you use for the clothes. After you wash them. I can't remember the name. Oh, and I know this word as well.
A: You mean an iron?
B: Yes, an iron! And also the thing that you put the clothes on when you use the iron.
C: Yeah, an ironing board. OK. What else?
A: Oh, for the bathroom we need a thing for the shower. You know, the plastic thing that stops the water from leaving the shower – and the metal thing that holds it.
C: A shower curtain and a shower rail. Yeah, I noticed there wasn't anything like that in the bathroom. It's crazy, isn't it? Why doesn't the landlord provide things like that? It's so basic.

B: I know!
A: We should charge the landlord for these things.
B: Oh, one more thing. Before I forget. We need the machine that makes hot water – to make tea and coffee.
C: Oh, yes, of course. A kettle! I can't live without a kettle! I need my tea in the morning!

▶ **TRACK 85**

I must remember to call her later.
You mustn't forget to set your alarm.
You can, if you must.
We mustn't leave it here.
You must be tired.
He mustn't do anything till the doctor's seen him.
I must speak to them later.

▶ **TRACK 86**

1 For my birthday this year, my big sister bought me my own website. She's really good with computers and I'm not, but the website has become something fun we work on together. I also loved the way she told me. She sent me an email where she gave me clues about the present for me to guess what it was, but I didn't know. Then she sent me another email with a link to a website. When I clicked on the link, I understood everything and I realised that the site was the present. I was really excited! It's my favourite ever gift because, as I said, it's something we do together.
2 I got a mountain bike for Christmas a few years ago and it's been one of the most useful presents ever. Over the last year, I've lived close enough to work to be able to cycle and so I've saved loads of money on petrol. A birthday present that also saves me money! Excellent. I'm also fitter and have lost weight.
3 One of my ex-boyfriends was the king of bad presents. One year, he gave me an iron for my birthday! An iron! I mean, what kind of message does that send about our relationship and the way that he saw me? The following year, he bought me a dress that HE really liked and told me that he wanted me to start wearing more clothes like that from then on – because they would make me more attractive. I couldn't believe it! A couple of weeks after that, we broke up!
4 A few years ago, I went out with a girl and as we were getting out of the taxi to go to dinner, she suddenly said, 'I got you a present.' I was quite embarrassed because it was our first date and I hadn't thought of getting her anything. Then she handed me a rock from a beach. I was confused. Why had she given me this thing? She said, 'I wanted to give you something you'd never forget and you could tell your children about'. I said thanks to be polite, but I actually thought it was a bit stupid and it was a bad start to the evening!
   Now, though, I use that rock to stop papers on my desk blowing away and that girl is my wife!

▶ **TRACK 87**

/e/, /ə/, /ɔː/, /ɜː/, /beˈ/, /bɜː/, /preˈ/, /pɔː/, /zənt/, /zɜːrv/, /drɔː/, /tɔː/

▶ TRACK 88

1. I burnt my hand on the cooker.
2. We found some money buried in the garden
3. You mustn't pour chemicals down the sink.
4. There's a torch in the drawer over there.
5. There are strict laws to protect the environment.
6. I didn't get any birthday presents this year.
7. The old church is perfectly preserved.
8. Where do you store all your food?

▶ TRACK 89

1. I've been wanting to see that for ages.
2. It's just one of those things that happen sometimes.
3. I don't have to work tomorrow, so I guess I can, yeah.
4. How long have you been working in the music industry?
5. He's one of those people who can always make you laugh.
6. There's been an accident on the crossroads in the city centre.

UNIT 15

▶ TRACK 90

L = Laima, A = Aidan

L: So how long have you been living here?

A: Almost two years.

L: Wow! You must like it.

A: Yeah, it's nice. I have a good quality of life here – warm climate, near the beach, not too much work.

L: It sounds fantastic.

A: Yeah, it's great, but I'm actually going back to Canada in a few months.

L: Forever?

A: Yeah, I think so.

L: Why? It sounds perfect here.

A: Well, the economy's doing quite badly at the moment. I mean, unemployment has gone up quite a lot over the last few months, so I'm not sure I'm going to have a job in a year's time.

L: Really?

A: Yeah, and also salaries aren't so high here, you know. I could get paid a lot more back home.

L: Sure, but I bet the cost of living's a lot higher in Canada as well. Everything's so cheap here. I mean, eating out is twice the price in my country. You can get a three-course meal for about six dollars here.

A: Yeah, that's true, but it used to be cheaper in the past. Inflation has gone up over the last two years and if it stays high, well, you know, it won't be so cheap.

L: I know, but it's still a big difference, no?

A: Yeah, maybe, but anyway, in the end, I miss my family and friends and maybe money isn't so important, but I'll still have more opportunities back home, I think, so work might be more interesting there.

L: I guess so. It seems a shame, though. It's so nice here. Won't you miss the heat?

A: Yeah, probably, but I don't mind the cold weather so much. You get used to it after a while.

L: Mmm.

A: So what about your country? How are things there? Is it a good place to live?

▶ TRACK 91

The lawyer continued reading. It seemed Dad had actually been a good salesman. He earned quite a good salary, but he just preferred to save it. And he had been good at investing money too. The most expensive technology he had was a radio, but he bought shares in some camera and electronic shops. In 1965, the shares cost eight pence each and he sold them 35 years later for £4.12 each.

Of the 2.7 million pounds he was leaving, he had decided to give two million to a charity that looked after teenagers with problems. The rest was divided between me and my sisters.

For a moment, I felt angry. Why hadn't he said anything? Why had we lived like poor people? Why was he giving the money to other children? But then I thought, it's stupid to think like that. Really, I had a happy childhood and I'm very happy now. I remembered my parents reading us books they'd borrowed from the library and the hours we played cards together. It was fantastic what my parents had done. The love we had was more important than money, but now maybe the money they saved can bring some love to others.

The only problem I have now is what to do with a quarter of a million pounds – when I honestly don't really need anything!

▶ TRACK 92

1. Two million pounds
2. Seven hundred and eighty-one thousand
3. Six hundred and fifty-three
4. Nineteen sixty-five
5. Four pounds twelve
6. Two point seven
7. A quarter

▶ TRACK 93

1. The minimum wage at that time was five pounds seventy-three an hour.
2. Inflation fell to three point four per cent last month.
3. The government is going to invest seven hundred million in schools.
4. Three-quarters of the population own a car.
5. The new factory will create eight hundred and twenty-five jobs.
6. The house cost three hundred and sixty thousand euros.
7. We borrowed a hundred and ninety-four thousand from the bank.
8. We'll finally pay back the mortgage in twenty fifty-one.

▶ TRACK 94

1

A: Yes, Sir?

B: Can we get the bill, please?

A: Certainly. One moment.

B: Thanks.

C: How much is it?

B: Don't worry. I'll get this. It's my treat.

C: Are you sure? I don't mind paying half.

B: No, really. It's fine. After all, I asked you out.

C: Thanks. It's really kind of you.

B: Oh no!

C: What's up?

B: I've just realised I left my wallet in my other jacket. It's got all my credit cards and cash in it! I'll have to go and get it.

C: Don't be silly. It's too far to go. I'll pay today.

B: Are you sure? I'll pay you back as soon as I can, I promise.

C: No, it's fine. Honestly. Oh! Wow! Right. That's a lot! I hope they accept my credit card!

2

D: That looks great on you.

E: Really?

D: Yeah. Really suits you.

E: Maybe. How much is it?

D: Well, it's vintage sixties.

E: Sorry?

D: It's very old. From the nineteen sixties. It's hard to find things like that in this condition.

E: Oh. Yes. So how much?

D: Let's call it 200.

E: Pounds?

D: Yes, of course pounds.

E: Two hundred pounds! But it's not in perfect condition. Look – there's a mark here.

D: OK. So let's say 180.

E: No, sorry. It's too much. Thank you.

D: OK, OK. The best price I can manage is 150. Any lower than that and I'll lose money.

3

F: But if I don't buy it, someone else will.

G: So you've said, but a thousand pounds is a thousand pounds.

F: I know, but if I don't have a car, then I'll have to keep getting the bus into town. And that's not cheap either. Fares have just gone up.

G: OK, OK. Look, you did well in your exams and we'd be happy to help, but it is a lot of money. You're working now, so why don't you pay half?

F: I would if I could, Mum, honestly, but I haven't managed to save much yet!

G: Well, maybe we can borrow some money from the bank.

F: Really? Oh, that'd be brilliant!

G: And you can pay us half back when you have the money, OK?

4

H: Your card was cancelled because of some irregular activity that we noticed.

I: Irregular activity? What do you mean?

H: Well, for instance, did you have lunch in Singapore last week?

I: No. I've never been there in my life.

H: Exactly. We suspect that your card was copied sometime last month and that someone then used it overseas.

I: Oh no! How did they manage to do that? And will I get a refund?

H: Everything is covered by your insurance and we're sending out a new card today. You'll receive your new PIN number after you get the card. They're sent separately for security reasons.

▶ TRACK 95

/ɪ/, /ɔɪ/, /ə/, /əʊ/, /rəʊ/, /ləʊ/, /rɪdʒ/, /gɪdʒ/, /rəns/, /ʃən/, /dʃɔɪ/, /plɔɪ/

▶ TRACK 96

1 What's the average salary?

2 Can I borrow fifteen euros?

3 I don't know what the local currency is.

4 They won't win the election.

5 It was a joint decision to go.

6 The interest on our mortgage is low.

7 Thanks. I owe you a favour.

8 Youth unemployment is almost 50%.

UNIT 16

▶ TRACK 97

1

A: Did you have a nice weekend?

B: Yes, it was great, actually.

A: Yeah? What did you do?

B: One of my oldest friends got married on Saturday, so I went to the wedding in the afternoon and then the reception later on. It was really good.

A: Oh yeah?

B: Yeah. They hired an old castle on the coast for it. It was an amazing venue. And they had a big buffet there, with really good food, and a DJ and everything.

A: That sounds great. What was the music like?

B: Excellent. I was expecting typical wedding reception music, but this DJ played lots of modern things as well. The dance floor was full all evening.

2

C: Did you do anything last night?

D: Yeah, I did, actually. I went to a friend's house-warming. She's just moved into this new place. It's an amazing flat – in a converted church. It's a really impressive place.

C: Oh, wow! So what was the party like? Was it good?

D: It was great to begin with, yeah. All the other guests were lovely. Everyone was really warm and friendly and very easy to talk to, but then my ex arrived with his new girlfriend.

C: Oh no!

D: Yes, and to make things worse, she was absolutely gorgeous!

C: Oh, you poor thing! That's awful.

D: I know. It ruined the night for me, to be honest. I didn't stay much longer after that.

3

E: So what did you do last night? Anything interesting?

F: Yeah, I had a little dinner party.

E: Oh really? What was the occasion?

F: There wasn't one. I just felt like inviting some friends round and cooking for them.

E: Nice. So how did it go? Was it good?

F: Yeah, it was lovely. It was nice to see people and chat.

E: How many people came?

F: Twelve.

E: Wow! That's a lot of cooking.

F: I know! It took me ages to get everything ready.

E: Did you cook everything yourself?

E: Yeah.

F: You must be a good cook.

E: I don't know about that! I just follow recipes.

F: So what did you do?

E: Well, for starters, I did grilled aubergines covered in yoghurt and served with a slightly spicy sauce and then ...

► TRACK 98

1 We call April the 21st Kartini Day. It's the day that Raden Ajeng Kartini was born in 1879. She's very important in Indonesia because she fought for women's rights and against sexual discrimination at a time when we were very much second-class citizens. She set up the country's first all-girls school and really helped to change the country for the better. There's still some way to go, sure, but it's important to remember her life and celebrate it every year.

2 My great-grandmother on my mum's side was Ukrainian. We never met, as she died before I was born, but a few years ago my mum and I decided to go on a trip to the village that she came from. We spent a night in the house she'd been born in, which was very moving. The people were very welcoming and I felt a real connection with the place. It was incredible – a day I'll never forget.

3 June the 25th will always be a very special day for me as it's the anniversary of the day that Michael Jackson died. His death in 2009 was a real tragedy and I still feel his loss today. I know he was a controversial figure, but he touched the lives of millions of people all over the world. One of my biggest regrets is that I wasn't able to go to Los Angeles for his memorial service. I wanted to be there, but I just couldn't afford to buy a ticket from Bulgaria.

4 When I was 23 or 24, I spent six months travelling round South East Asia. It was an amazing time in my life and I had lots of great experiences, but perhaps the day I remember best was when I climbed Mount Kinabalu in Malaysia, one of the highest mountains in the region. We started climbing at midnight, with a local guide, and we reached the peak just as the sun was coming up. It was incredibly beautiful.

5 March the 24th is a very special day for me as it's the anniversary of the day that my sight was restored. Thirteen years ago, my eyes were severely damaged in an accident at work and I was told I'd never see again. However, two years ago, I agreed to have this special new operation. It was still in the experimental stage, but amazingly, it worked, and thanks to my surgeon, I can now see my two kids. I'll always be grateful for that!

► TRACK 99

/graʊ/, /klɪə/, /skrɪ/, /stæ/, /blɪ/, /fre/, /pre/, /spaɪ/, /trə/, /aʊnd/, /end/, /əsts/

► TRACK 100

1 They played some nice background music.
2 The DJ almost cleared the dance floor.
3 Women still face a lot of discrimination in the workplace.
4 A new government was established after the war.
5 On my birthday, I had some friends round for dinner.
6 The organisation of the whole event was very impressive.
7 I cooked my special spicy chicken dish.
8 You should try the traditional breakfasts here.

► TRACK 101

1 To be honest, I avoid talking to him if I can help it.
2 I guess it'll take some time before I get used to it.
3 He's a computer programmer based in the States.
4 I'm going to go back as soon as I save enough money.
5 He always promises to help, but then he fails to keep all his promises.
6 I'm currently living at home, but I'm planning to leave after I graduate.

WORKBOOK

CAROL NUTTALL AND DAVID EVANS

PRE-INTERMEDIATE

OUTCOMES

CONTENTS

VOCABULARY
Illnesses and health problems

1 Read the clues. Then write the health problems in the grid.

ACROSS →
1 When body heat is higher than normal (11)
5 When blood runs from your nose (9)
6 A pain, when you can't swallow or speak easily (4, 6)
8 A negative reaction of the body to something that is normally harmless (7)
9 A sore head (8)

DOWN ↓
2 When your stomach hurts and you feel sick (12)
3 An allergy which appears in springtime, rather like a bad cold (3, 5)
4 An illness with a high fever, aching body, cold, etc. (3)
7 A medical condition that makes it difficult to breathe (6)

2 Choose the correct verb in each sentence.
1 When I get hay fever, my eyes *wash / water* all the time.
2 I've got a sore throat and I can't *sneeze / swallow*.
3 I feel hot and cold and I'm *sweating / swallowing* a lot.
4 If I go near a cat, I start *sneezing / hurting* and I can't breathe.
5 I've lost my appetite and my whole body *coughs / aches*.
6 I get these awful headaches that sometimes *last / make* up to an hour!
7 The pain's so bad that I can't *concentrate / swallow* on my work.
8 Have you got any throat sweets? My throat hurts when I *sweat / cough*.

GRAMMAR Giving advice
(*should, ought to, why don't you*)

3 Choose the correct phrase – *why don't you, ought to* or *should* – to complete the sentences.
1 A: I've got a bad back.
   B: I don't think you .... lift that heavy box, then.
2 Look, you've been working all day. .... take a break?
3 I know you don't want to upset him, but you .... tell him how you feel.
4 A: Ow! I've cut myself!
   B: You .... put a plaster on that.
5 What .... I do about my nosebleed? It won't stop!
6 .... put some lavender oil on that burn? It's good for the pain, and helps it get better.
7 You .... go to the doctor's about that rash. You've had it for a week now.
8 You .... complain! You've waited an hour for your soup.

Language note

1 *Should, ought to* and *why don't you* are all fairly polite ways of giving advice, but *should* and *ought to* are slightly more forceful. The speaker is certain that this is what the other person should do, e.g. *You ought to finish your work before you leave.*

2 *Why don't you* introduces a more gentle suggestion, as a possibility, e.g. *If you're worried, why don't you talk to the teacher about it?*

---

4 Correct the mistakes in the following sentences.
1 I think you shouldn't come to work if you're not well.
2 Maybe you should to put something on that cut.
3 He's got an awful cough. He oughts to stop smoking!
4 Katie looks awful! Why not you take her to see the doctor?
5 You ought stay in bed with that high temperature.
6 You don't ought eat chocolate when you've got an upset stomach.

DEVELOPING CONVERSATIONS
Common questions about illness

5 **Complete the conversations with the questions in the box.**

> Are you OK?
> Are you taking anything for it?
> Have you been to the doctor's about it?

1 A: .... ?
   B: No, not really. I've got an upset stomach.

2 A: .... ?
   B: No, not yet. I've got an appointment tomorrow, and I'll see what she says.

3 A: .... ?
   B: Well, I'm taking these tablets, but they make me sleepy.

4 A: .... ?
   B: Yes, I went this morning, and she told me to get some rest.

5 A: .... ?
   B: No, I'm not. I've had this terrible headache all morning.

6 A: .... ?
   B: Well, I've got this cough mixture and some throat sweets.

6 **Match the conversations (1–6) with the correct advice (a–f).**

1 A: So what did the doctor say about your hay fever?
   B: ....

2 A: Good news. My leg isn't broken! But it really hurts.
   B: Fantastic! So what did the doctor say?
   A: ....

3 A: What did the doctor say about the rash on your arm?
   B: ....

4 A: So, did the doctor say you weigh too much?
   B: Yes, she did! No surprise to me.
   A: And what advice did she give you?
   B: ....

5 A: What did the doctor tell you to do about your upset stomach?
   B: ....

6 A: The doctor told me my cough's got worse.
   B: Really? And what did she tell you to do about it?
   A: ....

a 'You should go to bed, drink lots of water and eat nothing but rice with some lemon in it.'

b 'Why don't you start jogging?'

c 'Why don't you take some throat sweets and gargle with salt water three times a day?'

d 'You ought to take it easy, put your leg up and rest for a few days.'

e 'You should take these tablets, and put some drops in your eyes three times a day.'

f 'You should wear cotton clothes and use this cream three times a day.'

LISTENING

7 🔊 **9.1 You are going to hear two conversations. In each case, one speaker has a problem. Listen, and decide what problem they have.**

1 ....
2 ....

8 **What advice does the other speaker give them?**

1 ....
2 ....

9 **In conversation 2, what does the man tell the woman to do at the end?**

....

10 **Match each conversation with one of the pictures.**

LISTENING

1 The child in the photo has Down's Syndrome (DS).
How much do you know about DS? Tick (✓) the best answer
to complete the sentences.
1 DS is:
  a mental illness
  b a condition babies are born with
  c a disease.
2 People with DS:
  a are usually physically disabled
  b cannot speak
  c can learn to read and write.
3 People with DS:
  a never have learning difficulties
  b have learning difficulties
  c sometimes have learning difficulties.
4 Many people with the condition lead:
  a active, semi-independent lives
  b inactive, dependent lives
  c inactive, semi-dependent lives.

2 🎧 9.2 Listen to the first part of an interview with a doctor talking
about people with DS and check your answers.

3 Read the statements and tick (✓) the sentences that are true.
Listen and check your answers.
1 In the UK one in every 1,000 babies is born with DS.
2 The general public now understands a lot about this condition.
3 DS occurs after a child is born.
4 A person with DS does not suffer from the condition.
5 People with DS are unable to play team games.
6 There are three football teams for children with DS.

4 🎧 9.3 In part two of the interview Dr Aziz talks about a woman
with DS who has done a lot in her life. Complete these notes as
you listen.
Ruth Cromer is an example of someone with DS who attended
¹..................... .
She succeeded in learning to ²..................... , and taught herself to
³..................... .
She became ⁴..................... , and has appeared on TV several times.
She also writes articles and gives ⁵.................... about DS.

VOCABULARY Phrases with *mind* and *matter*

5 Complete the conversations with the phrases in
the box.

it's a question of mind over matter
what's the matter? ·   I don't mind
it doesn't matter   never mind
to make matters worse   you don't mind
would you mind ·   I've got a lot on my mind
that's a matter of opinion

1 A: You look upset! ....?
   B: Oh, what with problems at work, and Kate not
      doing well at school, I guess ....
2 A: I know you're busy, but ....
      helping me with these bags? It'll only take a minute.
   B: Sure, no problem.
3 S: Do you want me to take you to the station, Val?
   V: Oh, that's kind of you, Sven. Are you sure
      ....?
   S: You know me, Val. .... helping a
      lady!
4 H: So, I have to go through my presentation again,
      and improve it. ...., I've lost
      some of my notes, and will have to start again.
   K: .... At least you won't look an
      idiot in front of the client.
   H: .... I'm not sure I'll be able to
      make a better job of it. I thought my ideas were OK.
5 C: Georges! So sorry we're late! The traffic was awful!
   G: .... because Ken and Gitty have
      only just arrived.
6 I: I can't do it, doctor! I hate needles!
   D: There's nothing to worry about, Ivan.
      ....

6 Match the sentences (1–6) with the responses (a–i).
There are more responses than you need.
1 How can you take that medicine? It tastes awful!
2 Would you like some help there?
3 That's a terrible cough you've got.
4 It's easy to become a vegetarian.
5 You look stressed. What's the matter?
6 I completely forgot your birthday!
  a That's a matter of opinion. I'm not sure I could
     stop eating meat.
  b Never mind. It's not difficult.
  c It doesn't matter. I didn't do much, anyway.
  d To make matters worse, I've got a temperature, too.
  e I don't mind doing it.
  f It's a question of mind over matter.
  g I've got a lot on my mind, and I'm exhausted.
  h Would you mind eating a salad?
  i If you're sure you don't mind.

PRONUNCIATION

7 **Underline** the stress on these words.

central   musical   industrial   physical
unbelievable   enjoyable   reliable   curable

8 ◈ **9.4** Listen and check your answers. Notice that the last syllable in each word is unstressed.

9 ◈ **9.5** Practise saying these sentences. Then listen and repeat.
1. The flat is really central.
2. Most kids are pretty musical.
3. That part of town is really industrial.
4. Rugby's a very physical game.
5. That's unbelievable!
6. The course was enjoyable.
7. The cars they make are very reliable.
8. A lot of diseases are curable.

DEVELOPING WRITING A webpage – fundraising

Language note

A *charity* is an organisation which collects money to help people or projects that need support, e.g. UNICEF, WWF, etc.
To *raise money for charity* is to do something in order to collect money for a particular organisation, e.g. *Andre is going to cycle from London to Paris to raise money for Greenpeace.* This is also known as *fundraising*.

10 Read the fundraising webpage and answer the questions.
1. What is Marianna going to raise money for?
   ....
2. Why is she raising money for this charity?
   ....
3. What is she going to do?
   ....
4. How much money is she hoping to raise?
   ....

11 Match the headings (1–6) to the parts of the webpage (a–f).
1. What I am going to do   ....
2. How much money I'm hoping to raise   ....
3. Why I'm interested in helping this charity   ....
4. Thanks   ....
5. Information about the health problem   ....
6. How much money I've raised until now   ....

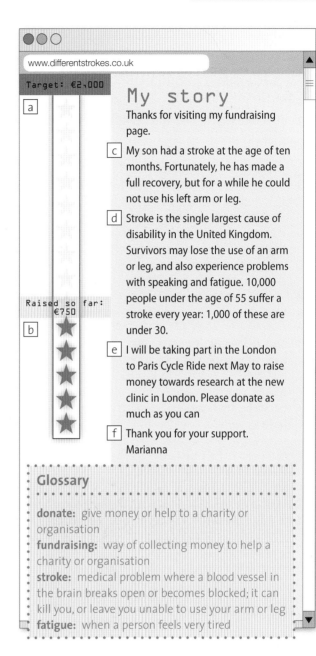

www.differentstrokes.co.uk

Target: €2,000

[a]

Raised so far: €750

[b] ★ ★ ★ ★ ★

My story
Thanks for visiting my fundraising page.

[c] My son had a stroke at the age of ten months. Fortunately, he has made a full recovery, but for a while he could not use his left arm or leg.

[d] Stroke is the single largest cause of disability in the United Kingdom. Survivors may lose the use of an arm or leg, and also experience problems with speaking and fatigue. 10,000 people under the age of 55 suffer a stroke every year: 1,000 of these are under 30.

[e] I will be taking part in the London to Paris Cycle Ride next May to raise money towards research at the new clinic in London. Please donate as much as you can

[f] Thank you for your support.
Marianna

Glossary

donate: give money or help to a charity or organisation
fundraising: way of collecting money to help a charity or organisation
stroke: medical problem where a blood vessel in the brain breaks open or becomes blocked; it can kill you, or leave you unable to use your arm or leg
fatigue: when a person feels very tired

12 Raoul has decided to do something to raise money for the charity Speakability. He is going to write a fundraising webpage, and has written some notes. Read Raoul's notes and write a webpage like Marianna's above.

1. Target: to raise €5,000
2. My reason for helping: accident in 2005, head injury, aphasia for two years. Speakability helped me speak again
3. Charity: Speakability UK.
4. Description: they help people who cannot speak, read or write after suffering a stroke, head injury, etc. Medical name for this problem — aphasia
5. What I'm going to do: walk from Edinburgh to Brighton

VOCABULARY Parts of the body

1 Complete the sentences with one of the words from the box.

| legs   face   stomach   feet   finger   lips   ear   hair |

1 After working on the computer for four hours, he went for a walk
  to stretch his ....
2 Tom threw the ball at me and it hit me in the .... My
  nose and mouth are still sore!
3 I hurt my hand playing volleyball, and I can't get my ring off my
  .... !
4 She's got really long, blond ....
5 Wear sunglasses when you ski and don't forget your ....
  can crack from the dry wind, so put sun protection on them.
6 While we were boxing, Jorge hit me on the left side of my head
  and my .... 's all red now!
7 You shouldn't swim on a full .... , so don't go after lunch.
8 Peter, your .... smell after wearing those football boots!

2 Choose the words or phrases that are not used in English.
1 have a black eye / an eyeball / eye hair / have good eyesight
2 hair style / yellow hair / a hairdryer / a hairdresser
3 broken arm / armband / armchair / armstand
4 backache / back arm / backside / back pain / back bone
5 have a mouthful / mouthwash / mouth ache / have a sore mouth

GRAMMAR Imperatives

**3 Complete the sentences with the imperative of one of the verbs
in the box. Make them negative where necessary.**

| eat   leave   drink   take   let   put   touch   call |

1 If you're not sure, ... the doctor.
2 .... the milk bottle back in the fridge after breakfast.
3 .... your shoes there! Someone will fall over them! Put
  them in the cupboard.
4 It says you should take these after a meal, so ....
  something first.
5 .... more than four tablets a day.
6 Here! You've got a bad back. .... me take those bags.
7 .... this juice, Katie. Go on, it's good for you.
8 .... that iron! It's hot! You'll burn yourself!

4 Match the sentences (1–8) in exercise 3 with their function (a–f) .
a encouragement   ....   d instruction   ....
b order   ....   e offer   ....
c warning   ....   f advice   ....

Language note

We use the imperative more frequently when we are giving advice
or instructions to friends and family.
We don't use the imperative in formal situations. We use the
more polite form of *should, ought to* and *why don't you*.

**5 You are the doctor looking at the people in the
picture. You have just walked into the waiting room.
Tell your patients what to do. Use the phrases below
to help you, and use negative forms where necessary.**

| eat   go to bed   put on some cream |
| take some painkillers   drink hot drinks and fruit juice |

1 ....
2 ....
3 ....
4 ....
5 ....

READING

**6 Read the webpage opposite, and match the three
types of therapy with the photographs.**

1 ....   2 ....   3 ....

**7 Match the words in bold in the text with their
meaning below.**
1 move your hand over a part of your
  body, pressing down slightly   ....
2 machine that heats a room in a house   ....
3 wash your mouth and throat with
  a liquid, without swallowing it   ....
4 methods for curing a health problem   ....
5 place a mixture over heat   ....
6 gas rising from hot water   ....
7 signs of an illness   ....
8 a small living thing that causes an
  illness that can be passed to other people ....

8 Read the text again. Which remedy / remedies …

1 fights the virus? ....
2 fight the symptoms? ....
3 do you swallow? ....
4 advise you to rub part of your body? ....
5 helps stop the virus affecting other people? ....

Holistic Health Answers Your Questions

Q Can you give me some advice about alternative remedies for the flu?

A There are several ways to treat the flu. The best method is to take echinacea as soon as you feel slightly unwell. This will stop the **virus** from developing. If the **symptoms** have already appeared, then you should try one or more of the following remedies.

a) Aromatherapy for colds and flu

Several essential oils help fight the virus. Mix basil, eucalyptus and pine in some almond oil and **rub** it on your chest to clear your blocked nose. If you have a chesty cough, put some basil, pine and tea tree in a bowl of hot water and breathe in the **steam**. Don't do this if you suffer from asthma. If you have a sore throat, try putting one drop of tea tree and one drop of lemon in a small glass of water and **gargle**. Don't swallow it, though! For children, you should add some honey. Finally, **burn** a mixture of the oils to keep the home atmosphere healthy, and stop other family members catching the virus. At night, place a slightly wet towel on the **radiator** in each bedroom, and put two drops of eucalyptus and tea tree on it. This helps sleepers' noses stay clear.

b) Nutrition for flu and colds

For a couple of days, you should swallow only liquids – water, juices, teas and soups. Freshly made juices and homemade soups are the most effective **remedy** for flu symptoms. Make chicken and rice soup, and add some garlic and ginger. Freshly-made fruit juice also helps lower a high temperature. Drink at least six to eight glasses of liquid a day, to make it easier for the body to fight the virus. Don't drink milk because it blocks the nose.

c) Hydrotherapy for flu

As well as following the advice above, why don't you take hot baths, or hot foot-baths followed by a 'cold mitten rub'? Keep your feet warm at all times. To warm your feet, sit them in a hot mustard bath for five to ten minutes. Put one large spoonful of mustard powder in four cups of hot water. After a hot bath, try the cold mitten rub. Wet a small towel or washcloth with cold water. Wrap this round your hand and rub your other arm hard, beginning with the fingers and finishing at the shoulder. Do this again, and then dry your arm with the towel. Repeat the action on your other arm, and then do your legs, feet and body.

Glossary

holistic health: health advice that includes diet and exercise as well as helping the particular health problem

alternative (medicine, therapy, treatment, remedy, etc.): different forms of treating health problems, which use plants, diet, massage, etc.

mitten: a kind of glove that covers the whole hand

Vocabulary Builder Quiz 9

Download the Vocabulary Builder for Unit 9 and try the quiz below. Write your answers in your notebook. Then check them and record your score.

1 Complete the sentences with the correct form of the word in CAPITALS.

1 I get .... easily. ANXIETY
2 His behaviour was not .... ! ACCEPT
3 She is physically .... DISABILITY
4 They're a very .... family. RELIGION
5 I want to learn more about Ivan's .... background. CULTURE
6 She felt .... after he left her. DEPRESSION
7 Thank you for your .... gift. GENEROSITY

2 Correct the errors in the collocations.

1 I ate some shellfish and now I've got a sad stomach.
2 Take a deep muscle through your nose.
3 She's made a speedy diarrhoea from the flu.
4 He broke out in a burn after touching the cat.
5 I lost my breath after shouting so much at the match.

3 Decide whether the statements are true (T) or false (F).

1 A *dose* of medicine is the amount you take. ....
2 If an injury *heals*, it gets worse. ....
3 If you *exceed* the correct amount of medicine, you take too much. ....
4 An *operation* is a kind of medicine. ....
5 A *prescription* is when your body is very hot. ....
6 A *scar* is a mark on your skin from an old wound or injury. ....
7 You have a *physical* disability when part of your mind does not work properly. ....

4 Cross out the word that does not form a collocation with the key word.

1 healthy / put on an / lose your / work up an appetite
2 head / back / throat / stomach ache
3 wise / severe / bouts of / mild depression
4 have a bad / bite my / a pain in my lower / flat on my back
5 emotional / allergic / first / back reaction
6 take a deep / hold your / suffer from / get out of breath

Score ___/25

Wait a couple of weeks and try the quiz again. Compare your scores.

10 PLACES TO STAY

VOCABULARY Places to stay

1 Make collocations with words from box A and box B.

A	
babysitting	provide
basic	put up
free	real
heated	reduced
including	share
low	shower

B	
fire	breakfast
a room	service
meals	rate
season	the tent
block	furniture
wi-fi	pool

2 Complete the collocations in the sentences.
1 The room only had basic ...., but it was only €30 a night including ....
2 We put up .... fairly quickly, and then I went to get cleaned up, but the water in the shower .... was cold!
3 It was great! There was a heated ...., which the kids spent all day in, and also a babysitting ...., so we were able to get out on our own a couple of nights.
4 They gave us the room at a reduced ...., as it was low ...., but I thought it was still quite expensive.
5 It had a huge double bed and a real ...., and with room service providing ...., we never left the room all weekend!
6 Well, six of us had to share .... in the hostel, but it was clean, and there was free ...., which was a nice surprise!

3 Circle the word in *italics* which does not normally collocate with the key word. Use a dictionary to help you.
1 service — *room / babysitting / low / self*
2 provide — *meals / price / help / information*
3 room — *double / tent / single / service*
4 tent — *put up / leave / take down / pitch*
5 season — *high / free / holiday / low*
6 block — *shower / apartment / campsite / office*

LISTENING

4 ✿ 10.1 You are going to listen to four people talking about the type of holiday accommodation they prefer. Listen and match two of the speakers with the photographs A and B. Write the type of accommodation the other two speakers mention.
Speaker 1: ....
Speaker 2: ....
Speaker 3: ....
Speaker 4: ....

A – a hostel

B – an apartment block.

5 ✿ 10.1 Listen again and complete the sentences with phrases that you hear.
1 Speaker 1 says the .... in his type of accommodation helps him to really relax.
2 He also likes having .... so that he can keep in touch with the office if necessary.
3 Speaker 2 likes the freedom from a .... so that she can get up when she wants.
4 She also likes going on holiday in the ...., as it's quieter.
5 Speaker 3 likes to know how many people she will .... with before she goes to her type of accommodation.
6 She also checks .... before deciding where to go.
7 Speaker 4 likes having facilities such as a .... where he goes, because he has children.
8 He also likes the fact that the place .... and so he doesn't always have to cook.

DEVELOPING CONVERSATIONS
Apologising

6 Answer the following questions with *I'm afraid so* or *I'm afraid not*.
1 Do you have a babysitting service?
....
2 Is it necessary to book in advance?
....
3 Can we order meals in our room?
....
4 Is there a cancellation fee?
....
5 Do you allow dogs?
....
6 Do we have to pay for the mirror we broke?
....

7 Answer the following questions. Begin with _I'm afraid_, and use the words in brackets to help you.

1 Do you take Visa?
I'm afraid ....
(not accept credit cards / but / can pay by cheque).

2 Do you have any rooms available from the 12th to the 15th of this month?
I'm afraid ....
(fully booked / until / end of month)

3 Where can I park my car?
I'm afraid ....
have to park / car park / down the road)

4 Is this the only room you have available?
I'm afraid ....
(wedding party / tomorrow evening / all guests / stay in hotel)

5 Do you have a pool?
I'm afraid ....
(yes / closed for repairs)

6 Can I book theatre tickets through the hotel?
I'm afraid ....
(not have / enough staff)

DEVELOPING WRITING
An online booking form

8 Read the hotel online booking form and answer the questions.

1 Who is making the booking enquiry? ....
2 Where do they want to go? ....
3 How many people are going? ....
4 When do they want to go? ....
5 How long do they want to stay? ....
6 Are they having a celebration? If so, for which occasion?
....
7 Will they get any discount? If so, what for?
....
8 Can they take their dog? ....

9 Match the words (1–8) with their definitions (a–h).

1 guest house
2 nights
3 rooms
4 type
5 board
6 your details
7 booking information
8 pets not allowed

a how many nights you want to stay
b kind of accommodation: bed and breakfast, or bed and two meals, etc.
c we do not accept animals in the hotel
d how many rooms you want to book
e special services offered when you book
f kind of room you want: single, double or family room
g small hotel with usually no more than 10 rooms
h the customer's personal information

10 You want to stay at the Willowmere Guest House with your family for the first two weeks of July. Complete the form below.

Booking Enquiry to: Applecote Guest House

arrival	2 Sept 2015	rooms	1
nights	8	type	family
adults	2	board	B&B
children	2		
age of children	16, 9		

Your details
name Jorg Oskarsson
email josk@kambia.com
phone 0046 784 331225

Booking information
Special celebrations:
Son's 16th birthday

Children under 12 pay £10 per night.

Pets not allowed

Booking Enquiry to: Willowmere Guest House

arrival	....	rooms	....
nights	....	type	....
adults	....	board	B&B
children	....		
number of children under 10	....		

Your details
name ....
email ....
phone ....

Booking information
Special celebrations: ....
Children under 10 pay £10 per night.
Dogs are allowed in some rooms – please request at time of booking.

Glossary
B&B: Bed and Breakfast – no other meals are available.

10

VOCABULARY Solving hotel problems

1 Complete the hotel guests' problems with phrases from the box.

noise outside	boiling
no record	more expensive than I expected
no toothbrush or toothpaste	an upset stomach
free for sightseeing	an early flight
get the jacuzzi to work	before you serve breakfast

1 G: Hello. I'm in room 206, and I can't .... I was really looking forward to a hydromassage.

 R: ....

2 G: Reception? This is Mrs. Dobbs here, room 403. The room is .... It's too hot!

 R: ....

3 G: Where should I go? I've only one day ....

 R: ....

4 G: There's .... of my booking, you say? But there must be!

 R: ....

5 G: I've got .... in the morning, and haven't got an alarm clock.

 R: ....

6 G: Excuse me. There's a lot of .... my room, and I can't sleep.

 R: ....

7 G: Erm, hello? I've got .... I must have eaten something.

 R: ....

8 G: Look here! This is .... I thought the bill would be about €230.

 R: ....

9 G: So, you see, we must leave .... , and the kids are sure to be hungry.

 R: ....

10 G: I forgot to pack my toilet bag, and I've got .... Do you have any?

 R: ....

2 Write the receptionist's response (a–j) to the problems in exercise 1.

a Let me have a look, sir, and tell you what it includes.

b I'll send someone up to turn down the heating right away, madam.

c Oh dear! Would you like to change rooms, sir?

d I'm afraid not, madam, but there's a shop next door.

e I could give you a wake-up call and book a taxi for you, sir.

f I'll send someone up to have a look at it immediately.

g I'm afraid I can't help, madam, but there's a chemist down the road. It's open 24/7.

h Don't worry, madam. I can get the cook to make you something to take with you.

i I could recommend a few places, sir, if you'd like.

j Let me check again ... No, I'm afraid there's no booking under the name Howe.

GRAMMAR Second conditionals

3 Put the words into the correct order to make sentences.

1 you first were, a I'd book I if room.

 ....

2 would you if happened do what it to you?

 ....

3 better would be it went home you if.

 ....

4 he listen him might you if called to you.

 ....

5 you think do better would it if left we be?

 ....

4 Make questions. Use the second conditional, and make any other changes necessary.

1 What / you do if / no hot water / your hotel bathroom?

 ....

2 If / I ask / you / marry me / what / you say?

 ....

3 you complain / if / it happen / to you?

 ....

4 If / I order / breakfast in my room / how much / it cost?

 ....

5 you think / I'm crazy / if / I buy / that hotel?

 ....

6 you know / what to do / if / you / on your own?

 ....

Learner tip

Remember to use the second conditional only for imaginary situations, or situations that cannot be changed. Although we use the past tense for this conditional, we are talking about the present or the future.

5 Give advice for the following situations. Begin with *If I were you* ...

1 The hotel breakfast was awful this morning!
If I were you, ...
(complain / chef)

2 There are no clean towels in my room!
....
(ask / maid)

3 I've never been to London before, and I want to book a hotel there.
....
(search / Internet)

4 The waiter in the hotel restaurant was really rude and unfriendly.
....
(complain / head waiter)

5 Our room is filthy, and there are no clean sheets on the bed!
....
(tell / manager)

6 I've checked my bill and they've charged me twice!
....
(ask / refund)

LISTENING

6 💿 **10.2 You are going to listen to three conversations with a hotel receptionist, about a guest's problem. Match the problem with the correct conversation.**

1 a door that won't open ....
2 the need to buy a present ....
3 faulty air conditioning ....

7 💿 **10.2 Listen again and answer the questions.**

1 In which conversation does the receptionist give the guest some advice? ....
2 In which conversation does the receptionist give the guest some instructions? ....
3 Which problem is not solved? ....

8 Complete the sentences.

1 In conversation 1, the receptionist tells Mr Wiseman to .... the air conditioning.
2 Mr Wiseman says he can't .... the switch.
3 He couldn't see it because he'd ....
4 In conversation 2, the problem is urgent because Mr Arnold is .... at a charity dinner.
5 In conversation 3, the man is celebrating his ....
6 The receptionist suggests he buys his wife ....

9 Complete the advice in the following conversations.

1 A: I don't know what to get my wife for her birthday.
   B: If I were you, ... (get / perfume)
2 A: My husband's stuck in the bathroom!
   B: If I were you, ... (call / hotel manager)
3 A: The air conditioning isn't working in my room.
   B: If I were you, ... (change room)
4 A: There's no hot water in my room!
   B: If I were you, ... (ask room service / call a plumber)
5 A: I'm late for an important meeting in the conference room!
   B: If I were you, ... (ask / receptionist / call and explain / problem)
6 A: I don't know where to eat tonight. I'm bored with the hotel dining room.
   B: If I were you .... (ask / receptionist / recommend a restaurant)

10 Put the conversation between the man and his wife in the correct order.

W: OK, I'll phone reception for help. I won't be a minute ... It's all right, Henri. They'll send someone up in a minute. Be patient. ....
M: Aaagh! ... It's no good! It won't move! ....
W: What? OK! I'm coming. Give me two seconds ... Right! You pull, I'll push. ....
M: Just a minute. I'm nearly ready ... Oh wait, Cherise! I can't open the door! ....
W: Right. One, two, three ... go! ....
M: Wait. Just one second ... OK, ready! ....
W: Hurry up, Henri! We're going to be late! ....

READING

1 Read the passage below. Decide where it comes from.
a a travel brochure, advertising holidays in Greece
b a newspaper
c a blog on the Internet

2 Choose the best ending for each sentence.

1 The writer says he didn't travel much as a child because he lived
   a   in the mountains.
   b   in Greece.
   c   by the sea.

2 The writer remembers his childhood holidays as being
   a   adventurous.
   b   good fun.
   c   boring.

3 One reason the family stayed at the same place every year was that
   a   it was on the beach.
   b   the owners didn't mind guests.
   c   dogs were allowed.

4 As a boy, the writer used to find the bouzouki
   a   pleasant.
   b   annoying.
   c   uninteresting.

5 Today the writer
   a   realises the value of such experiences.
   b   appreciates music.
   c   wishes he was still a boy.

Learner tip

Sometimes in reading tasks like the one in exercise 2, more than one option seems possible. Read the text carefully and choose the *best* answer.

PRONUNCIATION

3 Match the <u>underlined</u> vowel sounds to the correct column in the table.

us<u>ua</u>lly	b<u>eau</u>tiful	<u>u</u>ninteresting
s<u>u</u>mmer	s<u>u</u>ntan	<u>u</u>seful
c<u>u</u>te	<u>u</u>sed to	d<u>o</u>ne
<u>u</u>mbrella		

/juː/	/ʌ/

4 ◐ 10.3 Listen and check. Practise saying the words in exercise 3.

5 ◐ 10.4 Listen and practise speaking.

1 Practise saying the telephone numbers.
   0030 2510 36754
   24210 89567
   6979 010259

2 Practise spelling these names.
   Mr Kendall. That's K – E – N – D –A – L – L.
   Mrs Tsiakos. That's T – S – I – A – K – O – S.
   Miss Pandhi. That's P – A – N – D – H – I.

6 ◐ 10.4 Listen again and check.

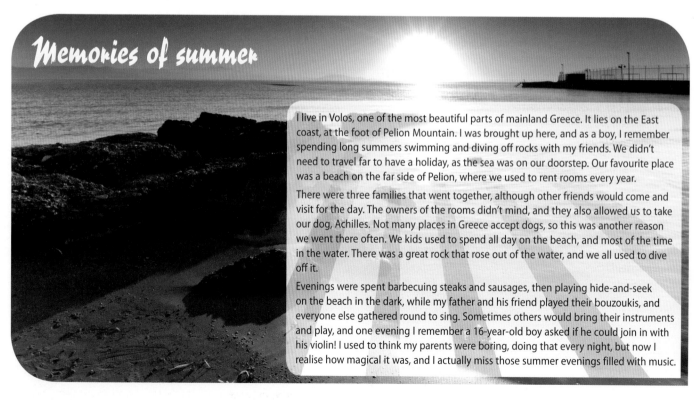

Memories of summer

I live in Volos, one of the most beautiful parts of mainland Greece. It lies on the East coast, at the foot of Pelion Mountain. I was brought up here, and as a boy, I remember spending long summers swimming and diving off rocks with my friends. We didn't need to travel far to have a holiday, as the sea was on our doorstep. Our favourite place was a beach on the far side of Pelion, where we used to rent rooms every year.

There were three families that went together, although other friends would come and visit for the day. The owners of the rooms didn't mind, and they also allowed us to take our dog, Achilles. Not many places in Greece accept dogs, so this was another reason we went there often. We kids used to spend all day on the beach, and most of the time in the water. There was a great rock that rose out of the water, and we all used to dive off it.

Evenings were spent barbecuing steaks and sausages, then playing hide-and-seek on the beach in the dark, while my father and his friend played their bouzoukis, and everyone else gathered round to sing. Sometimes others would bring their instruments and play, and one evening I remember a 16-year-old boy asked if he could join in with his violin! I used to think my parents were boring, doing that every night, but now I realise how magical it was, and I actually miss those summer evenings filled with music.

GRAMMAR *used to*

7 **The sentences a–d are taken from the Reading text.**

1 Which three sentences talk about past habits? ....
....

2 Which sentence talks about a change of opinion? ....

a Our favourite place was a beach on the far side of Pelion, where we used to rent rooms every year.

b There was a great rock that rose out of the water, and we all used to dive off it.

c I used to think my parents were boring, doing that every night, but now I realise how magical it was ...

d We kids used to spend all day on the beach ...

8 **Rewrite the sentences below with *used to*.**

1 When I was young, I walked to school every day.

....

2 When I was a kid, I never went on holiday with my parents, so now family holidays are special to me.

....
....

3 We went to North Wales every summer, until I went to university.

....

4 My dad went fishing with his friend every morning.

....

5 We stayed in the same place every year, so we made lots of friends there.

....

6 I swam in the sea every day of the holidays.

....

9 **Find five mistakes and correct them.**

1 I didn't never used to like singing round camp fires, but I do now.

2 I used to travel abroad with my parents as a boy, so now I enjoy exploring Britain.

3 We use to like going to the outdoor swimming pool.

4 When I was at school, we usually go on skiing trips every February.

5 I didn't use to play much sport, but I'm in a football team now.

6 Last weekend, I used to have to get up early for a hockey tournament.

7 We usually visit my cousins in the summer holidays.

8 Rob used going to summer camp every August.

> **Learner tip**
>
> When you use *used to* in a sentence, it is easy to make mistakes. Always check what you have written!

Vocabulary Builder Quiz 10

Download the Vocabulary Builder for Unit 10 and try the quiz below. Write your answers in your notebook. Then check them and record your score.

1 **Make nouns ending in *-ment* or *-ing* from the verbs in brackets.**

1 Malik goes .... (climb) every weekend.

2 The hotel offers organised .... (entertain) every Tuesday and Thursday.

3 They made an .... (arrange) to meet outside the restaurant.

4 The hotel has a .... (babysit) service.

5 .... (park) facilities are at the back of the cinema.

6 Passing your driving test first time is quite an .... (achieve).

2 **Match the sentence halves.**

1 The hotel's in a convenient ....

2 They could find no record ....

3 On the way, we had a close ....

4 They finally managed to put ....

5 It has an indoor heated ....

6 I'd like to welcome you on ....

7 I have many fond ....

a up the tent after an hour.

b encounter with a bear.

c pool and a gym, too.

d behalf of all the staff of the Kent Hotel.

e location, near the town centre.

f memories of our trip to Tunisia.

g of her booking, so she had to leave.

3 **Decide whether the statements are true (T) or false (F).**

1 A hotel with childcare *facilities* can look after your kids for you. ....

2 If you pay the *standard rate*, you pay the normal amount. ....

3 A *demanding* hotel guest is always happy with the service. ....

4 You *doubt* something when you believe it is true. ....

5 A *chemist's* is a place where you can buy medicine. ....

6 If you *reject* an invitation to dinner, you agree to go. ....

4 **Complete the sentences with the correct form of a verb from the box.**

mess	turn	climb	take	send	warn

1 Don't worry, madam. I'll .... your dog out for a walk.

2 We need to .... people about that awful restaurant.

3 I'll .... someone up to deal with the problem, sir.

4 She had to .... down his invitation as she got sick.

5 The lift wasn't working so we .... the stairs to the fourth floor.

6 The kids .... around by the pool all day.

Score ___/25

**Wait a couple of weeks and try the quiz again.
Compare your scores.**

VOCABULARY Science and nature in the news

1 Match the verbs 1–6 to the phrases they collocate with (a–f).

1	investigate	a	*a new product / an attack / a rocket / an*
2	find		*application*
3	lunch	b	*research / a project / development*
4	spread	c	*news / disease / the word / lies / gossip*
5	conduct	d	*experiments / research / business / an interview*
6	fund	e	*an accident / the effect of something / a crime*
		f	*a cure / a solution / an answer*

2 Choose the correct word in *italics* to complete the sentences.

1   Scientists are working hard to *find / investigate* a cure for the virus.
2   The news soon *launched / spread* that the iPhone 7 was on the market.
3   Is it true that the Yangtze river dolphin has *found / become* extinct?
4   The Government has agreed to *fund / ban* research into an ocean clean up project.
5   When the storm *hit / spread* the small coastal town, the residents were totally unprepared.
6   Scientists and engineers at the CERN Institute spent years *conducting / building* the Large Hadron Collider (LHC).
7   NASA *launched / funded* the New Horizons space probe in 2006, and it reached Pluto in 2015.
8   The space probe will *spread / investigate* the planet Pluto.
9   The council has decided to *hit / ban* all vehicles from the centre of town, in an effort to reduce pollution.
10 Scientists are looking for ways to *conduct / build* experiments without using animals.

3 Complete the collocations in the sentences with the words in the box.

diseases	extinct	science block	research	coast
product	effect	smoking	experiments	cure

1   The company launched its new .... onto the market just in time for Christmas.
2   The Research Centre has banned .... in the building. Employees must go outside.
3   The government should fund .... into the causes of Alzheimer's disease, so that it can be treated.
4   Scientists are conducting .... on chimpanzees to study their behaviour when frightened or angry.
5   We must try harder to save the bees, and stop them from becoming ....
6   Sick pets can sometimes spread .... to people.
7   Scientists are investigating the .... of parents' lifestyle on their children's DNA.
8   Some researchers believe they have found a .... for Parkinson's disease.
9   The forecast said that the storm is going to hit the south .... of England this evening.
10 The university is going to build a new .... next year.

LISTENING

4 🔊 11.1 You are going to hear three news stories. Before you listen, talk to a partner about the cartoons. Then listen and match each story to a picture.

5 🔊 11.1 Listen again and choose the best answer.

1   The first story is about a student who has made a
    a   recycled car.   b   refrigerator.
2   Emily's design uses
    a   electricity.   b   the sun's energy.
3   In the second story, people were worried that Tommy
    a   had had an accident.   b   had run away.
4   Tommy's mother says that she was going to
    a   sell the dogs.   b   lock the garden gate.
5   The weather forecast tells us that heavy rain
    a   fell yesterday.   b   is expected today.
6   Drivers are told to
    a   phone for more   b   stay at home.
        information.

6 Use one of the words from the box to complete each sentence.

invented	shed	energy	recycled	puppy	flooding

1   Three days of heavy rain caused .... in the village of Hartington yesterday.
2   Clara loved her dog when it was a cute little .... but was not so happy when it grew!
3   The plane was .... by Wilbur and Orville Wright in 1903.
4   I've built a .... in the back garden to keep my tools in.
5   20% of this new car is made from .... materials.
6   Turn the lights off. We're trying to save ....

DEVELOPING CONVERSATIONS Responding to news and comments

7 Five of the responses to the sentences below are not correct. Correct them.

1 A: Kate's just had a baby!
　B: Really? That's terrible!
　...

2 A: It's great to hear some good news for a change.
　B: Absolutely!
　...

3 A: Hey! They're testing a new drug to treat cancer and the results are very good.
　B: Really? That's great news!
　...

4 A: They're going to pull down those old buildings by the river and create a park there.
　B: Definitely.
　...

5 A: They should do something about the rubbish outside.
　B: Really? That's awful!
　...

6 A: I've passed my exams! We should celebrate!
　B: Great idea!
　...

7 A: We should take boys' old clothes to the children's home.
　B: Really? That's interesting.
　...

8 A: This article says that goats are really useful animals.
　B: Absolutely!
　...

8 Match the responses below with the gaps in conversations 1 and 2.

| No. So is it going to snow? |
| Really? That's amazing! |
| They should do more |
| Really? That's awful! |
| Maybe we should |

Conversation 1
A: I heard on the radio that a 21-year-old designed a fridge in her grandad's shed.
B: [1] ....
A: Yes, I know. It works without electricity, using the sun. She's shared her idea with people in Africa, and helped to build more out there.
B: [2] .... to help people in Africa.
A: Definitely.

Conversation 2
C: Did you hear the weather forecast for tomorrow?
D: [3] ....
C: No, but there's going to be heavy rain all over this area.
D: [4] ....
C: I know. There are warnings of floods, too. And we're going out for the day!
D: Yeah, well I'm not sure. [5] .... stay at home, and go another day.
C: Yeah, good idea.

PRONUNCIATION Word stress

9 How many syllables do the words below have? Mark the syllable which is stressed.

1 population .... 　2 research .... 　3 invent .... 　4 experiment .... 　5 pollution .... 　6 energy ....

10 Write the words from the box in the correct stress list.

| study | research | population | extinct | energy | experiment | explore | shortage |
| solution | investigate | natural | pollution | participant | invent | resources | protect |

2 syllables, stress on first syllable	2 syllables, stress on second syllable	3 syllables, stress on first syllable	3 syllables, stress on second syllable	4 syllables, stress on second syllable	4 syllables, stress on third syllable

11 ◈ 11.2 Listen and practise saying the words.

VOCABULARY Animals

1 Write the animals from the box below in the correct column. Some animals belong in more than one category.

dog	cat	rabbit	sheep	hen	lion
cow	shark	dolphin	whale	pigeon	horse
parrot	tiger	eagle	panther		

pets	farm animals	marine animals	birds	wild cats

2 Complete the article with words from the box.

dogs	less	bones	ground	workers
success	excited	school		

HERO RATS

Bart Weetjens trains giant rats in Tanzania to find unexploded land mines and bombs in the [1].................. . Weetjens says that rats are better at doing the job than [2]................... because they have a very keen sense of smell, and they don't get as nervous or [3].................. as dogs. Also, they weigh much [4].................. , so they are less likely to cause the mines to explode and be killed.

Weetjens has already had some [5].................. in Africa with his team of rats. They cleared the area round a [6].................. in Mozambique, and made it safe for the children to return to the classroom. At the beginning of the year, they also cleared 5000 m² of land at Pfukwe, after [7].................. bringing electricity to the area had found mines there. During the clearance, the rats discovered 32 unexploded mines, and found the [8].................. of people and animals that had died in the minefield over the years.

Glossary

mine: a type of bomb that is placed in the ground and explodes when someone touches it
bomb: an object made of materials that explode and cause great damage

READING

3 Read the texts. In the table, tick which environmental problems each idea helps to solve.

	magnetic fridge	methane farming	green machine	floating wind turbines
air pollution				
water shortage				
energy resources				

Cool *green* solutions for our **warm** planet

A Magnetic Fridge
Refrigerators and air conditioners eat up more electricity in the home than any other machine. Now there is a new cooling method that works using a system of magnets to make metals cool down. Camfridge, the UK company that is designing this new system, says that its fridges and air conditioners will reduce the use of electrical power by up to 40%.

B Methane Farming
The world's largest biogas factory in Penkun, Germany, makes fuel from animal waste. It produces 84,000 tonnes of the gas methane every year. This natural gas is then used as a fuel which produces enough heat for the 50,000 people who live in the town.

Glossary

biogas: gas that comes from dead plants or animals, or animal waste
fuel: any substance like coal, or gas, that can be burnt to produce heat or energy

4 Which idea(s)

1 reduce the amount of electricity used? ....
2 produce electricity? ....
3 saves water? ....
4 use natural sources of power? ....
5 performs two tasks? ....

5 Match the words (1–5) with the definitions (a–e).

1 magnet   a   a country's national electricity
2 emission   network
3 offshore   b   in the sea
4 float   c   sit on top of water
5 grid   d   a piece of metal which pulls other
                metals towards it
           e   when gases are released into the air

C Green Machine

Washing machines also require a lot of energy, as well as huge amounts of water. Now, a new company called Xeros has developed the world's first 'almost waterless' washing machine. Small magnetic metal balls attract dirt from clothes, and leave them dry. The machine uses 90% less water and 40% less electricity than normal washing and drying machines. If all households in the world change to this machine, annual CO_2 emissions will fall by 28 million tonnes.

D Floating Wind Turbines

At present, most offshore wind turbines stand on a base that is fixed to the sea floor. This means that they can only be placed in shallow water, close to land. However, the strongest winds are often further out at sea, where the water is deep. Norway has solved this problem by developing the world's first floating wind turbine. Hywind floats on the water like a boat, and is anchored ten kilometres off the Norwegian coast. It will begin feeding power into the national electricity grid this month.

GRAMMAR Past perfect simple

6 Underline the actions in the sentences below. Then decide which action happened first and which happened second.

1 The biologist checked the results of the experiment and called his boss.
2 The chemistry student realised she had followed the wrong instructions.
3 Ayodele had already finished his physics exam when the teacher told them there were 30 minutes left.
4 Dr Mukabe looked at the bones and knew she had discovered a dinosaur.
5 Night had fallen by the time they got home from their trip to the Science Museum.

7 Complete the sentences below with the past perfect of the verb in brackets.

1 She decided to leave after she .... the experiment. (finish)
2 When they found the cat, it .... by a car. (be hit)
3 Before he met her, he .... in love. (never be)
4 I suddenly realised I .... to tell Sarah about the party. (forget)
5 They soon learnt that the experiment .... successful. (not be)
6 When police got to the bank, the thieves .... (already leave)
7 The scientist realised that he .... to time his experiment. (forget)
8 Archaeologists studied the skeleton and realised they .... a dinosaur. (discover)

8 Put the verbs in brackets into the past simple or the past perfect simple to complete the article.

200 million year-old skeleton looks like the Loch Ness monster

A young couple have found the remains of a Loch Ness-style creature that [1]................. (live) in the English Channel 200 million years ago. Scientists say that the skeleton, which is 70% complete, belongs to a 12-foot-long plesiosaur. This creature [2]................. (exist) during the Jurassic period of 150 to 200 million years ago, and looked like the Loch Ness monster with its long neck and tail.

Tracey Marler and Chris Moore, who [3]................. (discover) the remains on a beach last week, said that many of the bones were in the correct position when they found them, so they could see what the dinosaur [4]................. (look) like when it was alive. It was also possible to see how it [5]................. (die), said Mr Moore, an expert in fossils. There were teeth marks on some bones from another animal. So it seemed that another creature [6]................. (eat) the plesiosaur.

Scientists are still examining the remains, and it is hoped that the skeleton will go on public display at the Lyme Regis Museum.

GRAMMAR Passives

1 Rewrite the following sentences with the correct form of the passive.

1 Michael Reynolds developed the first earthship in the 1970s.
The first earthship ....

2 People can build earthships from available recycled materials.
Earthships ....

3 They use worn out car tyres to build the external walls.
Worn out car tyres ....

4 They fill the tyres with rammed earth to make the walls.
The tyres ....

5 They built the first earthship in the UK in Fife, in Scotland.
The first earthship ....

6 Could you use glass bottles to build walls?
Could glass bottles .... ?

7 Can you heat the earthships naturally?
Can the earthships .... ?

8 They heat the buildings with solar panels.
The buildings ....

2 Choose the correct phrase (a or b) to complete the sentences.

1 Seven new species of tiny frog .... recently in the Brazilian rainforest.
a were discovered   b discovered

2 Scientists believe that dinosaurs .... about 65 million years ago.
a disappeared   b were disappeared

3 Playing video games can .... people's brain activity.
a improve   b be improved

4 Scientists say that 3D printing can now .... to print human body parts.
a use   b be used

5 Recently, people in southern Australia .... by hundreds of spiders falling from the sky.
a rained on   b were rained on

6 'Spider rain', also known as 'ballooning', is how spiders .... in groups from one place to another.
a move   b are moved

7 There are only five northern white rhinos left in the world. Can they .... ?
a save   b be saved

8 Great white sharks can .... to 15–20 feet (4.6–6.1 metres) long.
a grow   b be grown

DEVELOPING WRITING
An email – expressing an opinion

3 Anagele is a Kenyan student at a college in Brighton. Below is an email he wrote yesterday to his friend at home. Read the email and match the headings below (1–5) to each paragraph (a–e).

1 The weather   ....
2 Closing   ....
3 His flatmate   ....
4 Opening   ....
5 The town   ....

4 We use the words in the box below to connect our ideas. Use them to complete the email.

| but | one thing | although | secondly | however | another |

From   Anagele K
To   kitunzi@gmail.afr
Subject   First impressions of Brighton

a) Hi, Kitunzi!

How are things? I've been in Brighton for two weeks now, and I want to tell you how I'm getting on.

b) The town's really nice. ¹................... I like about it is that it's a holiday town, so there are lots of tourists. This makes it lively. ²................... , there are some great bars and restaurants to go to in the evenings, ³................. they're rather expensive. We usually eat at home, and then just go out for a drink.

c) My flatmate is an Italian guy, called Fabio. He's crazy, but great fun. When we go out, he talks to everyone, so we've already met lots of people. ⁴................. thing I like is my college. The teachers are really enthusiastic, and I'm enjoying the course – except for the homework!

d) The English weather is not so good! Grey skies every day! I haven't seen the sun since I got here! ⁵................. the buildings are comfortable and very warm inside, ⁶................. the dark atmosphere outside sometimes makes me miserable. I really miss the African sun. In general, though, I like it here.

e) Write and tell me how you're getting on.

Bye for now,

Anagele

Language note

Although and *but* connect opposite ideas, such as a good point and a bad point. Look at how they are used in a sentence.

Although I like living in Italy, I don't like the heat in the summer.

I like living in Italy, but I don't like the heat in the summer.

5 Connect the sentences in the pairs below. Use *although, but* or *another thing*.

1 I like most animals. I don't like rats.

....

2 I know that more homes are needed in the city centre. There should be parks.

....

3 Paris is a beautiful city, with wide streets. I like the cafés on street corners with tables outside.

....

4 It's a good thing that governments are talking about climate change. They should do more.

....

5 I like living by the sea. It gets cold in the winter.

....

6 I like sweets. They're not healthy.

....

6 Write an email to a friend in another country. Describe your town, and say what the weather is like there. Think of two things you like, and something that you don't like. Use the words from exercises 4 and 5 to connect your ideas.

Vocabulary Builder Quiz 11

Download the Vocabulary Builder for Unit 11 and try the quiz below. Write your answers in your notebook. Then check them and record your score.

1 Complete the sentences with the correct form of a verb in the box.

investigate	conduct	fund	witness	ban

1 Margot .... a nasty accident outside her home last night.
2 The organisation has agreed to .... research into Alzheimer's.
3 The hospital has .... the use of mobile phones within the building.
4 Scientists are .... experiments to see how people react to the drug.
5 Police are .... the disappearance of a ten-year-old boy.

2 Choose the correct word.
1 Divers stand in a *net / cage* to watch the sharks underwater.
2 Scientists have *suspected / detected* signs of life on Mars.
3 There is not enough *effect / evidence* to arrest the woman for the crime.
4 *Freezing / Windy* temperatures are expected this weekend.
5 Bernard Morin lost his *weight / sight* aged six, but still became a mathematician.

3 Match the sentence halves.
1 I dropped my phone and used sticky
2 Maria G. Mayer was awarded
3 Doctors Without Borders save
4 Taking echinacea can boost
5 This morning they launched

a your health.
b the rocket into space.
c tape to hold it together.
d the Nobel prize for Physics in 1963.
e hundreds of lives in war zones.

4 Complete the sentences with the correct preposition.
1 Anil was witness .... the birth of his twin boys.
2 Magda insisted .... staying for the experiment.
3 They were always nice to each other .... public.
4 The dog barked loudly .... the postman.
5 He appeared .... court as a witness yesterday.

5 Complete the sentences with the correct form of the word in CAPITALS.
1 I .... broke my mother's favourite vase yesterday.   ACCIDENT
2 Ananya talked for an hour about .... problems.   ENVIRONMENT
3 The boy's act of .... made the old woman smile.   KIND
4 She stood up and looked at her classmates ....   CONFIDENT
5 Children need the .... of a loving family.   SECURE

Score ___/25

Wait a couple of weeks and try the quiz again. Compare your scores.

12 ON THE PHONE

VOCABULARY Using phones

1 Choose the correct words to complete the sentences.

1 I'm sorry, he's not here at the moment. Can he call you *through* / *back* later?
2 Can you put me *through* / *off* to the sales department please?
3 The receptionist put me *up* / *on* hold for over ten minutes.
4 I couldn't ask him about his plans because we got cut *up* / *off* in the middle of our conversation.
5 He was really angry with me and hung *back* / *up* before I could explain.
6 She's out of the office today. You could *shout* / *call* her on her mobile.
7 I keep calling them but I can't get through. The line's *busy* / *full*.
8 I don't want to phone him. He talks for hours. It's easier to *text* / *type* him.

2 Choose the correct word to fill the gaps.

coverage	text	signal	busy	line

I've been trying to phone you all morning. The first time I called, the ¹ .... suddenly went dead. The second time it was ² .... Then I couldn't get a ³ .... on my mobile. I don't know why. Maybe there's no ⁴ .... in that area. Anyway, in the end I decided to send you this ⁵ .... message instead.

Language note

Mobile phone (or mobile) is used in British English. In American English, people say cellphone.

DEVELOPING CONVERSATIONS
Explaining where people are

3 Complete the phone conversation with these phrases.

from home	sick	the factory
a meeting	on business	visiting a client

Caller: Could I speak to Ali Khalil, please?
Secretary: I'm afraid he's away ¹ .... He won't be back in the office until Monday now.
Caller: Is Sukhi Pandhi available, then?
Secretary: Certainly. Hold the line, please. No, I'm sorry. She's in ² ....
Caller: OK. How about Vicky Reece?
Secretary: She's off ³ .... today. Would you like to leave a message?
Caller: No, I'd like to speak to someone. Is Mike Jones there, then?
Secretary: One moment, please. I'm afraid he's out ⁴ .... I'm not sure what time he'll be back.
Caller: I don't believe this! What about Rob Downey? Surely he's there?
Secretary: I'm terribly sorry, but he's working ⁵ .... today. Can I help you?
Caller: This is John Carpenter, the managing director! I'm at ⁶ .... and my car's broken down. Is there anyone who can come and pick me up?

4 Write replies to the questions by putting the sentences (a–c) into the right order.

1 Hello. Is that Simon?
   a Simon's not up yet. ....
   b No, it's Joe. ....
   c Is it urgent? ....
2 Hi, is Christine there?
   a She'll be back next week. ....
   b She's away on holiday. ....
   c No, I'm afraid she isn't. ....
3 Hi, Boris?
   a Boris is in a meeting at the moment. ....
   b Can I take a message? ....
   c No, it's Dima actually. ....
4 Hello. Could I speak to Ms. Seidel, please?
   a She'll be back at about 3 o'clock. ....
   b I'm afraid not. ....
   c She's out of the office this morning. ....

5 Match the sentence halves.

1 I'm afraid he's been off	a a meeting at the moment.
2 I'm sorry but she's in	b available right now.
3 I'm afraid that he's just walked out	c of the door.
4 I'm sorry but he's working at	d home today.
5 I'm afraid that he's on	e away from her desk.
6 Unfortunately she's	f sick all week.
7 I'm sorry, he's not	g line's engaged at the moment.
8 Can she call you back? Her	h holiday this week.

LISTENING

6 🔊 **12.1 Listen to the phone conversation and underline the five mistakes in this message.**

> ══════ **MESSAGE** ══════
>
> *Tina Morrison called about your meeting next Tuesday. She's going to be away on holiday that day, so can you change the meeting to Thursday? Two o'clock at her office. If there are any problems, please call her mobile on 08857 678548.*

AN IMPORTANT MESSAGE? OK...YEP... I'M TAKING IT DOWN RIGHT NOW...

SPORTS

RECEPTION

7 🔊 **12.1 Listen again and rewrite the message correctly.**

> ══════ **MESSAGE** ══════
>
> ....
> ....
> ....
> ....
> ....

GRAMMAR *yet, already, still* and *just*

8 **Complete these sentences with *yet, already, still* or *just*.**

1 A: What was that noise?
   B: I think someone has .... dropped a plate.
2 A: Can I see your most recent essay?
   B: I'm sorry, I haven't finished it ....
3 A: Can you write to Mr Hudson to apologise for the mistake?
   B: There's no need. I've .... emailed him.
4 A: Have you managed to get Samira on the phone?
   B: No, I haven't but I'm .... trying.

9 **Use the words in brackets to write answers to these questions, using *yet, already, still* or *just*.**

1 A: What is this terrible mess?
   B: I'm sorry. ....
   (I / spill my coffee)
2 A: Can you phone Mr Thorsen please?
   B: There's no need. ....
   (I / call him)
3 A: Is Anita in the office today?
   B: I don't know. ....
   (I / not see her)
4 A: Has the delivery arrived?
   B: No. ....
   (We / wait for it)
5 A: Have you told them we're going to be late?
   B: No. ....
   (I / not speak to them)
6 A: Where's Roger?
   B: He was here a second ago. I think ....
   ....
   (he / go out for a moment)
7 A: Has she found her mobile phone?
   B: No. ....
   (She / look for it)
8 A: Will you send them an invoice for those goods we sent them?
   B: I don't have to. ....
   (They / pay us)

Language note

Just, still and *already* normally go between the auxiliary and main verbs. *Yet* normally comes at the end of the sentence.

READING

1 Quickly read the article. Tick (✓) the best summary.

a Mobile phone companies are now making big profits from poor people in Africa and Asia.

b The mobile phone is helping poor people to earn money and improve their living conditions.

c Schools are facing serious problems because teenagers are wasting too much time on their mobile phones.

d The spread of the mobile phone is worrying governments in many countries.

How Mobile Phones are Changing the World

1 When mobile phones first appeared in the early 1990s, they were status symbols for wealthy businesspeople. Phones were big and heavy, and the signal was usually poor, so people often shouted when they used them. Over the next ten years, technology improved and prices fell considerably. In many rich countries the mobile phone became the teenager's favourite toy. In just 20 years, mobiles have changed the way people do business and socialise in rich countries. But mobile technology is having a dramatic impact on life in the developing world too.

2 In Africa, arrival of inexpensive mobile phones in areas where there are no landline telephones has already helped many people to start small businesses. Before mobile phones, starting a business often meant renting a shop or an office, which was expensive. If customers called when the owner was out, business was lost. Now business owners can write their mobile number on an advertisement, put it on a noticeboard and wait for customers to call them. As a result, thousands of people can find a market for their goods or services.

3 In India, fishermen now use their mobiles to find the best market for their fish before they return to shore. A few quick calls on their mobile phones can tell them which ports to visit to find the best price for their fish and avoid unnecessary waste.

4 Farmers, too, are using mobile phones. Around the world, new mobile services provide local weather forecasts to help them plan their work. They can also have advice on farming methods and up-to-date information about prices for their crops sent to their mobile.

5 As mobile phones make business easier, they improve living conditions for hundreds of thousands of people around the world. And as they spread, becoming cheaper and more popular, it seems likely that they will change the world in ways that we can't imagine yet.

2 Match the words and phrases (1–8) to their definitions (a–h).

1	status symbol	a	fruit and vegetables produced by a farm
2	socialise	b	big effect
3	dramatic impact	c	poorer countries which are growing economically
4	developing world	d	something which shows you are rich and successful
5	market	e	something that cannot be used.
6	crops	f	the way something is done
7	method	g	meet friends and acquaintances
8	waste	h	a place where things are bought and sold

3 Read paragraph 1 again and answer these questions.

1 When did mobile phones first appear?

....

2 Why did people often shout when they used them?

....

3 What happened to the price of mobiles over the next ten years?

....

4 Whose favourite toy did they become?

....

5 What have mobile phones changed in rich countries?

....

6 Where else are mobile phones having an impact now?

....

4 Read paragraph 2. Decide whether the statements are true (T) or false (F).

1 Mobile phones are very expensive in Africa at the moment. ....
2 Mobile phones have helped many Africans start businesses. ....
3 It has always been cheap to rent shops and offices in Africa. ....
4 Business owners often leave their mobile phone numbers on noticeboards. ....
5 At the moment, mobile phones are only being used to sell services and not goods. ....
6 There are places in Africa where there are no landline telephones. ....

5 Read paragraphs 3 to 5 and complete these sentences.

1 Fishermen in India use their mobiles to find
....
2 This helps them to avoid ....
3 There are now mobile phone services for farmers which provide ....
4 This helps farmers to ....
5 They can also get advice on ....
6 In the future mobiles will change the world in ways
....

VOCABULARY Forming negatives

6 Make negative adjectives using the words in the box. Write them in the correct column.

wise	legal	appropriate	fortunate
polite	happy	expected	practical
fair	comfortable	common	patient
convenient	possible	natural	rational
pleasant			

un-	
im-	
in-	
il-	
ir-	

7 Replace the words in *italics* with negative adjectives from exercise 6.

1 He's been *miserable* since he lost all his money.
....
2 The way you spoke to her was *not suitable*.
....
3 They were *very rude* to the waiter in the restaurant.
....
4 It is *against the law* to park your car outside the Town Hall. ....
5 He was *very unlucky* to fall over and break his leg.
....
6 It is *not clever* to feed animals in a zoo. ....
7 Her father gets *angry easily*. ....
8 I know it's a little *crazy*, but I'm scared of butterflies.
....
9 The result was *not predicted*. ....
10 I'm afraid this is an *awful* time to call, as he's sleeping. ....

PRONUNCIATION Same or different?

8 🔊 12.2 Listen to the underlined vowel sounds in these pairs of words. Decide whether they are the same (S), or different (D).

1 p<u>o</u>lite — p<u>o</u>ssible
2 p<u>o</u>ssible — c<u>o</u>mmon
3 c<u>o</u>mmon — c<u>o</u>mfortable
4 <u>o</u>btain — <u>o</u>pinion
5 h<u>o</u>le — h<u>o</u>ld
6 <u>o</u>peration — rem<u>o</u>te

DEVELOPING WRITING Text and email – abbreviations

1 **Look at the text message and find abbreviations for these words and phrases.**

1	are	....	8	meeting	....
2	as soon as possible	....	9	possible	....
3	documents	....	10	see	....
4	evening	....	11	text	....
5	for	....	12	to	....
6	later	....	13	you	....
7	message	....	14	your	....

From: Brian

Hi Steve. Thanks 4 yr msg. R u coming 2 the meet this eve? If so, can u bring the docs we discussed? Please let me know by txt msg if this is poss asap. C u l8r. Brian

Language note

You don't have to use abbreviations in text messages and there are no rules about how to write them. The abbreviations in this activity are quite common but are not always used.

2 **Read Steve's email reply. Rewrite the text message as an email without abbreviations.**

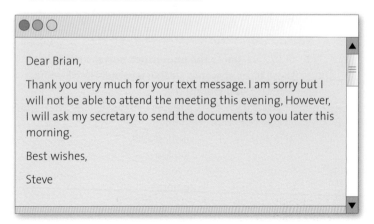

Dear Brian,

Thank you very much for your text message. I am sorry but I will not be able to attend the meeting this evening, However, I will ask my secretary to send the documents to you later this morning.

Best wishes,

Steve

VOCABULARY Reporting crimes

3 **Complete the three phone calls reporting crimes with the correct form of the words from the box.**

steal	make	kick	crash	hack	get	come	kick
grab	text	have	hit	threaten	follow	run	buy

Caller 1: It was horrible! I ¹ .... home from work and discovered that someone had ² .... my front door down. Two guys were in my living room, and they started ³ .... me. They wanted money, but I don't keep any at home. Then one of them just started ⁴ .... and ⁵ .... me for no reason. I screamed for help, but our neighbours were ⁶ .... a party and ⁷ .... a lot of noise, so no one heard me. Suddenly, the other guy ⁸ .... my bag, and they both ⁹ .... off.

Caller 2: I'm not sure how it happened, but I ¹⁰ .... something online last week, and I can only think they ¹¹ .... my bank details from there. Anyway, they ¹² .... into my account, and ¹³ .... €5,000. That's almost all my savings! I need to cancel everything immediately!

Caller 3: I couldn't believe it! This guy asked me the way to the M4, so I told him to ¹⁴ .... me, as I was going that way. Anyway, we came to the junction and he just ¹⁵ .... into the back of my new car! He was ¹⁶ ...., of course, and so didn't see the red light.

LISTENING

4 🔊 **12.3 Listen to the recorded message and answer these questions.**

1 What kind of organisation has the caller phoned?
....
2 How many options are there? ....
3 What can you do if you press 1? ....
4 Which number do you press for technical support?
....
5 Which option does the caller choose? ....
6 How long is the wait time? ....

5 🔊 **12.3 Listen again and complete the sentences. Then listen again and check your answers.**

1 For information about opening ...., press two.
2 Your call .... to us.
3 A member of our dedicated customer services team .... to speak to you shortly.
4 Please note that calls may be recorded for ....
5 Unfortunately we are currently experiencing a .... calls.
6 You may find it .... to call back later.

GRAMMAR Reporting speech

6 Choose the correct verb tense in these sentences reporting speech.

1 I'm helping my friend with her homework.
You said you *helped / were helping* your friend with her homework.

2 I haven't seen the new James Bond movie.
You said you *weren't seeing / hadn't seen* the new James Bond movie.

3 I phoned you twice on Friday.
You said you *have phoned / had phoned* twice on Friday.

4 We're going to the theatre this evening.
You said you *have been going / were going* to the theatre this evening.

5 We've seen them twice this month.
You said you *had seen / have seen* them twice this month.

6 We didn't hear from them yesterday.
You said you *haven't heard / hadn't heard* from them yesterday.

7 Put these sentences into reported speech.

1 Anna posted the letter on Tuesday.
She said Anna ....

2 I'm sending you the books today.
You said you ....

3 We haven't been to the office all day.
You said you ....

4 I didn't bring my notes with me.
You said you ....

5 They haven't delivered the letters yet.
They told us they ....

6 I'm going to the post office right now.
You said you ....

8 Complete the sentences with *said, asked* or *told*.

1 The woman I spoke to .... that there weren't any left in my size.

2 The guy on reception .... me what the reason for my visit was.

3 The secretary .... me he was in a meeting.

4 She .... me if I would like to leave a message.

5 Mr. Stevens .... me to send in my report the next day.

6 He .... it was urgent.

Language note

When you are writing sentences in reported speech, remember to check the personal pronouns. They will sometimes (but not always!) have to change.

Vocabulary Builder Quiz 12

Download the Vocabulary Builder for Unit 12 and try the quiz below. Write your answers in your notebook. Then check them and record your score.

1 Match the sentence halves.

1 Can you confirm ....
2 Certainly, sir. Hold ....
3 One moment and I'll put ....
4 The line's busy. Can she call ....
5 My battery's low. I'll have to ....
6 The signal's poor. We may get ....

a the line, please.   d your password?
b you back?   e cut off.
c hang up.   f you through.

2 Complete the sentences with the correct form of the word in CAPITALS.

1 There's no .... for my mobile in this area.   COVER

2 I've no milk left and the shops are closed.
How ....!   CONVENIENT

3 I accidentally deleted your message.
Can you .... it?   SEND

4 Her decision to leave was ....
I can't understand it.   RATIONAL

5 Your arrival is ....; I thought you were coming tomorrow!   EXPECT

6 He made a good impression ....   INITIAL

3 Decide whether the statements are true (T) or false (F).

1 A *domestic drill* is a household tool.   ....
2 A *fine* is a gap or space in something.   ....
3 If something is *scary*, it is exciting.   ....
4 A *leaflet* is a piece of paper which gives information about something.   ....
5 A *signal* is a small animal with eight legs.   ....
6 If something is *urgent*, it is very important and you need to do it immediately.   ....
7 If you *misuse* something, you use it efficiently.   ....
8 If you are *fair*, you behave well.   ....

4 Complete the sentences with a word from the box.

| continuously threatening campaign transfer relatively |

1 Wait a moment and I'll .... you to the Complaints department.

2 They decided to .... against the use of mobile phones in theatres.

3 I've been calling ...., but I can't get through.

4 Setting up the account was .... easy.

5 He started making .... phone calls, and so she called the police.

Score ___/25

Wait a couple of weeks and try the quiz again.
Compare your scores.

13 CULTURE

VOCABULARY Films

1 Each group of words (1–6) describes a kind of film. Write down the kind of film in the box.

```
1              C
2              I
3              N
4              E
5            M
6              A
```

1 special effects, costumes, space
2 the past, costumes, family, society
3 car chases and explosions, special effects
4 complicated plot, scary, violent
5 funny, laughter, happy ending
6 violent, special effects, kung fu

2 Choose the most suitable word or phrase.
1 A scary, violent film is called *an action / a horror* movie.
2 A science-fiction film usually has a lot of *violence / special effects*.
3 A historical drama is a film that is set in the *past / future*.
4 Romantic comedies are often quite *predictable / scary*. You know what's going to happen in the end.
5 Jackie Chan stars in lots of *war / martial arts* movies set in Hong Kong.
6 Musicals usually have *scary / romantic* plots.

3 Answer the quiz. If you don't know the answer, guess!

LISTENING

4 You are going to hear two people talking about three films. Match the title to the kind of film you think it will be.
1 *Run and Hide*   a drama
2 *The Mansford Saga*   b comedy
3 *Mr Pickles*   c thriller

5 🔊 13.1 Listen and check your answers.

6 🔊 13.1 Listen again. Match the films to the names below.
A *The Mansford Saga*   B *Run and Hide*   C *Mr Pickles*

1 Thierry Dumand   ....
2 Jeffrey Hinds   ....
3 Antonio Torres   ....
4 Catherine Pickard   ....
5 Andreas Dumas   ....
6 Zena Williams   ....

7 Decide whether the statements are true (T) or false (F).
1 Abha is searching the Internet to find out what's on at the cinema.   ....
2 Antonio Torres is the star of *Run and Hide*.   ....
3 Brad has already seen *Run and Hide*.   ....
4 Abha wants to see *The Mansford Saga*.   ....
5 They decide to go and see the Thierry Dumand film.   ....
6 *The Partygoer* is on at the Palace Cinema.   ....

Film Quiz

1 The first proper cinema showing only films opened in ...
A Paris in 1897   B New Orleans in 1902
C Los Angeles in 1895

2 The best-paid actor in 2008 was ...
A Johnny Depp   B Will Smith
C Heath Ledger

3 A historical drama is sometimes called a ...
A costume drama   B effects drama   C hat drama

4 The movie capital of India is called ...
A Hollywood   B Bollywood   C Dollywood

5 The most successful movie in the world until now is ...
A Avatar
B Harry Potter and the Philosopher's Stone
C Casablanca

6 The first films with sound were called ...
A singing movies   B talking movies
C laughing movies

7 The most famous prizes for film actors are called ...
A Homers   B Oscars   C Basils

8 The biggest film industry outside the USA is based in ...
A Egypt   B Brazil   C India

DEVELOPING CONVERSATIONS

supposed to

8 **Match the following statements (1–6) with the subjects (a–f).**

1 I'd love to hear Keiko Matsui play. She's supposed to be magical. ....
2 I've never been, but it's supposed to be a beautiful place. ....
3 They're supposed to have an excellent selection of wines. ....
4 I haven't read it, but the plot is supposed to be quite complicated. ....
5 I haven't seen it, but Daniel Day Lewis is supposed to be superb in it. ....
6 There's an exhibition of his work at the Tate Gallery at the moment. It's supposed to be impressive. ....

a New Zealand
b film
c a painter
d a musician
e a restaurant
f a book

9 **Complete the mini-dialogues with a suitable phrase from the box.**

| why don't you | what are you doing | amazing | are supposed to |
| do you fancy | really talented | would you like | is supposed to |

1 A: Jen, ¹.. this afternoon? Have you got any plans?
   B: I'm thinking of going to see a film. ².. to come?
   A: I don't know. What's on?
   B: The new Johnny Depp film, at the Hippodrome. It ³... .... be really good.
   A: OK. I like Johnny Depp. What time does it start?

2 C: Have you got any plans for tomorrow, Tom?
   D: Not really. Why?
   C: I'm thinking of going to the new Magdalena Abakanowicz exhibition. Would you like to come?
   D: Isn't she the sculptor who designed the *Agora* figures in Grant Park?
   C: That's the one. I think she's ⁴.. .
   D: They're supposed to be ⁵.. ! Nine feet high, or something like that. OK, I'll come.

3 E: Are you doing anything this evening, Despina?
   F: Actually, I'm thinking of going to the Kool Kats concert. ⁶.. come with me?
   E: Kool Kats? They're that teenage band, aren't they? They ⁷.. be very good.
   F: So, ⁸.. it?
   E: OK, then.

GRAMMAR *-ed / -ing* adjectives

10 **Choose the correct adjective in each sentence.**

1 The film was all right, but I got a bit *bored / boring* at the beginning.
2 It had an *interested / interesting* plot, but the acting was rather poor.
3 I'm quite *exciting / excited* about going to see the Michael Jackson film. It's supposed to be really good.
4 I was *shocking / shocked* by the amount of violence in that film.
5 I'd read the book and really enjoyed it, but the film was *disappointing / disappointed*.
6 I find that actress so *annoying / annoyed* ! She's the same in every role.
7 We've had a *tired / tiring* day shopping in town, so let's watch a DVD at home tonight.
8 I was *confused / confusing* by the ending. Why did he leave like that?

11 **Rewrite the sentences with the correct adjective form of the verb in *italics*.**

1 Can you stop that? It's starting to *annoy* me.
   Can you stop that? It's becoming ....
2 Jeffrey Hinds' performance really *surprised* me.
   I was .... by Jeffrey Hinds' performance.
3 Ian's behaviour *worries* me. He's been acting really strange lately.
   I'm .... about Ian's strange behaviour lately.
4 That fight scene *disgusted* me. It was too violent.
   I found that fight scene .... It was too violent.
5 Too much talking in a film *bores* me. I want action and suspense!
   I find films with a lot of talking and not much action ....
6 The dialogue *amazed* me. It was so clever!
   It was .... how clever the dialogue was.

GRAMMAR Noun phrases

1 Make a list of noun phrases using a word from box A with one from box B.

A	
film	film
fashion	cinema
photo of	
works of	

B	
my family	director
cameraman	audience
industry	art

2 Match one of the phrases from exercise 1 with each of the pictures below.

1

2

3

4

3 Complete the sentences with one of the noun phrases from exercise 1.

1 There's a lot of competition in the ...., and it's hard for designers to become successful.
2 The .... told the actors to do the scene again.
3 Thieves stole some valuable .... from the local gallery last night.
4 The film has delighted .... all over the world.
5 This .... is my favourite, as everyone's here, even Uncle Joe.
6 I'd love to be a .... for National Geographic one day.

4 Choose the correct phrase (a or b) to complete the sentences.

1 My dream is to become a ....
  a designer of fashion   b fashion designer
2 Money is not as important to me as a good ....
  a quality of life   b life of quality
3 My kids love watching .... , as it's got some really interesting documentaries.
  a Discovery Channel   b Channel of Discovery
4 I don't often go to the theatre, as the .... is rather high in this country.
  a tickets cost   b cost of tickets
5 I once went on a .... , but didn't win anything.
  a show of quizzes   b quiz show
6 People often disagree about the ....
  a issue of violence in films   b violence of films issue
7 I hate getting stuck in a .... on a Friday evening, when everyone's leaving the city for the weekend.
  a traffic jam   b jam of traffic

8 James paints beautiful pictures and shows a real ....
  a fine art interest   b interest in fine art
9 Have you read any of ....? She's written five.
  a the books of Kate   b Kate's books
10 I'm thinking of becoming .... the local gym. How much does it cost to join?
  a a gym member of   b a member of

PRONUNCIATION -ed

5 Place the following past participles in the correct column.

excited	bored	tired	disappointed
interested	starred	amazed	treated
played	surprised	directed	recorded

/ɪd/	/d/
excited	bored

6 🔊 13.2 Listen and check.

7 Practise saying the words.

Language note

Where a verb ends in *-d, -de, -t* or *-te*, we pronounce the *-ed* ending of the past participle /ɪd/.

READING

8 Read the movie blog below. Decide which film is

1 a fantasy ....
2 a drama ....
3 a romantic comedy ....

9 Which film(s)

1 is frightening? ....
2 is amusing? ....
3 have a complicated plot? ....
4 is about human kindness? ....
5 contain some violence? ....
6 is surprising? ....

10 Make a list of adjectives that end with -*ing* from the reviews below. Add the verb form.

adjective	verb
moving	*move*

My favourite film!

A Amélie   star rating: ★★★★★

Kylie from Australia wrote:
I've seen a number of good movies in the last few years, but none as moving as this simple French story about the life of an ordinary girl. There are few special effects, and no exciting car chases, but the audience is taken on a magical bike ride with the heroine through the streets of Paris. Amélie is a funny, imaginative young woman, who tries to bring a little happiness to the people around her. As she does this, she falls in love. The director has captured the beauty of the simple things in life in this wonderful story, and shows us the extraordinary side of ordinary people's characters. Audrey Tautou is excellent as Amélie. I saw this film in the cinema when it first came out, and have watched it five times on DVD since then.

B Pan's Labyrinth   star rating: ★★★★★

Dino from Brazil wrote:
I had heard a lot about this film before I saw it, so I was worried that I would find it disappointing. However, it was amazing! Critics have been calling it *Alice in Wonderland* for adults, and I think this is true. The story is set in post-Civil War Spain, during a time of violence and hatred. A young girl called Ofelia, played by Ivana Baquero, escapes from a cruel reality into a fantasy world. *Pan's Labyrinth* is the best film that director Guillermo del Toro has ever made. He moves the action easily between Ofelia's imaginary and real worlds. The violence in Ofelia's real life is shocking, but necessary, for it shows her desperate need for escape and makes her dream world seem even more magical. The scenery inside the labyrinth is fantastic, the monsters are scary, the acting is superb, and all this is accompanied by a wonderful musical score.

C Slumdog Millionaire   star rating: ★★★★☆

Margarhita from Spain wrote:
Slumdog Millionaire is a film that both shocked and surprised me. Set on the violent streets of Mumbai, it tells the story of Jamal, a young boy who gets the chance to play the TV game show *Who Wants To Be A Millionaire*. He does well, but the show's host say's he has been cheating. Jamal gets arrested, and begins to tell the police officer the story of his life on the streets. Simon Beaufoy's screenplay is a clever adaptation of the novel *Q&A* by Vikas Swarup, and Danny Boyle's creative direction provides surprising twists and turns. The picture of life on the streets is not a pleasant one, and the way the children are treated is upsetting. It is a powerful story, and the emotional ending made me cry, along with others in the cinema.

Glossary

labyrinth: a place with many paths, so that it is difficult to understand where you are
get arrested: to be taken to the police station by the police, because they think you've done something wrong

VOCABULARY Music, art and books

1 Fill the gaps with a word from the box.

albums	composer	singer	concert
instruments			

I go to a music college in northern Italy, and I play three [1] ....

I started playing the piano when I was five, and the guitar at eight. Ennio Morricone is my favourite [2] ...., and I've got nearly all his [3] .... I sometimes play music from the film 'The Mission' on the piano. For the last four years, I've been learning the violin, and I'm now in the college orchestra. We gave a [4] .... last month. My girlfriend, Christina, is a [5] ...., and she sang soprano. It was a great success.

sculptures		paintings	landscape
portrait photographer		exhibition	

In my job as a [6] ...., I meet lots of interesting people. I was lucky enough to photograph the Hungarian sculptor, Laszlo, last year. His bronze [7] .... of political figures are superb. I met him at an [8] .... of his work in Madrid, and was impressed by the range of styles. My favourite modern artist, however, is the [9] .... painter, Vitali Komarov. His [10] .... are full of the rich countryside colours he sees around him.

novel	authors	comedy	crime fiction	poetry

At book club we choose a [11] .... to read each month, and then all discuss it. This month we're doing a [12] ...., but I don't find it very funny, I'm afraid. I prefer [13] ...., and one of my favourite [14] .... is Ian Rankin. His books about Inspector John Rebus are great, but unfortunately, not many of the other club members want to read detective stories. Someone asked if we could try [15] .... next, and suggested a long poem about a cat. I don't think I'll be a member for long!

GRAMMAR Present perfect continuous

2 Complete the sentences with *for* or *since*.
1 I've been playing the piano .... five years.
2 He's been working on that project .... two months now, and he still hasn't finished!
3 You've been working on the computer .... six this morning. Have a break!
4 We've been going to Latin American dance classes .... 2004, and we're quite good at the tango now.
5 I've been reading this book .... three weeks now.
6 We've been waiting here .... hours!

Learner tip

Use the present perfect continuous when you are interested in the action and how long it has been going on.
Use the present perfect simple to talk about the result of that action until now, i.e. how much / how many.
e.g. *I've been writing emails all morning*: action and how long
I've written ten so far: result of that action and how many

3 Choose the correct form.
1 She's *been acting / acted* for ten years, and has *been starring / starred* in six films.
2 He's *directed / been directing* several films, including *Love Me Forever*, and for the last six months he has *worked / been working* on a film in Africa.
3 She *started / has started* painting in 1980, and *held / has held* exhibitions in several countries since then.
4 Mandy *is playing / has been playing* the drums since she was eight and *is having / has had* her own drum set for three years.
5 Laura's *known / knowing* Ian for two years, and they *are going / have been going* out together for six months.
6 The book has *been becoming / become* very popular, and has been *published / being published* in 27 languages.

4 Complete the text with the present perfect continuous or the present perfect simple of the verbs in brackets.

Nobuya Sugawa is one of Japan's leading saxophonists. He [1] .... (play) the saxophone since he was a young boy, and [2] .... (gain) admirers all over the world.

Sugawa studied at the Tokyo University of Fine Arts and Music. He performs in around 100 concerts a year and [3] .... (record) more than 20 CDs, including Takashi Yoshimatsu's Saxophone Concerto Cyber-bird with the BBC Philharmonic, and Made In Japan. He [4] .... (work) with most of Japan's major orchestras and several leading international orchestras.

For the last few months, Sugawa [5] .... (tour) Europe, giving masterclasses and concerts. He will be appearing at the Royal College, London in November, and then at the Conservatory in Madrid.

DEVELOPING WRITING
Blog entry – a book review

5 Carla reads a lot of online book reviews. The books blog of a local newspaper has asked readers to choose their favourite book of this year. Read Carla's entry below, and complete it with the correct adjective form of the verbs in brackets (1–3).

posted by Carla, 06 Dec:

MY BOOKSHELF

a I have chosen *The Secret Scripture* by Sebastian Barry as my favourite book of the year. I found it very [1] .... (move) and read it in one day.

b The heroine, Roseanne, is nearly 100 years old, and has been living in a mental hospital for 60 years. Her psychiatrist, Dr Grene, is [2] .... (interest) in her, and wants to learn about how she came to be there. The story is told through the journals of these two characters. Through Roseanne's memories, the writer allows us to gradually see pieces of the truth, and her story is a [3] .... (surprise) one.

c The story develops in a clever way and Sebastian Barry's beautiful prose touches the reader's heart. Definitely worth reading!

Glossary

prose: written language using normal sentences; not poetry

6 Match the headings (1–3) with the paragraphs in Carla's entry (a–c).
1 opinion of the book ....
2 name of my chosen book ....
3 description of the plot ....

7 The underlined phrases in the text can be used to express your opinion about a book or a film. The phrase *beautiful prose* can become *wonderful screenplay / script* for a film.
Write a similar blog entry for your own favourite book or film. Try to use some of the underlined phrases and descriptive adjectives to help you.

Vocabulary Builder Quiz 13

Download the Vocabulary Builder for Unit 13 and try the quiz below. Write your answers in your notebook. Then check them and record your score.

1 Complete the sentences with the correct preposition.
1 I'm .... a band. I sing and play the guitar.
2 Her films focus .... social issues.
3 He wants to make people aware .... what's happening in his country.
4 The books are aimed .... teenagers who are interested in science.
5 The story is set .... a remote village in Scotland.

2 Complete the sentences with the correct form of the word in CAPITALS.
1 Mozart is one of my favourite .... COMPOSE
2 Her music is loved by people from different .... backgrounds. SOCIETY
3 The plot was complicated, and the ending was .... PREDICT
4 There was a loud .... and the lights went out. EXPLODE
5 She's got the .... role in a play opening next week. LEAD
6 James Cameron is the .... of the movie *Avatar*. DIRECT
7 Many Hollywood actors are very .... WEALTH
8 He's the .... of the local school orchestra. CONDUCT

3 Choose the correct word.
1 They're busy *rehearsing / publishing* a new play at the Royal Court theatre.
2 They're trying to *invade / promote* Bollywood by showing Indian movies on TV.
3 He's taking part in the Arts *Festival / Exhibition* in Edinburgh this summer.
4 She has a *talent / taste* for capturing human emotion in a photograph.
5 I thought the film was rather *surprising / depressing*, and had a really negative attitude towards the issue.
6 YouTube is a wonderful *source / element* of entertainment.

4 Match the sentence halves.
1 He never raises his
2 The paintings will be put up
3 The band are busy recording
4 He was fined for illegally
5 I was impressed by the special
6 The film looks at the issue

a for auction next month.
b downloading films.
c of the homeless in Athens.
d effects in *Life of Pi*.
e voice when he's angry.
f their new album.

Score ___ /25

Wait a couple of weeks and try the quiz again. Compare your scores.

14 STUFF

VOCABULARY Things in the house

1 Read the clues 1–8, and write the things in the house in the grid.

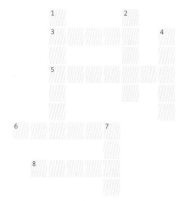

Across
3 You dry yourself with this after a bath.
5 You put this on when you cut yourself.
6 You use a needle to repair clothes with this.
8 You use a hammer to bang these into a piece of wood.

Down
1 You use this to join pieces of paper together.
2 You wipe surfaces clean with this.
4 This helps you see in the dark.
7 You work here on your computer.

2 Fill the gaps in these words and match them to the pictures.
1 mop and b _ _ _ _ t.   3 dustpan and b _ _ _ h.
2 n _ _ _ _ e and thread.   4 h _ _ _ _ r and nails.

DEVELOPING CONVERSATIONS
Explaining where things are

3 Complete these conversations with the phrases in the box.

Yes, there are some in the fridge.
Can I make a drink?
Have you got a needle and thread?
There's a first aid kit in the kitchen cupboard.
Have you got today's paper?
Where do you keep the plasters?
Yes, the coffee is on the shelf.
Have you got any snacks?
There's a sewing box on the shelf.
There's one on the bathroom wall.
Can I borrow a hairdryer?
It's on the table by the TV.

1 A: I'd like to wash my hair. ....
   B: ....
2 A: I've just cut my finger. ....
   B: ....
3 A: I'm feeling hungry. ....
   B: ....
4 A: A button has come off my shirt. ....
   B: ....
5 A: I'm thirsty. ....
   B: ....
6 A: I'd like to check the sports news. ....
   B: ....

4 Fill the gaps in these sentences with the prepositions in the box.

on	under	in	in	next	in	at	on

1 You'll find a mop in the cupboard .... to the kitchen door.
2 There's a needle and thread .... the drawer.
3 There's a torch on the table .... the side of the bed.
4 You'll find some towels .... the shelf in the bathroom.
5 There's a rubbish bin .... the desk in the study.
6 You'll find a vacuum cleaner .... the corner of the garage.
7 There's a notebook .... the table.
8 There's a clean shirt .... the wardrobe.

GRAMMAR Relative clauses

5 Complete these sentences by joining them to a phrase in the box using *which*, *who* or *where*.

helps you to get dry	horse racing takes place
cleans carpets	you can watch the latest movies
hold water	prepares food in a restaurant
you can keep fit	make things from wood

1 A gym is a place ....
2 A chef is a person ....
3 A vacuum cleaner is a thing ....
4 Carpenters are people ....
5 A cinema is a building ....
6 A towel is a piece of cloth ....
7 A racecourse is an area ....
8 Buckets are containers ....

Language note

In relative clauses you will sometimes see *that* used instead of *who* or *which*. For example:
He's the man that drives the bus. = *He's the man who drives the bus.*
It's a machine that drills holes. = *It's a machine which drills holes.*

6 Choose the correct word in *italics* in these sentences.
1 She's the woman *which / who* sold me her car.
2 It's a place *where / which* you can go to be alone.
3 They're the people *who / when* saw the robbery.
4 It's the time of day *who / when* people relax after work.
5 Here comes the man *when / who* knows all the answers.
6 This is the room *which / where* we keep the records.
7 We're the people *which / who* are paying for the party.
8 This is the day *who / when* we remember the great successes of the past.

7 Complete the conversation with *who* or *which*.
A: What's the name of that restaurant [1] .... does Moqueca?
B: I don't remember. And what's Moqueca!?
A: It's a famous Brazilian dish [2] .... is made of fish.
B: Oh, now I remember. And all the people [3] .... work there are Brazilians, right?
A: Yes, that's the place.
B: It's the Carnicero.
A But a Carnicero is a person [4] .... prepares different cuts of meat! A butcher, in English. That's a funny name for a fish restaurant.
B: It's not a fish restaurant. It's a place [5] .... serves everything.

LISTENING

8 🌐 **14.1 Two cleaners are starting their day's work at a hotel. Listen to their conversation. Put a tick next to the four things that they have to do.**

TO DO
Clean carpets in lobby   Wipe mirrors
Tidy reception area   Sweep front steps
Clean marble floor in   Polish glasses in bar
   dining room   Put up picture

9 🌐 **14.1 Listen again and make a list of the things they need to do each job.**
1 ....
2 ....
3 ....
4 ....

10 Where can they find the things that they need? Match these places to the things you have listed above.
1 in the drawer in the staff room
....
2 in the cupboard behind the reception area
....
3 in the cellar
....
4 under the stairs
....

11 At the end of the conversation one of the cleaners can't find the right word. What is it? ....

VOCABULARY Containers

1 Choose the word that does not collocate with the container.

1	a can of	cola / beer / shampoo
2	a packet of	biscuits / bread / sweets
3	a jar of	fish / honey / jam
4	a carton of	milk / orange juice / butter
5	a bar of	soap / cheese / chocolate
6	a box of	sausages / cereal / tissues
7	a pot of	yoghurt / crisps / tea
8	a tin of	eggs / baked beans / tomatoes

2 Match the words (1–6) to the clues (a–f).

1 metal ....
2 glass ....
3 plastic ....
4 cardboard ....
5 cloth ....
6 paper ....

a this material is often made from wool or cotton
b you can make many things from this material including bags and bottles and sheets.
c a material which you can see through
d this is made from layers of paper stuck together
e iron and aluminium are examples of this material
f this is made from wood or rags

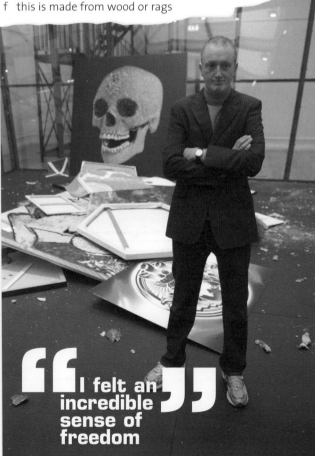

I felt an incredible sense of freedom

READING

3 Quickly read the article. Which of these sentences is the best summary?

a The article is about a man who destroyed his home and family life because he couldn't stop buying things.
b It's about a man who destroyed everything he owned as a work of performance art.
c It tells the story of a man who lost everything that he owned because of bad luck.
d It's about a man who was always breaking things, including some very valuable objects.

THE MAN WHO DESTROYED EVERYTHING

In February 2001, the artist Michael Landy destroyed everything he owned. He rented an empty shop on London's busiest shopping street, Oxford Street. He took all his possessions there and with the help of ten assistants, started to make a list of everything – his car, his books, his works of art, his photographs, his clothes, his passport, his driving licence, his toothbrush – absolutely everything! When they had written all 7,227 items onto huge cards Landy and his assistants started the serious business. One by one, they placed Michael Landy's things onto a conveyer belt which took them to a machine that destroyed them.

Why did Landy do this? For him, it was a work of performance art, which he called *Break Down,* and he even invited the public to come along and watch. During the two weeks that it took to destroy all his possessions, 45,000 people visited the shop in Oxford Street. Landy believed that *Break Down* could make people think again about the consumer society that they live in and reflect on their shopping habits and possessions.

At the end of the process, Michael Landy was left with nothing except his cat. So how did he feel?

'I felt an incredible sense of freedom,' he said, 'the possibility that I could do anything.'

Since then, Michael Landy has become one of the most respected artists in the UK but he certainly took an unusual route to career success!

Glossary

conveyer belt: a moving strip which carries things from one place to another
performance art: a live work of art in which the artist plays a part
consumer society: a society in which shopping is very important

4 Read the article again and answer the following questions.

1 Where did the event happen?

....

2 How many assistants did Michael Landy have?

....

3 How many things did he own?

....

4 What was the event called?

....

5 What did he want people to think about?

....

6 What one thing did he have at the end?

....

7 How did he feel at the end of the event?

....

8 What has happened to Michael Landy since 2001?

....

5 Decide whether the statements are true (T) or false (F).

1 Oxford Street is London's busiest shopping street.
....

2 Michael Landy didn't own a car. ....

3 His things were destroyed by a conveyer belt. ....

4 Michael Landy didn't want publicity. ....

5 The event lasted two weeks. ....

6 He saved his works of art. ....

6 Fill the gaps in the conversation with these sentences.

> We all have too many possessions these days.
> I think he made a good point.
> You're always going shopping.
> It was so wasteful!
> But he could have given them to charity.
> Why do you think that?

A: I think Landy's *Break Down* was a stupid idea.

B: 1 ....

A: He didn't need to destroy his things.

2 ....

B: I disagree.

3 ....

A: What point was he trying to make?

B: I think he was trying to say something about the consumer society.

4 ....

A: 5 ....
It would have been more useful. And I don't think I have too many possessions!

B: Yes you do!

6 ....

GRAMMAR *must, mustn't*

7 Match the sentences with the same definitions.

1 There is a law that tells you to do this. ....

2 There is no law. ....

3 There is a law that tells you not to do this. ....

a You mustn't do this.

b You don't have to do this.

c You must do this.

8 Complete this hotel information sheet with *You must, You mustn't* or *You don't have to*.

Information for Guests

1 .... return the keys to reception when you leave.

2 .... smoke in the children's play area.

3 Check out time is 11.00 am. ....
leave your room before then on your last day.

4 .... use your mobile phones in the quiet room.

5 The coffee is free. .... pay for it.

6 If you want to check out late, ...
tell reception the day before.

7 Towels are available at the swimming pool.
.... bring your own.

8 You can use the sauna any time ....
book in advance.

9 The swimming pool is very shallow.
.... dive into it.

10 .... wear your swimming costume in the dining room.

GRAMMAR Verbs with two objects

1 Choose the correct word.
1 She bought the shirt *for / to* me.
2 He sent the parcel *for / to* them.
3 They brought the books *for / to* our house.
4 He cooked roast beef *for / to* her.
5 Can you lend your bike *for / to* me for the afternoon?
6 Will you give that plate *for / to* him?
7 Will you read the letter *for / to* us?
8 Can you pour some orange juice *for / to* her?

2 Change the order of the two objects in these sentences.
1 He gave the books to me.
   He gave ....
2 I bought you a cup of coffee.
   I bought ....
3 He poured a glass of milk for me.
   He poured ....
4 I sent you a postcard.
   I sent ....
5 She made a sandwich for me.
   She made ....
6 He read them the report.
   He read ....
7 The lent their car to us.
   They lent ....
8 We cooked dinner for them.
   We cooked ....

PRONUNCIATION
/g/ and /k/, /b/ and /p/

3 🔊 14.2 Say these pairs of words. Then listen and tick (✓) the word you hear.

1	glass	class	6	good	could
2	gave	cave	7	ban	pan
3	bin	pin	8	bad	pad
4	bear	pair	9	goal	coal
5	gold	cold	10	boring	pouring

LISTENING

4 🔊 14.3 Listen to the conversation. Decide whether the statements are true (T) or false (F).
1 Rachel has just returned from Scotland.   ....
2 She brought back a present which is a bit like a handbag.   ....
3 You wear it over your shoulder.   ....
4 In Scotland the men wear them.   ....
5 It has four tassels on the front.   ....
6 It's called a kilt.   ....

WRITING

5 Read this paragraph about haggis, a famous Scottish dish. In which order do you read these things? Number them 1 to 4.
The writer's opinion of haggis   ....
The writer's recommendation   ....
A definition of haggis   ....
The writer's first experience of haggis   ....

6 Write a description of one of these things. Use the notes to help you organise your writing.
- Your favourite place
- Your favourite food
- A movie you've seen recently
- Your favourite piece of music
- Your favourite book.

Haggis is a huge surprise

The dictionary definition of haggis is 'a Scottish dish made from the organs of a sheep which are mixed with oatmeal and boiled and then served in the sheep's stomach'. It isn't a very attractive description - maybe it doesn't make you want to choose haggis from a menu. But that definition doesn't give you a true idea of how delicious haggis really is. When I first tried haggis in Edinburgh two years ago, I didn't know what to expect, but my Scottish friends told me to try it. I loved its rich texture and peppery taste. Now I understand why the Scottish poet Robert Burns wrote a famous poem to a haggis! I think haggis is probably my favourite food of all time, although I don't think I could eat it every week. Don't take my word for it, though. You really have to try haggis for yourself!

The guide books say that ...
The dictionary definition of X is ...
The newspaper reviews say that ...
Most people think that ...

But that does not give you a true idea of how *amazing / delicious / special, etc.* X really is.

When I first *saw / heard / tried etc* X, I thought ...
(Describe your first experience of X.)

I think that X is ... (Give your opinion of X.)

But don't take my word for it, you really have to *see / try / taste, etc.* X for yourself.

Vocabulary Builder Quiz 14

Download the Vocabulary Builder for Unit 14 and try the quiz below. Write your answers in your notebook. Then check them and record your score.

1 Complete the sentences with a word from the box.

> sack spilt rid consumed clue shame

1 We got .... of all our rubbish last weekend.
2 I've no idea. Can you give me a .... ?
3 Can you buy some bread, milk and a .... of potatoes?
4 It's a .... they're moving! They're such good neighbours.
5 Oh no! I've .... coffee all over my new shirt!
6 We .... so much food last night! It's embarrassing!

2 Decide whether the statements are true (T) or false (F).

1 A *shelf* is something that you put things like books on. ....
2 A *sticker* is a small piece of material that you put over a cut on your skin. ....
3 You use *a plaster* for boiling water. ....
4 A *mortgage* is an amount of money you borrow to buy a house. ....
5 A *site* is a place that we use for a particular purpose. ....
6 You put stuff you want to keep in a *bin*. ....
7 You can buy a *carton* of jam and a *jar* of milk. ....

3 Complete the sentences with the correct form of the word in CAPITALS.

1 We made a big .... in spending last year.   REDUCE
2 I feel .... about all the rubbish I produce.   GUILT
3 Adverts try to persuade .... to buy more stuff all the time.   CONSUME
4 It was very hard to .... of all their rubbish.   DISPOSAL
5 The system was .... so she upgraded it. EFFICIENCY
6 We need to increase the amount of .... that we do.   RECYCLE

4 Choose the word that does not form a collocation with the key word.

1 *rubbish / waste paper / clue*   bin
2 *petrol / kitchen / desk*   drawer
3 *excellent / exhausted / poor*   record
4 *gold / coal / soap*   mine
5 *biscuit / jam / cake*   tin
6 *plaster / door / wooden*   handle

Score ____/25

Wait a couple of weeks and try the quiz again.
Compare your scores.

15 MONEY

VOCABULARY The economy and quality of life

1 Find the words and phrases from the list below hidden in the box. The missing words read up ↑, down ↓, to the left ← or to the right →.

C	O	T	D	E	R	U	K	A	E	W	N	P	U
X	Y	O	O	A	O	N	I	D	Q	W	X	Y	L
W	C	L	C	B	T	E	S	C	E	T	N	T	E
T	N	L	X	T	I	M	E	O	F	F	P	I	V
A	E	U	I	Y	N	P	K	S	A	L	A	R	Y
S	R	E	N	A	W	L	Z	T	M	H	J	U	T
Z	R	T	F	I	Q	O	V	O	I	C	E	C	R
Q	U	A	L	I	T	Y	O	F	L	I	F	E	O
S	C	M	A	K	L	M	B	L	Y	A	R	S	P
T	R	I	T	E	U	E	M	I	R	C	H	B	S
Y	P	L	I	C	I	N	Z	V	Q	D	U	O	N
P	W	C	O	I	W	T	P	I	Y	F	G	J	A
U	L	O	N	S	T	R	O	N	G	G	O	W	R
Q	I	M	A	V	E	R	A	G	E	R	S	A	T

1	average	6	family	11	strong
2	climate	7	inflation	12	time off
3	cost of living	8	job security	13	transport
4	crime	9	quality of life	14	unemployment
5	currency	10	salary	15	weak

2 Choose the correct word or phrase to complete the sentences.
1 One of the biggest problems at the moment is *unemployment / inflation*. Many skilled people are out of work.
2 The *pace of life / cost of living* is quite fast in this city, and a lot of people suffer from stress.
3 While the economy is doing badly, most people are interested in having *job security / a high salary*.
4 More and more people are moving out of the city to find a better *average salary / quality of life*.
5 People are becoming more and more worried about *climate change / crime* as temperatures rise and there is less rain than in the past.
6 Our currency is *weak / strong* at the moment, so it's not a good time to travel abroad.
7 The rate of *inflation / crime* is rising at the moment, and the cost of living is high.
8 Although Gina has a good *currency / salary*, she doesn't have much job security.

LISTENING

You're going to listen to Carlos and Yelena speaking. Carlos is a native Argentinian, and Yelena is from the Czech Republic.

3 🔊 **15.1** Listen and answer the questions.
1 Does Yelena like living in Argentina?
....
2 Is the economy doing well?
....
3 Why does she want to leave?
....
....

4 🔊 **15.1** Listen again and complete the sentences with one word.
1 According to Carlos, the cost of living in Prague is .... than it is in Argentina.
2 Yelena says that unemployment is .... in Prague than it is in Argentina.
3 According to Yelena, houses are .... in the Czech Republic.
4 Carlos says that eating out is less .... in Argentina.
5 Yelena says that salaries are .... in the Czech Republic.
6 Yelena thinks it is important for Miguel and her to decide where they will both feel .... to live.

5 Tick (✓) the arguments Yelena gives to support her decision to move to Prague.
1 It is important for Miguel to understand her culture and language.
2 Prague is a better place to bring up children.
3 They will find a better paid job easily.
4 Cars are cheaper in the Czech Republic.
5 She doesn't have a good quality of life in Argentina.
6 They need to live in both countries to decide where to raise a family.

GRAMMAR Time phrases and tense

6 Match the sentence halves.

1 House prices are currently ....
2 Unemployment has fallen ....
3 According to the government, the economy will ....
4 The cost of living has gone up over ....
5 Rents used to be a lot cheaper ....
6 The government is going to announce ....
7 According to newspaper reports, inflation is falling ....
8 The pace of life used to be much ....

a improve over the next few months.
b the last two years.
c slower when I was a child.
d at the moment.
e rising and many people can't afford to buy their own home.
f since this time last year.
g when I was a student.
h the new budget in two weeks' time.

7 Put the words in the sentences into the correct order.

1 used to / on education / the government / spend more

2 a new shopping centre / yesterday / they opened / on the ring road

3 she's going to / next week / in advertising / a new job / start

4 three jobs / he's had / in the last two years

5 improving / at the moment / the economy is

6 in the last five years / three loans / she's had / from the bank

8 The tense is wrong in the sentences below. Correct the mistakes.

1 Unemployment used to rise over the last few months.

2 The average salary has been higher when I was at school.

3 Inflation will fall since last year.

4 The price of petrol has risen again in the next few weeks.

5 The cost of living used to fall at the moment, and prices are lower.

6 I think the economy has improved next year.

DEVELOPING CONVERSATIONS
Comparing prices

9 Below are lists of average prices for certain items in two countries, Celtonia and Faroland. Compare the prices and complete the sentences about them. Use phrases such as *more / less expensive than, cheaper than, much cheaper than*, etc.

	Celtonia	Faroland
three-bedroom house	€200,000	€300,000
four-door saloon car	€20,000	€25,000
petrol	€1 per litre	€1.20 per litre
computer (PC)	€750	€1000
iPod	€200	€200

1 Houses are .... to buy in Celtonia than in Faroland.
2 In Celtonia petrol is .... in Faroland.
3 Cars are .... in Faroland than they are in Celtonia.
4 Computers are .... in Celtonia.
5 An iPod, however, costs .... in Celtonia as in Faroland.
6 Generally, the cost of living in Celtonia seems to be .... it is in Faroland.

10 Complete the replies to the following statements with an example from the lists in exercise 9.

A: Clothes are cheaper in Faroland than in Celtonia.
B: I know. You can buy designer jeans for €60, whereas they cost €70 in Celtonia.

1 A: Houses are much cheaper in Celtonia.
B: I know. You can buy a three-bedroomed house for €200,000 there, whereas

2 A: Cars are more expensive in Faroland.
B: I know. A four-door saloon costs €25,000 in Faroland, whereas

3 A: However, petrol is only slightly more expensive in Faroland.
B: I know. It costs €1.20 there,

4 A: If you want a new computer, you should go to Celtonia. They're much cheaper there.
B: I know. They cost only €750 in Celtonia,

READING

1 Read the newspaper article about Professor Muhammad Yunus and complete the sentences.

1 Professor Yunus used to work as

....

2 In 1983, he formed

....

3 In 2006, Professor Yunus was awarded

....

2 Decide whether the statements are true (T) or false (F).

1 Professor Yunus was a university student in 1974. ....

2 Professor Yunus was upset by the famine in Bangladesh. ....

3 The woman's story showed him how traders took advantage of the poor. ....

4 Professor Yunus helped the woman and other workers by offering them a loan. ....

5 He did not expect them to pay back the money. ....

6 Everyone paid back the money they had borrowed. ....

7 In 1983, Professor Yunus started a bank to help poor people. ....

8 The bank is not very successful. ....

3 Complete the sentences with a word or phrase from the box.

| loan | micro-credit | borrowed |
| lend | interest | pay back |

1 People usually pay a lot of .... on a business loan, and it often takes them a long time to pay back the money.

2 Riko, can you .... me £50? I haven't got enough money to pay the bill.

3 Several banks are setting up .... systems for small businesses to help the economy improve.

4 Hi, Camille! Look, I'm sorry for the delay. I'll .... the money I owe you at the end of the week, OK?

5 I'm fed up! Ming .... £100 from me three months ago, and he still hasn't paid it back!

6 Right, David! Here's £1,000 towards your car. Remember it's a .... , so I expect to be paid back!

Nobel Prize Winner receives Medal of Freedom

Professor Muhammad Yunus has many reasons to be proud. He was awarded the Nobel Peace Prize in 2006, and has just been presented with the Medal of Freedom by United States President, Barack Obama.

When famine hit Bangladesh in 1974, Professor Yunus was teaching Economics at Chittagong University. He was deeply shocked by the number of people dying in the streets, and wanted to do something to help.

He mixed with villagers, learning about their lives and their problems. One woman made bamboo stools. She was skilled and hardworking, but did not have the money to buy the bamboo. She was forced to borrow from a trader who then paid a low price for the stools, which he would then sell for a good profit. The woman's profit was just a penny a day! Professor Yunus discovered that this was true for many villagers. Together with one of his students, he made a list of 42 people who worked like this woman. He decided to lend them the total amount they needed to become independent in their work – about £1 per person – and told them it was a loan, but without interest. The Professor then persuaded a bank to provide such loans, with him as guarantor. The bank was not enthusiastic, but the system worked, and all the loans were paid back.

Professor Yunus realised that a new bank was needed; a bank that was owned by the people. In October 1983, the Grameen (Village) Bank was formed. Over the next few years, it made small loans to some of the poorest people in Bangladesh, so that they could become self-employed and escape poverty. It was a huge success. Since then, the bank has grown so much that it now has almost 8 million members, and 96% of them are women. Grameen's system of micro-credit is one of the most successful banking systems in the world, with 98% of all loans paid back in full.

Professor Yunus has given the people of Bangladesh hope and a sense of pride.

Glossary

famine: period when large numbers of people have little or no food and they die

stool: a seat with legs but no support for the back

guarantor: person who promises to make sure a loan is paid back

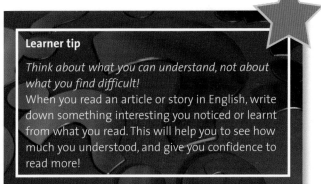

Learner tip

Think about what you can understand, not about what you find difficult!
When you read an article or story in English, write down something interesting you noticed or learnt from what you read. This will help you to see how much you understood, and give you confidence to read more!

VOCABULARY Money verbs

4 Choose the best word in *italics* to complete the sentences.

Ming Woo had no money, and he ¹ *left / owed* €5,000 to the bank. He ² *borrowed / lent* €5 from his brother and bought a lottery ticket. Fortunately, he ³ *won / saved* €10,000! Ming paid the money to the bank, and ⁴ *left / gave* his brother €1,000. Then he bought a second-hand car for €3,000. That ⁵ *left / saved* him with €1,000. He decided to ⁶ *lend / save* it, and put it in the bank. Ming Wu is more careful with his money now. He is worried that he might ⁷ *drop / lose* his job. He saves €100 every month. But he still ⁸ *plays / spends* the lottery every week!

5 Complete the sentences with the most suitable word(s) from the box.

credit card	attention	bill	interest
to do it	paid	back	

1 Sinead didn't have much cash, so she paid for the meal by ....
2 Ameet spent too much money last month and couldn't afford to pay the electricity ....
3 Can I borrow €50? I promise I'll pay you .... !
4 Our TV needed repairing and we paid the technician €65 ....
5 The sales manager talked for an hour at the meeting, but few people paid much ....
6 Oh, no! I've spent all my wages and I'll have to wait another two weeks until I get .... !
7 I don't want to ask the bank for a loan, as I'll have to pay a lot of ....

LISTENING

6 🍩 15.2 Listen to two people talking, and answer the questions.
1 What is Isabel doing?
2 Does she say it is easy or difficult?
3 Does Primo like the idea?

7 🍩 15.2 Listen again. Choose the most suitable answer.
1 Isabel is
  a writing out a cheque.   c paying bills through the Internet.
  b writing an email.
2 How does Primo feel about what she is doing?
  a Surprised.   b Uninterested.   c Enthusiastic.
3 Isabel says this system
  a saves you money.   c is complicated.
  b is good for the environment.
4 Primo worries about
  a security.   b expense.   c wasting time.
5 Isabel agrees that
  a it's expensive.   c it is difficult.
  b there are some risks.
6 When he goes to pay bills in Scotland, Primo sometimes finds it difficult to
  a work out the money.   c remember his ID number.
  b understand the cashier's accent.
7 Isabel says her way
  a wastes money.   b is slower.   c saves time.
8 Finally, Primo
  a thinks it's a good idea.   c doesn't like the idea.
  b is uncertain.

PRONUNCIATION

8 Say the words. Choose the word in each group that does not belong.

/aɪ/	price	online	bill	buy	twice
/əʊ/	loan	grow	owe	owl	own
/aʊ/	amount	through	pound	round	sound
/eɪ/	save	paid	said	sales	wage

9 🍩 15.3 Listen to the sentences, and practise saying them. Stress the words in bold.
1 **Buy** a house when the **price** is **right**, and pay your bills on**line**.
2 Take out a **loan** to buy your **own home**, then **owe** the bank money until you **grow old**.
3 Twenty-five **pounds** for a meal may not **sound** much but is a large **amount** for a pizza.
4 I got **paid** a good **wage** for my job in **sales**, and was able to **save** for a holiday in **Wales**.

15

GRAMMAR Time clauses

1 Six of these sentences contain mistakes. Find and correct them.

1 I'll pay back the money I owe you as soon as I'll be able to.
2 Call me after you'll transfer the money. OK?
3 I lend you the money until you get paid.
4 I'm going to talk to the manager as soon as he arrives at the bank.
5 When I find a job, I open a savings account.
6 I'm going to invest in Dave's company after I retire.
7 As soon as I'll get confirmation of payment, I'll let you know.
8 When I'll have enough money, I'll buy a new car.

2 Choose the correct word in *italics* to complete the sentences.

1 I'll leave home *when / until* I finish college.
2 Oliver is going to pay me back *before / as soon as* he comes home.
3 Don't buy a flat *after / until* you're sure where you're going to live.
4 I'm going to see what different banks offer *before / after* I take out a mortgage.
5 You'll be able to pay bills online *until / after* you register.
6 Don't forget to pay the bill *as soon as / until* it arrives.

3 Complete the sentences with the correct form of the verb in brackets.

1 We .... (cancel) your credit card as soon as we get home.
2 Don't buy that laptop until you .... (have) enough money to pay for it.
3 Inflation .... (not fall) until the government takes action.
4 When the economy .... (recover) unemployment will fall.
5 I .... (not invest) any money until the price of shares .... (fall).
6 As soon as I .... (win) the lottery, I .... (take) you to Hawaii.
7 Before you .... (take out) a bank loan, always .... (check) how much interest you will have to pay.
8 After I .... (finish) university, I .... (come) to work for you.

VOCABULARY Dealing with banks

4 Complete the sentences with one of the verbs in the box.

change	make	charge	transfer	pay	cancel	open	take out

1 Farouq and Heba want to buy their first house, and so they are going to .... a mortgage.
2 I'm afraid my credit card has been stolen, so I need to .... it.
3 Yes, my husband and I would like to .... a joint account, please.
4 The banks are planning to .... us £2.40 every time we take cash from a cash machine!
5 Yes, I'd like to .... a complaint. You've overcharged me for this meal.
6 I want to .... some money into my account, please.
7 Could you .... €1,000 from my account to Ms Yoko Wong in Tokyo, please? Just a moment and I'll give you her account number.
8 Just a moment, Vikram! I haven't got any euros! I need to .... some money.

5 Look at the situations and write what you will do.

e.g. You are travelling to the USA, but you haven't got any dollars.
I will change some money.

1 You want to send some money to your brother, who lives in Prague.
....
2 Your parents have sent you some money for your birthday. You take it to the bank. ....
3 Someone asks you to translate an article. You want to be paid for this.
....
4 You want to buy a flat, but need to borrow some money from the bank.
....
5 You've just started your first job and want to put your money in a bank.
....
6 You think someone has stolen your credit card details.
....

Language note

Some verbs can go with more than one noun to form collocations.
e.g. *take out ~ a loan*; *~ a mortgage*; *~ some money*
When you see a verb + noun collocation, use your dictionary to see if the verb can form other collocations, and make a list.

DEVELOPING WRITING
Email – giving information and advice

Sanjida is going to be a foreign exchange student at Edinburgh University. She has written to the university asking about the cost of living for students there. Below is the reply from the International Office.

6 Read the reply, and fill the gaps with one of the following words and phrases.

cost	spend	pay	expenses	cost of living	charges

○○○

From	info@internat.office.ed.uk
To	Sanjida Beiz
Subject	re: cost of living in Edinburgh

Dear Sanjida,

1) You asked about the ¹.................... in Edinburgh. Edinburgh is quite an expensive city, so as a student here, you'll need to budget carefully.

2) You will ².................... £170 per week to stay in a university hall of residence. This includes the ³.................... of electricity, hot water, Internet access and your breakfast. The university canteen ⁴.................... students £13 a week for lunches. Then you will need to think about social ⁵.................... , such as a cinema tickets, haircuts, clothes, drinks and so on. So, you can expect to ⁶.................... at least £210–220 per week.

3) We look forward to welcoming you here. Don't hesitate to write again if you have any more questions.

Best wishes,

Gavin Stewart

7 What do the following amounts refer to?
£170:..
£13:...
£210–220:...

8 Place the paragraph headings in the correct order.

a) information and advice ....
b) closing statement and offer of extra help ....
c) reason for writing ....

9 Paco is a foreign exchange student who is coming to study in your city. He is going to stay in your house. He has written an email asking you for information about the social life. Read the notes you have made below. Then write Paco an email with some information. Use paragraphs like the model above.

college student centre - films, parties, discount prices at bar
local cinema / theatre - student prices
art gallery - free
sports facilities - some are expensive
eating out - expensive!

Vocabulary Builder Quiz 15

Download the Vocabulary Builder for Unit 15 and try the quiz below. Write your answers in your notebook. Then check them and record your score.

1 Decide whether the statements are true (T) or false (F).
1 *Inflation* is an increase in prices. ....
2 *Goods* are things that are bought and sold. ....
3 A *bill* is a card with numbers or pictures on it. ....
4 An *election* is when people in a country vote to choose a new government. ....
5 The *minimum* is the largest amount possible. ....

2 Correct the error in the collocations.
1 It's an old motorbike so it doesn't worth much.
2 Our insurance concerns fire and flooding.
3 It cost us €10,000 to repair the harm to the house.
4 In times of recession, people want more job safety.
5 She decided to buy shame in the company.

3 Choose the correct word.
1 My father took out a *will / loan* to build his factory.
2 The President's *population / popularity* has decreased.
3 We discovered he *earned / owed* 35,000€ to the bank.
4 Our *salary / currency* is strong now, so it's a good time to go abroad.
5 He left all his money to a children's *charity / company*.

4 Match the sentence halves.
1 The second-hand car was in ....
2 It will take the economy a long time to recover ....
3 Luciano took out a ....
4 The government has promised to invest ....
5 The bank charges an interest ....

a rate of 8%.
b more money in schools.
c immaculate condition.
d loan to pay for his car.
e from the recession.

5 Complete the phrasal verbs.
1 The cost of living has gone .... again, and it's becoming difficult to afford the basics.
2 I'm cold! Can you turn .... the air conditioning?
3 You're driving too fast! Please slow ....
4 Samir was too shy to ask Marianna ....
5 She turned old dresses .... skirts to save money.

Score ___/25

Wait a couple of weeks and try the quiz again. Compare your scores

VOCABULARY Describing parties and events

1 Fill the gaps in these sentences with the words in the box.

leaving	launch	housewarming
surprise	reception	dinner

1 To celebrate a marriage, there is often a wedding ....
2 When a new book or product is introduced there is sometimes a .... party.
3 If you don't know a party is going to happen, it's a .... party.
4 A .... party happens when someone moves to a new job.
5 When people move to a new house or flat they sometimes have a .... party.
6 If you have friends round to your house to eat in the evening, it's a .... party.

2 Match the sentence halves.

1 There wasn't much food, just a few bowls ....
2 I couldn't hear anyone because the background ....
3 The party was held in a converted ....
4 The DJ played such bad music that he cleared ....
5 They met each other at a birthday ....
6 They had a terrible argument and ....
7 I wasn't very hungry and just picked ....
8 The buffet was amazing and everyone ....

a party last year.
b ruined the whole evening.
c of olives and nuts.
d helped themselves to as much as they wanted.
e warehouse near the river.
f at a few crisps.
g the dance floor in five minutes.
h music was much too loud.

3 Choose the word or phrase in italics which does not complete the answer.

1 A: So where did you go last night?
   B: I was at a *leaving / launch / host / dinner* party.
2 A: What were the other guests like?
   B: They were all very *easy to talk to / comfortable and convenient / warm and friendly / cold and distant.*
3 A: Did you like the venue?
   B: Oh, yes. It was *impressive / amazing / backward / elegant.*
4 A: What kind of food did they have?
   B: It was mostly *spicy / grilled / general / cold.*
5 A: What was the wedding like?
   B: Well, it was very *modern / traditional / formal / full.*
6 A: Where did they hold the event?
   B: It was on the *past / ground / top / dance* floor.

DEVELOPING CONVERSATIONS Linked questions

4 Fill the gaps in the conversation with these questions.

Was anyone I know there?	And what was the venue like?
Did you have a good time?	Was there anything to eat?
Or did you hang out with your friends?	What time did you leave?
Is he the person you went to school with?	What's he like?

A: How was the party last night? [1]...
B: Yes, it was pretty good actually.
A: [2]... Did you stay really late?
B: No. It was probably about midnight.
A: [3].. Was it a nightclub?
B: Yes, it was that new place in the middle of town, near the river. Do you know it?
A: I know the one you mean, but I've never been inside. So what about the food? [4]..
B: Not really. Most of it had gone by the time I arrived.
A: Oh, that's a shame. So did you meet any new people?
   [5]..
B: With friends mostly.
A: Who was there? [6]..
B: Yes, Peter was there. Do you remember him?
A: Have I met him? [7]..
B: That's him, yes. Anyway, he introduced me to a friend of his, who was rather nice.
A: Really? [8]..
   Are you going to see him again?
B: Well, it's a long story ...

LISTENING

5 🔊 **16.1 Listen to the conversation. Tick (✓) the best description.**
a Two people discussing a party the night before.
b Someone complaining to a friend about her neighbour's noisy party.
c Two people planning a surprise party for a friend.
d Someone talking about a party with a professional party planner.

6 🔊 **16.1 Listen to the conversation again and correct the mistakes in these notes.**

Kind of party	18th birthday
Atmosphere	Fun and noisy
Venue	Nightclub in shopping mall
Food	Hot buffet
Music	Live band
End time	1.00-2.00 am

7 Fill the gaps in these questions with the phrases in the box. Then listen again to check.

| would you like | what kind of | what time | can you think |
| sort of venue | have you got | are you going to | |

1 .... party is it going to be?
2 What .... do you want?
3 .... any suggestions?
4 .... of anywhere else?
5 And .... serve any food?
6 What kind of music .... ?
7 .... would you like the party to finish?

PRONUNCIATION

8 🔊 **16.2 Listen to these three extracts from the listening activity. Mark where the intonation rises or falls at the ends of the sentences.**

1 A: With lots of people? ↗

   B: Oh, yes, at least a hundred.

2 A: How about a cold buffet?

   B: Yeah, a cold buffet's good.

3 A: Shall we say three to four in the morning?

   B: Yeah, that's great.

9 🔊 **16.3 Will these sentences have rising or falling intonation? Mark them with rising or falling arrows, then listen and check.**

1 Where did you go last night?

2 Did you see what she was wearing?

3 Why were you so rude to him?

4 Have you been here before?

5 How many people here do you know?

6 Are you going to eat something?

7 Who's that man in the sunglasses near the bar?

8 Do you have the time?

Language note

Rising intonation means that the pitch increases and is often used in *Yes / No* questions. Falling intonation means that it decreases and is often used in *wh-?* questions. Intonation is often marked with an arrow pointing up ⟶ or down ⟶.

VOCABULARY Historical events

1 Read the clues 1–8 and write the answers in the grid.

1			R			
2			E			
3			P			
4			U			
5			B			
6			L			
7			I			
8			C			

1 In the nineteenth century, the British … included India, Canada and Australia.
2 A king or government … a country; they run and control it.
3 A country that is not controlled by another country is ….
4 When a foreign power enters and then controls a country, they … it.
5 When you start something that you hope will last a long time, you … it.
6 When you make someone die, you … them.
7 When a foreign power enters a country in order to control it, they … it.
8 When groups of people within a country fight against each other, there is a ….

2 Choose the correct word in *italics* in these sentences.

1 India became *independent / invaded* from the UK in 1947.
2 The city of New York was *occupied / established* by the Dutch in 1614.
3 The Ottoman *Empire / Republic* controlled the lands around the Mediterranean for six centuries.
4 Greece was *occupied / established* by the Axis powers in the second world war.
5 The first French *Empire / Republic* was founded on 22nd September, 1792.
6 The Italian army first *invaded / ruled* Greece in 1940, but did not gain control until the following year.

3 Complete the sentences with the words in the box.

ruled	killed	Civil	Union	king	lasted

1 The North and South of the USA fought each other in the American .... War.
2 Finland became a member of the European .... in 1995.
3 The French Revolution .... for ten years.
4 Queen Victoria .... the British Empire for 64 years.
5 Felipe VI became .... of Spain in 2014.
6 Henry VIII's wife Anne Boleyn became Queen in 1533, and was .... three years later.

READING

4 This is an extract from a history of a state in the USA. Quickly read the text. Tick (✓) the state that it describes.
a California
b Florida
c Hawaii
d Texas

THE LONG HISTORY
OF THE
NEWEST STATE

Glossary

settlers: people who move to live in a new area of the world
missionaries: people who try to persuade others to become Christians
territory: in the USA, an area controlled by the government that is not a state
naval base: a place where navy (fighting) ships are kept

5 **Read the extract again and complete this timeline.**

500	*The first settlers arrived.* ....
1778	....
1779	....
1805	....
1820	....
1893	....
1898	....
1941	....
1959	....
1961	....

This American state is famous for its beautiful beaches and volcanoes and, of course, was also the childhood home of US President Barack Obama who was born here in 1961. But the newest state in the union (it became the 50th state in 1959) has a long and fascinating history.

The first settlers arrived on the islands around AD 500 but little is known about them until 1778, when the British explorer Captain James Cook stayed here on his way to Australia. At first the people of the islands were generous to him and may have thought he was a representative of their god. But when he returned a year later, Cook argued with the local rulers and was killed.

At the end of the 18th century, the rulers of the islands were continually fighting each other for power, but in 1805 Kamehameha I became the islands' first king and established a monarchy which ruled successfully for many years.

The fate of Cook did not discourage other Westerners. In 1820 the first Christian missionaries arrived and before long European and American sailors and traders were a familiar sight in the streets of the islands' main ports such as Honolulu. However, as Western influence grew during the 19th century, the monarchy became weaker. In 1893 a group of American businessmen seized power in a revolution. Five years later, the islands were made a territory of the USA.

Under American rule, the economy continued to grow during the 20th century and Pearl Harbor became one the USA's most important naval bases. It was here that the Japanese launched their surprise attack in December 1941 which brought the USA into the Second World War.

GRAMMAR Articles

6 **Choose the correct answer *the / a / an / -* to complete the sentences.**

1 After winning *the / an* last election, *the / -* President Obama introduced a series of reforms.
2 *The / A* Prime Minister has promised to reduce *the / -* income tax.
3 *The / -* Buckingham Palace is *a / the* most famous of the / - Britain's palaces.
4 *A / The* country like *the / -* France or *the / -* USA which does not have *a / the* king or queen is called *a / -* republic.
5 *The / -* British women gained *the / a* vote for *the / a* first time in 1918.
6 *The / A* majority of *the / -* population are against *the / a* new law.
7 *The / -* India was ruled by *the / -* British until *the / -* 1947.
8 We're having *a / the* party to celebrate *the / -* moving to *a / -* new home.

7 **Delete the unnecessary articles in the following sentences. There may be more than one in each sentence.**

1 There was a major scandal involving the President which led to the civil war.
2 The war led to thousands of the people becoming the refugees.
3 The discovery of the oil resulted in lots of oil companies buying the land.
4 The settlers depended on the farming to live.
5 This raised the issue of the unfair taxation laws in the country.
6 Britain and France went to a war against the Germany on 3rd. September, 1939.
7 The earthquake off the Japanese coast in the 2011 caused a tsunami which left more than the 28,000 people dead or missing.
8 Tsar Nicholas II ruled over a huge empire until 1917, when he fell from the power.
9 Florence Nightingale became a nurse in 1853, and went to care for the soldiers in the Crimean war in 1854.
10 She became known as 'The Lady of the Lamp', and one of her biggest fans was the Queen Victoria.

8 **Complete the text below with *a, an, the* or -.**

In [1] .... 18th century, [2] .....*the*..... British East India Company controlled all tea trading between [3] .... India and [4] .....*the*..... British colonies. [5] .....*the*..... British government had created [6] .... tea tax, so [7] .....*the*..... American colony refused to buy [8] .....*the*..... British tea. On December 16th, 1773, three British ships were moored in [9] ....*a*...... Boston harbour. [10] .... group of men calling themselves 'The Sons of Liberty' climbed onto [11] .... ships and threw forty-five tonnes of tea into [12] .... sea. This event became known as [13] .... Boston Tea Party and eventually led to [14] .... American War of Independence.

DEVELOPING WRITING

1 Read the text and put these events into the right order.

The Normans sailed across the English Channel.   ....
William was crowned king.   ....
King Harold was killed.   ....
The Normans established a camp.   ....
The Normans and the English fought a battle.   ....
William marched to London.   ....

2 Look at the text again.

1 Why is the date 1066 important?

....

2 What is the connection between William and modern Britain?

....

3 Underline these words in the text: *First, Next, Meanwhile, After*

4 Which word means 'at the same time as'? ....

3 Write a paragraph about an important event in the history of your country.

- Write a sentence to introduce the subject
- Include at least three steps in the story. Link them together with expressions such as *First, Next, Meanwhile* and *After*.
- Finish with a concluding sentence.

LISTENING

4 🔊 **16.4 Listen to a tour guide talking about the Bayeux Tapestry. Decide whether the statements are true (T) or false (F).**

1 The Bayeux Tapestry shows the events leading to the Norman invasion of England.   ....

2 The Normans walked to England.   ....

3 The tapestry shows the Battle of Hastings.   ....

4 The tapestry doesn't show the death of King Harold.   ....

5 The tapestry was made in 1070.   ....

6 Queen Matilda was King Harold's wife.   ....

7 The tapestry was definitely made by King William's brother.   ....

8 There is a copy of the tapestry in Reading, England.   ....

The Norman Conquest

In the UK, every schoolchild knows the date 1066. That was the year of the Norman invasion of England, which changed British history forever. William, Duke of Normandy, left France with his army in September of that year.

First, the Normans crossed the English Channel, landing at Pevensey Bay on the south coast of England. Next, William established a camp near the town of Hastings. Meanwhile, the new English king, Harold Godwinson, was marching towards Hastings with his army.

The two armies met on 14 October and fought a fierce battle in which Harold was killed. After the battle, William marched north to London where he was crowned king on Christmas Day.

William the Conqueror became the first in a long line of British kings and queens which includes the current monarch, Elizabeth II.

GRAMMAR Verb patterns (-ing or infinitive with to)

5 In each pair, match the sentence halves.

1 I forgot — telling her to go home early.
  I remember — to post the letter.

2 He spent two weeks — doing nothing.
  She decided — to review all the work.

3 They hated — to play tennis.
  They persuaded us — going to the theatre.

4 I'd like — watching TV this evening.
  I don't feel like — to help my parents with their business.

5 She enjoyed — to help with her assignment.
  She asked me — taking her brother to school.

6 Her new boss offered — to help her sort out the accounts.
  The new job stopped — her spending so much time at home.

6 Use the prompts to write answers to the questions.

1 A: Do you always drive to work?
  B: Yes. *I / hate / take the bus.*
  ....

2 A: Do you still smoke?
  B: *No. I / stop / smoke / last year*
  ....

3 A: What are you doing for your holiday next year?
  B: *I'd like / go / Hawaii*
  ....

4 A: Do you want to come to the cinema this evening?
  B: No, thanks. *I / feel like / watch TV at home*
  ....

5 A: Why doesn't your phone work any more?
  B: *Because / I forget / pay my bill*
  ....

6 A: What was the last thing you remember before the accident?
  B: *I remember / see / my brother's face*
  ....

7 A: What did you do between school and university?
  B: *I / spend a year / work for my father's business*
  ....

8 A: Have you had a meeting with your boss yet?
  B: Yes. *I manage / speak to her yesterday*
  ....

Learner tip

Now that you have come to the end of the Workbook, look through it again and make a list of any language points that you are uncertain about. Ask your teacher to help you with them.

Vocabulary Builder Quiz 16

Download the Vocabulary Builder for Unit 16 and try the quiz below. Write your answers in your notebook. Then check them and record your score.

1 Complete the sentences with a word in the box.

unique	settled	ceremony	independent
converted	venue		

1 Our family .... in the USA 100 years ago.
2 The old church was .... into a private home.
3 We need to find a suitable .... for Nick's 21st birthday party.
4 Nothing is quite like Gaudi's .... architecture.
5 The wedding .... was held in a hotel.
6 India became .... from British rule in 1947.

2 Complete the sentences with the correct form of the word in CAPITALS.

1 The view from the top of the mountain is very .... IMPRESSED
2 The 15th August is a major .... festival in Greece. RELIGION
3 Water .... is now a major global issue. SHORT
4 After World War 2, several countries had .... problems. ECONOMY
5 The .... of the right-wing party walked out of the meeting. LEAD
6 He kept trying to .... her to marry him. PERSUASION

3 Decide whether the statements are true (T) or false (F).

1 A *buffet* is a fight between two armies. ....
2 If you *convert* something you change it into something else. ....
3 A *battle* is a period of ten years. ....
4 A *citizen* is someone who performs operations on patients. ....
5 If something is *distant* it is far away. ....
6 If you *establish* an organisation you start it. ....
7 *Grass* is a green plant that covers the ground in gardens. ....

4 Choose the word that does not form a collocation with the key word.

1 background — *colony / noise / music*
2 trade — *route / union / parade*
3 civil — *war / region / rights*
4 oil — *rule / company / exports*
5 nomadic — *bowl / tribe / society*
6 gorgeous — *dress / agriculture / cake*

Score ___ / 25

Wait a couple of weeks and try the quiz again. Compare your scores.

Unit 09

🎧 9.1

Conversation 1

W = woman; M = man

W: Hello, there! Are you OK?

M: No, not really. I've got a terrible headache, and a sore throat. It hurts when I swallow.

W: Oh, you poor thing! Have you taken anything for it?

M: Well, I took an aspirin, but it still hurts.

W: Maybe you should go to see a doctor.

M: Mm, I don't like going to the doctor's.

W: Well, you ought to go if your headache's still bad. And why don't you take some throat sweets? Here, I've got some in my bag … Go on, try them.

M: Thanks. Mmm, yeah, that's nice.

Conversation 2

M = man; W = woman

M: Hey! Are you OK?

W: Aah! Oh dear! I feel really dizzy!

M: Here, why don't you sit down for a minute? Shall I get you a glass of water?

W: What…? Oh, yes, please. Thanks.

M: Here you are. Is that better?

W: Mm, yes, a little, thanks. I don't know what happened. I just suddenly felt very weak, and couldn't stand up.

M: Perhaps you ought to see the nurse. Have you eaten anything today?

W: Well, I had a piece of toast on the way to the office.

M: And it's now five in the afternoon! You should eat something!

🎧 9.2

I = Interviewer, A = Dr Aziz

Part 1

I: I'm delighted to welcome to the programme today Dr Emil Aziz, who specialises in Down's Syndrome research.

A: Thank you for inviting me.

I: Thank you for coming. Now, Dr Aziz, I've read that one in every 1,000 babies born in the UK will have Down's Syndrome or DS.

A: Yes, yes, that's correct. About one in every thousand.

I: And do you think that people … well, that *most* people really understand this condition?

A: Well, Georgia, one of the problems is that people often think that Down's Syndrome is a mental illness. It is not. It is a condition that occurs before birth. It is *not* a disease, the person is not *ill*, and so does not *'suffer'* from the condition.

I: But they do have learning difficulties, don't they?

A: Well, that's not an easy question to answer. Yes, a person with Down's Syndrome will have *some* difficulty in

learning. But some people will have more problems and some people will have less. *Most* people will learn to talk, read and write, and *many* go to ordinary schools and lead enjoyable, semi-independent lives.

I: That's important to know. And how about physical problems? People with Down's Syndrome usually have physical disabilities, don't they?

A: Ah, another mistaken belief! They *do* have certain physical characteristics that make them look different. For example, their faces may look different. So, people often think this means they are also stupid.

I: Really?

A: And people sometimes think they can't do things like walk and play games. But the public need to realise that people with DS just *look* different. They are *people*, however, like you and me. Most of them are very healthy, active and strong.

I: Yes, that's important to know. And … talking of being healthy, active and strong, can you tell us about these football clubs here in London?

A: Yes, there are three football teams in London: the Fulham Badgers, QPR Tiger Cubs and Charlton Upbeats. They are all doing very well, and the players are enthusiastic and hardworking. I've been told that they're the only teams whose players are never late for training!

I: That's fantastic! So, doesn't anyone with DS ever have a physical disability?

A: Yes, sometimes, but this is often caused by another problem, not by DS itself. Thanks to research, and the wonderful work done by many charities and support groups throughout the UK, children with Down's Syndrome can get the right care and education to lead active lives, and an increasing number are able to then work in the community.

🎧 9.3

Part 2

I: Can you give us an example, Dr Aziz, of someone who has done just that?

A: Certainly! The story of Ruth Cromer is well-known to anyone involved with DS. She attended school, succeeded in learning to read and write, did not listen to teachers who told her she couldn't do things, and taught herself to type. She became an actress, and has been on TV several times. She also writes articles and gives speeches about the condition.

I: Amazing! Dr Aziz, that was extremely interesting. Thank you for coming to talk to us, and making us more aware that people with Down's Syndrome are *people*, first and foremost.

A: Thank *you* for inviting me, Georgia.

🎧 9.4

central
musical
industrial
physical

unbelievable
enjoyable
reliable
curable

🎧 9.5

1
The flat is really central.
2
Most kids are pretty musical.
3
That part of town is really industrial.
4
Rugby's a very physical game.
5
That's unbelievable!
6
The course was enjoyable.
7
The cars they make are very reliable.
8
A lot of diseases are curable.

UNIT 10

🎧 10.1

Speaker 1
I want to relax on holiday, and not run around after the kids all the time, so a place with a babysitting service is my first choice. To be honest, I'm not the outdoor type who likes sitting in a tent. I prefer the comfort of a hotel bar and heated pool. Free wi-fi access is also useful, so that I can check my messages from work.

Speaker 2
We like a certain amount of comfort, but don't want the fixed timetable of hotel breakfasts, as we like sleeping in. So we rent an apartment in a small block about 100 metres from the beach. We always go in the low season, so it's cheaper, and as regular customers we get a reduced rate. It's also quieter, which is nice. The furniture's fairly basic, but the cooking facilities are good, and there's a barbecue outside.

Speaker 3
It's a great way to travel around and see different places without spending too much money. Of course, the quality of the facilities differs from one hostel to another, but they're usually fairly clean. I look at online forums before going, to see what other travellers say about a place; you know, whether the showers are clean, how many people you have to share a room with, what the kitchen's like ... Things like that. Then I make a plan of which ones to go to, and which to avoid.

Speaker 4
There's nothing like sleeping in a tent, and it's actually quite comfortable. OK, you need to prepare your equipment beforehand, but it's worth it. We go to an organised campsite, as we're a family, and there's a shower block and washing facilities there. There are usually other families there, so the kids find other children to play with. The place we usually go to also provides meals on site, so if I don't feel like cooking one evening, there's that option.

🎧 10.2

Conversation 1
R = Receptionist, M = Mr Wiseman
R: Reception. Can I help you?
M: Hello. Mr Wiseman here ... Room 214. I'm not happy with my room. Could you give me another one?
R: I would if there was one available, sir, but I'm afraid we're fully booked this weekend. What seems to be the problem? Perhaps we can sort it out.
M: The air conditioning's on too high. It's freezing in here.
R: No problem, sir. Just turn it down.
M: I might be able to if I could find the switch!
R: It's on the wall by the door.
M: Well, I can't ... Oh, wait ... just a second. Yes, found it! I'd put my coat over it! Thanks very much.

Conversation 2
R = Receptionist, W = Mrs Arnold
R: Reception.
W: Oh, hello. I'm Mrs Arnold, from room 304. Could you send someone up, please? My husband's stuck in the bathroom.
R: Oh, dear! Is the door locked, madam?
W: No, it's stuck. I've tried pushing it but it won't move.
R: Right. Wait a moment. I'll see if someone's available ... Jeff? Can you send someone up to 304? The bathroom door's stuck ... Really? Well, can't you go? ... I see. Well, as soon as you can, then ...
Mrs Arnold?

W: Yes?

R: I'm afraid my colleague's very busy right now. It'll be about ten minutes.

W: But what are we going to do? My husband's the main speaker at the charity dinner, and it starts in five minutes! Call the manager, please!

R: I'll see what I can do, Mrs Arnold.

Conversation 3
R = Receptionist, M = Mr Dominguez

R: Hello, Reception.

M: Oh, er, hello. It's Mr Dominguez here, in the executive suite. I wonder if you could help me.

R: If I can, sir, certainly. What's the problem?

M: Oh, no problem exactly. It's our wedding anniversary, and I didn't have time to buy my wife a present. Is there anything I could order from here?

R: If I were you, I'd order a big bouquet of red roses. We have an arrangement with a local flower shop. I could phone them for you.

M: Lovely idea. Could you order them for me then and have them sent up to the room?

R: Certainly, sir.

M: Great! Thanks a lot.

🞖 10.3
used to
usually
useful
beautiful
cute

umbrella
uninteresting
summer
suntan
done

🞖 10.4
Double 0 – 3 – 0   2 – 5 – 1 – 0   3 – 6 – 7 – 5 – 4
2 – 4 – 2 – 1 – 0   8 – 9 – 5 – 6 – 7
6 – 9 – 7 – 9   0 – 1 – 0 – 2 – 5 – 9
Mr Kendall. That's K– E – N – D –A – L – L
Mrs Tsiakos. That's T – S – I – A – K – O – S
Miss Pandhi. That's P – A – N – D – H – I

UNIT 11

🞖 11.1
... And on a happier note, a young scientist from Yorkshire has discovered a clever way to help people in the poorer countries of Africa. Emily Cummins, aged 21, has invented a fridge that works without electricity, and she did it in her Grandad's garden shed!

The fridge works using the sun's energy. Emily won £5,000 from York Merchant Adventurers for her design and took a year off from her studies to go to Africa and test out her idea. She helped make more than 50 electricity-free refrigerators during the trip, using such materials as recycled car parts, and the locals named her 'The Fridge Lady'. Emily said that she hopes to continue inventing, and making changes for a better world.

More good news now on the little boy who went missing yesterday. Four-year old Tommy Jones has been found alive and well. He went missing from his home near Burnham Woods yesterday afternoon with his two Labrador puppies. His family were worried that he had run away. However, searchers found both him and the dogs safe this morning. They were fast asleep under a tree. Tommy told his mother that the puppies had kept him warm all night. He is now resting at home. His mother, Anna, said that she's delighted he's safe, but she's going to lock the garden gate in future.

... And finally, the weather forecast. Heavy rain will spread across the south of England today. Floods are expected in some parts so if you are driving, be very careful. Telephone the Environment Agency Floodline for the latest warnings.

🞖 11.2
study   shortage
extinct   explore   invent   protect   research
energy   natural
solution   pollution   resources
experiment   investigate   participant
population

UNIT 12

🞖 12.1
R = Receptionist, T = Tina Morrison

R: Hello, the Ashley Corporation.

T: Could I speak to Mr Khalil please?

R: Who's speaking, please?

T: It's Tina Morrison.

R: Oh, I'm sorry, Mr Khalil is working at home today. Can I take a message?

T: Yes, please. Could you tell him that I called? It's Tina Morrison. It's about our meeting next Thursday. I'm sorry but I'm going to be away on business that day, so can we change the meeting to Friday? The same time, three o'clock at my office. He knows where it is. If there are any problems, tell him to call my mobile on 08897 6576548. Thanks.

R: I'll pass that message on to him.

T: Thanks, bye!

🞖 12.2
1   polite possible
2   possible common
3   common comfortable
4   obtain opinion
5   hole hold
6   operation remote

⚫ 12.3

Thank you for calling Lucibello Bank. You now have four options. To check your current bank balance, press one. For information about opening a new account, press two. For technical support with our internet banking services, press three. For all other queries or to speak to an adviser, press four.

[beep]

Thank you for calling Lucibello Bank. Your call is important to us. A member of our dedicated customer services team will be available to speak to you shortly. Please note that calls may be recorded for training purposes. Unfortunately, we are currently experiencing a high volume of calls and your call is being held in a queue. Your wait time at the moment is approximately 12 minutes. You may find it more convenient to call back later. Thank you for calling Lucibello Bank. Your call is important to us.

UNIT 13

⚫ 13.1

B = Brad, A = Abha

B: Have you found the website, Abha?

A: Yes, here it is. Now, let's see what's on... Films showing now ... There's that new thriller, *Run and Hide*, directed by Antonio Torres. Andreas Dumas is in it. It's supposed to be good.

B: Mm, I've heard it's nothing special. Kate went and saw it last Friday, and she said she was bored. It was too predictable, she said. She knew who the killer was long before the end.

A: OK ... Well, then how about *The Mansford Saga*? Jeffrey Hinds is in it. Mm, I like him!

B: What's it about?

A: It's a family drama, set in 1860. They're rich but they lose their money, and then have to struggle to survive. Sounds interesting. Zena Williams is in it too.

B: It sounds boring to me! Isn't there anything lighter on, like a comedy, for instance?

A: Right! Here's one. *Mr Pickles*, starring Thierry Dumand and Catherine Pickard. Wasn't he in that film we saw a couple of weeks ago?

B: *The Partygoer*, yes. He's good. Shall we go and see that, then?

A: OK. It's on at the Palace, in Walker Street.

B: That's not far. We can walk there. What time does it start?

A: The first showing is at 3, and then there's another one at 5.30.

B: Let's go to the 5.30 one. Then I'll take you to that nice Italian place afterwards. They do a great carbonara.

A: OK, Brad. Great.

⚫ 13.2

excited
bored
tired
disappointed
interested
starred
amazed
treated
played
surprised
directed
recorded

UNIT 14

⚫ 14.1

A: Morning! Have you got everything ready?

B: Of course not. I've only just arrived... What do we need today?

A: Well we have to clean the carpets in the lobby, so we'll need the vacuum cleaner.

B: Where's that, then?

A: Usual place. Under the stairs.

B: Right.

A: And we've got to clean the marble floor in the dining room ...

B: ... so we'll need the mop and the bucket.

A: That's in the cupboard behind the reception area. And we'll also need a cloth because we've got to wipe all the mirrors.

B: And remind me – where do we keep the cloths?

A: In the drawer in the staff room, of course.

B: Oh yeah.

A: And we also need a hammer and some nails because we have to put up a picture.

B: And where do we keep those?

A: Down in the cellar.

B: Oh yes, it's dark down there isn't it? We'll need ... we'll need ... what do you call it? A ... A ...

A: What are you talking about?

B: Well, the light doesn't work down there so we'll need a ... You know. We'll need a ... a ...

🎵 14.2

1 class
2 gave
3 bin
4 pair
5 gold
6 could
7 ban
8 pad
9 goal
10 pouring

🎵 14.3

G = Gianni; J-P = Jean-Paul

G: Hi Jean-Paul! So how was Rachel's trip to Scotland?

J-P: Oh, hi Gianni! Yeah, she had a great time. But she brought me back this really strange present.

G: Really? What's it like?

J-P: Well, it's a bit like a handbag but you wear it round your waist.

G: Round your *waist*?

J-P: Yes. It's made of leather and apparently in Scotland men wear them.

G: Oh I know what it is. Does it have three tassels on the front?

J-P: Tassels?

G: Yes, extra bits of leather that hang down.

J-P: Yes, it does.

G: It's called a sporran. It's a traditional part of Scottish dress. You wear it with a kilt.

J-P: A *sporran*? How do you know that?

UNIT 15

🎵 15.1

C = Carlos; Y = Yelena

C: So, you're moving to Prague. But I thought you liked living here.

Y: I do, but if Miguel and I get married, I want him to know something about my country, and to understand the culture, the language, and so on.

C: Can't you just go for a holiday?

Y: You don't learn much from a holiday, Carlos! No, we've decided to go for two or three years, and then see where we'd prefer to live and bring up a family.

C: OK, but the cost of living's really high in Prague, isn't it?

Y: Not much higher than it is here in Argentina. Also, unemployment has fallen there in the last few years, and is lower than it is here. So, I think we'll find jobs fairly easily.

C: But the economy's doing better here now, though, and you get paid quite well, don't you?

Y: Yes, Carlos. It's not that I don't like it here. I'm happy, and have a good quality of life, but things are getting more expensive, and it's not easy to buy a house here. In the Czech Republic, house prices are generally cheaper, and so are cars.

C: Perhaps, but eating out is cheaper here, and as you told me, you can't beat the night life here!

Y: True, but I'm thinking more of the future. The salaries are higher in Prague. I could get paid more for doing the same job as I'm doing now.

C: Do you think Miguel will like it there?

Y: I have no idea! That's why I want him to try it. Don't worry, Carlos! You're not going to lose your best friend! I just think it's important for us to see where we are both happier, and we can't do that if we don't try living in both countries. Anyway, you can come and visit!

C: Yeah, I suppose you're right.

🎵 15.2

P = Primo, I = Isabel

P: What are you doing, Isabel?

I: Oh, just paying some bills.

P: What, you're paying them online? I didn't know you could do that.

I: Yes, it's easy, too. You can do it through your bank, or the service itself. I pay my phone bill to the phone company's bill payment service on its website.

P: Really? It must save you a lot of time!

I: Yes, and it's good for the environment, too. You don't use any paper! I pay my mortgage and electricity through the online banking service. I just order the bank to transfer the amount each month.

P: Is it safe, though? I mean, don't you worry about someone stealing your bank details and then taking all your money?

I: Well, there are some risks, but we change ID numbers and security codes fairly often, so they're difficult to copy. You should try it, Primo. It would be much easier for you.

P: Mm, perhaps I'll try it myself. I hate standing in the queue for hours waiting to pay the electricity bill! And then I often can't understand what the cashier says! The Scottish accent is not easy!

I: I know! This way it only takes you a few minutes, and no need to talk!

P: Sounds great!

🎵 15.3

1

Buy a house when the price is right, and pay your bills online.

2

Take out a loan to buy your own home, then owe the bank money until you grow old.

3

Twenty-five pounds for a meal may not sound much but is a large amount for a pizza.

4

I got paid a good wage for my job in sales, and was able to save for a holiday in Wales.

Unit 16

16.1

A: So what kind of party is it going to be? It's your birthday, isn't it?

B: Yes, it's my 21st birthday, so I want something big and noisy.

A: With lots of people? How many do you want to invite?

B: Oh, at least a hundred.

A: OK. And what sort of venue do you want? Have you seen somewhere you like?

B: Hmm. I don't know. Have you got any suggestions?

A: I know a really good new nightclub in a shopping mall just out of town.

B: Oh no. I don't think so. Can you think of anywhere else?

A: Well, there's also a really good converted warehouse near the beach. You can get at least a hundred people in there.

B: That sounds great.

A: And are you going to serve any food? How about a cold buffet?

B: Yeah, a cold buffet's good.

A: And what kind of music would you like?

B: Well, definitely not background music. I want a really good DJ and I want it to be loud.

A: No problem. And what time do you want the party to finish? It will be late, won't it?

B: No earlier than three.

A: Shall we say three to four in the morning?

B: Yeah, that's great.

16.2

1

A: With lots of people?

B: Oh yes, at least a hundred.

2

A: How about a cold buffet?

B: Yeah, a cold buffet's good.

3

A: Shall we say three to four in the morning?

B: Yeah, that's great.

16.3

1 Where did you go last night?

2 Did you see what she was wearing?

3 Why were you so rude to him?

4 Have you been here before?

5 How many people here do you know?

6 Are you going to eat something?

7 Who's that man in the sunglasses near the bar?

8 Do you have the time?

16.4

Now, this room contains the famous Bayeux Tapestry. As you can see, at this end it shows the events leading to the Norman invasion of England in 1066. As we walk round, you'll see the Normans' sea journey to England, the Battle of Hastings itself and the death of King Harold. We are not sure exactly when the tapestry was made but it dates from the 11th century. One legend says that it was made by William the Conqueror's wife, Queen Matilda. However, many historians now think that King William's brother paid for the tapestry to be made. This is the original tapestry, but there is also a copy at the Museum of Reading in England. Right, are there any questions so far?

ANSWER KEY

UNIT 09

VOCABULARY Illnesses and health problems

1

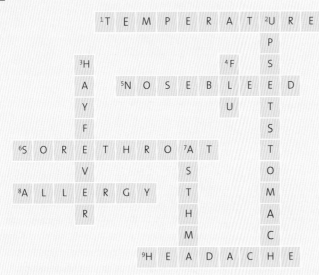

2

1 water;
2 swallow:
3 sweating;
4 sneezing;
5 aches;
6 last;
7 concentrate;
8 cough

GRAMMAR
Giving advice (*should, ought to, why don't*)

3

1 should;
2 why don't you;
3 you ought to;
4 should;
5 should;
6 why don't you;
7 should;
8 you ought to

4

1 I *don't* think you should …;
2 Maybe you should *put* …;
3 … He *ought* to stop …;
4 Why *don't* you …;
5 You ought *to* stay …;
6 You *oughtn't to / shouldn't* eat …

DEVELOPING CONVERSATIONS
Common questions about illness

5

1 Are you OK?
2 Have you been to the doctor's about it?
3 Are you taking anything for it?
4 Have you been to the doctor's about it?
5 Are you OK?
6 Are you taking anything for it?

6

1 e;   2 d;   3 f;   4 b;   5 a;   6 c

LISTENING

7

1 He has a headache and sore throat.
2 She feels dizzy and weak (because she hasn't eaten).

8

1 You should go to the doctor; take some throat sweets.
2 You should sit down; you ought to go to see the nurse.

9

He tells her to eat something.

10

1 b;   2 a

LISTENING

1

1 b;   2 c;   3 b;   4 a

3

1, 4, 6

4

1 school;
2 read and write;
3 type;
4 an actress;
5 speeches/talks

VOCABULARY Phrases with *mind* and *matter*

5

1 What's the matter, I've got a lot on my mind;
2 would you mind;
3 you don't mind. I don't mind;
4 To make matters worse, Never mind, That's a matter of opinion;
5 It doesn't matter;
6 It's a question of mind over matter

6

1 f;   2 i;   3 d;   4 a;   5 g;   6 c

PRONUNCIATION

7

unbe**lie**vable   **mu**sical   en**joy**able   in**dus**trial
re**li**able   **phy**sical   **cur**able

DEVELOPING WRITING A webpage – fundraising

10

1 research at the new clinic in London
2 Her son had a stroke when he was small, and Different Strokes helped them.
3 She's going to take part in the London to Paris Cycle Ride.
4 She's hoping to raise €2,000.

11

1 e;   2 a;   3 c;   4 f;   5 d;   6 b

12

Example answer:
Target: £5,000
Raised so far: £1,140
Donate now!
My Story
In 2005, I had a car accident and suffered a bad head injury. Afterwards I discovered that I could not speak. The medical name for this is aphasia. I suffered from this for two years. During this time, I received a lot of help and support from Speakability. Their speech therapists helped me to speak again. I decided that I wanted to help other people with this problem. I'm going to walk from Edinburgh to Brighton next month to raise money to help fund training for Speakability's speech therapists. Thank you for your support.

VOCABULARY Parts of the body

1
1 legs;
2 face;
3 finger;
4 hair;
5 lips;
6 ear;
7 stomach;
8 feet

2
1 eye hair;
2 yellow hair;
3 armstand;
4 back arm;
5 mouth ache

GRAMMAR Imperatives

3
1 call;
2 put;
3 Don't leave;
4 eat;
5 Don't take;
6 Let;
7 Drink;
8 Don't touch

4
1 f; 2 d; 3 b; 4 d; 5 c;
6 e; 7 a; 8 c

5
Example answers:
1 Take these painkillers three times a day.
2 Go to bed and rest.
3 Don't eat so many sweets. Eat more fruit.
4 Drink hot drinks and fruit juice.
5 Stay at home and put on this cream twice a day.

READING

6
1 hydrotherapy;
2 aromatherapy;
3 nutrition

7
1 rub;
2 radiator;
3 gargle;
4 remedy;
5 burn;
6 steam;
7 symptoms;
8 virus

8
1 a; 2 b,c; 3 b; 4 a,c; 5 a

VOCABULARY BUILDER QUIZ 9

1
1 anxious;
2 acceptable;
3 disabled;
4 religious;
5 cultural;
6 depressed;
7 generous

2
1 I've got an upset stomach;
2 Take a deep breath;
3 She's made a speedy recovery from the flu;
4 He broke out in a rash after touching the cat;
5 I lost my voice after shouting so much at the match.

3
1 T; 2 F; 3 T; 4 F; 5 F; 6 T; 7 F

4
1 put on an;
2 throat;
3 wise;
4 bite my;
5 back;
6 suffer from

UNIT 10

VOCABULARY Places to stay

1
babysitting service; basic furniture; free wi-fi; heated pool; including breakfast; low season; provide meals; put up the tent; real fire; reduced rate; share a room; shower block

2
1 furniture, breakfast;
2 the tent, block;
3 pool, service;
4 rate, season;
5 fire, meals;
6 a room, wi-fi

3
Students should circle:
1 low;
2 price;
3 tent;
4 leave;
5 free;
6 campsite

LISTENING

4
1 hotel;
2 pic B – apartment;
3 pic A – hostel;
4 campsite

5
1 babysitting service;
2 free wi-fi;
3 fixed timetable;
4 low season;
5 share a room;
6 online forums;
7 shower block;
8 provides meals

DEVELOPING CONVERSATIONS Apologising

6
1 I'm afraid not;
2 I'm afraid so;
3 I'm afraid not;
4 I'm afraid so;
5 I'm afraid not;
6 I'm afraid so

7
1 I'm afraid we don't accept credit cards, but you can pay by cheque.
2 I'm afraid we're fully booked until the end of the month.
3 I'm afraid you'll have to park in the car park down the road.
4 I'm afraid so. There's a wedding party tomorrow evening and all the guests are staying in the hotel.
5 I'm afraid not. It is currently closed for repairs.
6 I'm afraid not. We don't have enough staff to offer that service.

DEVELOPING WRITING An online booking form

8
1 Jorg Oskarsson;
2 Applecote Guest House;
3 four (two adults, two children);
4 2 September 2015;
5 eight nights;
6 yes – son's 16th birthday;
7 yes – £10 per night for the one child under 12;
8 no

9
1 g; 2 a; 3 d; 4 f; 5 b; 6 h;
7 e; 8 c

VOCABULARY Solving hotel problems

1
1 get the jacuzzi to work;
2 boiling;
3 free for sightseeing;
4 no record;
5 an early flight;
6 noise outside;
7 an upset stomach;
8 more expensive than I expected;
9 before you serve breakfast;
10 no toothbrush or toothpaste

2
a 8; b 2; c 6; d 10; e 5; f 1; g 7;
h 9; i 3; j 4

GRAMMAR Second conditionals

3
1 If I were you, I'd book a room first. / I'd book a room first if I were you.
2 If it happened to you, what would you do? / What would you do if it happened to you?

3 It would be better if you went home.
4 He might listen to you if you called him. / If you called him, he might listen to you.
5 Do you think it would be better if we left?

4
1 What would you do if there was no hot water in your hotel bathroom?
2 If I asked you to marry me, what would you say?
3 Would you complain if it happened to you?
4 If I ordered breakfast in my room, how much would it cost?
5 Would you think I was crazy if I bought that hotel?
6 Would you know what to do if you were on your own?

5
Answers may vary. Possible answers:
1 If I were you, I'd complain to the chef.
2 If I were you, I'd ask the maid.
3 If I were you, I'd search on the Internet.
4 If I were you, I'd complain to the head waiter.
5 If I were you, I'd tell the manager.
6 If I were you, I'd ask for a refund.

LISTENING

6
1 2;   2 3;   3 1

7
1 3;   2 1;   3 2

8
1 turn down;   4 the main speaker;
2 find;   5 wedding anniversary;
3 put his coat over it;   6 roses

9
1 I would get her some perfume.
2 I would call the hotel manager.
3 I would change room.
4 I would ask room service to call a plumber.
5 I would ask the receptionist to call and explain that there's a problem.
6 I would ask the receptionist to recommend a restaurant.

10
W: Hurry up, Henri! We're going to be late!
M: Just a minute. I'm nearly ready ... Oh, wait, Cherise! I can't open the door!
W: What? OK! I'm coming. Give me two seconds ... Right! You pull, I'll push.
M: Wait. Just one second ... OK, ready!
W: Right. One, two, three ... go!
M: Aaagh! ... It's no good! It won't move!
W: OK, I'll phone reception for help. I won't be a minute ... It's all right, Henri. They'll send someone up in a minute. Be patient.

READING

1
c

2
1 c;   2 b;   3 c;   4 c;   5 a

PRONUNCIATION

3

/juː/	/ʌ/
used to	umbrella
usually	uninteresting
useful	summer
beautiful	suntan
cute	done

GRAMMAR *used to*

7
1 a, b, d;   2 c

8
1 When I was young, I used to walk to school every day.
2 When I was a kid, I never used to go on holiday with my parents, so now family holidays are special to me.
3 We used to go to North Wales every summer, until I went to university.
4 My dad used to go fishing with his friend every morning.
5 We used to stay in the same place every year, so we made lots of friends there.
6 I used to swim in the sea every day of the holidays.

9
1 I **never used** to like singing round camp fires, but I do now.
3 We use**d** to like going to the outdoor swimming pool.
4 When I was at school, we **used to** go on skiing trips every February.
6 Last weekend, I **had** to get up early for a hockey tournament.
8 Rob **used to go** to summer camp every August.

VOCABULARY BUILDER QUIZ 10

1
1 climbing;   4 babysitting;
2 entertainment;   5 Parking;
3 arrangement;   6 achievement

2
1 e;   2 g;   3 b;   4 a;   5 c;   6 d;   7 f

3
1 T;   2 T;   3 F;   4 F;   5 T;   6 F

4
1 take;   4 turn;
2 warn;   5 climbed;
3 send;   6 messed

UNIT 11

VOCABULARY Science and nature in the news

1
1 e;   2 f;   3 a;   4 c;   5 d;   6 b

2
1 find;   6 building;
2 spread;   7 launched;
3 become;   8 investigate;
4 fund;   9 ban;
5 hit;   10 conduct

3
1 product;   6 diseases;
2 smoking;   7 effect;
3 research;   8 cure;
4 experiments; 9 coast;
5 extinct;   10 science block

LISTENING

4

Emily Cummins 2; Tommy Jones 3; weather forecast 1

5

1 b;   2 b;   3 b;   4 b;   5 a;   6 a

6

1 flooding;   3 invented;   5 recycled;
2 puppy;   4 shed;   6 energy

DEVELOPING CONVERSATIONS
Responding to news and comments

7

Suggested answers:
1 Really? That's great news / fantastic / wonderful!
2 No change
3 No change
4 Really? That's good news / great / really good.
  Yes, I know. It's really good.
5 Definitely / Absolutely.
6 No change
7 Good idea.
8 Really? That's interesting.

8

1 Really? That's amazing!
2 They should do more
3 No. So is it going to snow?
4 Really? That's awful!
5 Maybe we should

PRONUNCIATION   Word stress

9

popu**la**tion – 4 syllables
re**search** – 2 syllables
in**vent** – 2 syllables
ex**per**iment – 4 syllables
pol**lu**tion – 3 syllables
energy – 3 syllables

10

2 syllables, stress on first syllable	2 syllables, stress on second syllable	3 syllables, stress on first syllable	3 syllables, stress on second syllable	4 syllables, stress on second syllable	4 syllables, stress on third syllable
study shortage research* natural*	extinct explore invent protect research*	energy natural*	solution pollution resources	experiment investigate participant	population

* both pronunciations are acceptable

VOCABULARY   Animals

1

pets	farm animals	marine animals	birds	wild cats
dog cat rabbit horse parrot	sheep hen cow horse	shark dolphin whale	eagle parrot pigeon	lion tiger panther

2

1 ground;   5 success;
2 dogs;   6 school;
3 excited;   7 workers;
4 less;   8 bones

READING

3

	magnetic fridge	methane farming	green machine	floating wind turbines
air pollution		✓		✓
water shortage			✓	
energy resources	✓	✓	✓	✓

4

1 a, c;   2 b, d;   3 c;   4 b, d;   5 c (washes and dries)

5

1 d;   2 e;   3 b;   4 c;   5 a

GRAMMAR   Past perfect simple

6

1 checked, called;   4 looked at, had discovered;
2 had followed, realised;   5 had fallen, got home
3 had already finished, told;

7

1 had finished;   4 had forgotten;   7 had forgotten;
2 had been hit;   5 had not been;   8 had discovered
3 had never been;   6 had already left;

8

1 lived;   3 discovered;   5 had died;
2 existed;   4 had looked;   6 had eaten

GRAMMAR   Passives

1

1 The first earthship was developed by Michael Reynolds in the 1970s;
2 Earthships can be built from available recycled materials;
3 Worn out car tyres are used to build the external walls;
4 The tyres are filled with rammed earth to make the walls;
5 The first earthship was built in the UK in Fife, in Scotland;
6 Could glass bottles be used to build walls?;
7 Can the earthships be heated naturally?;
8 The buildings are heated with solar panels

2

1 a;   2 a;   3 a;   4 b;   5 b;   6 a;
7 b;   8 a

DEVELOPING WRITING
An email – expressing an opinion

3

1 d;   2 e;   3 c;   4 a;   5 b

4

1 One thing;   3 but;   5 However;
2 Secondly;   4 Another;   6 Although

5

Answers may vary slightly. Suggested answers:
1 *Although* I like most animals, I don't like rats.
2 *Although* more homes are needed in the city centre, there should be parks.
3 Paris is a beautiful city, with wide streets. *Another thing* I like are the cafés on street corners with tables outside.
4 It's a good thing that governments are talking about climate change, *but* they should do more.
5 *Although* I like living by the sea, it gets cold in the winter.
6 I like sweets but they're not healthy.

1

1 witnessed;	3 banned;	5 investigating
2 fund;	4 conducting;	

2

1 cage;	3 evidence;	5 sight
2 detected;	4 Freezing;	

3

1 c; 2 d; 3 e; 4 a; 5 b

4

1 to; 2 on; 3 in; 4 at; 5 in

5

1 accidentally;	3 kindness;	5 security
2 environmental;	4 confidently;	

UNIT 12

VOCABULARY Using phones

1

1 back;	4 off;	7 busy;
2 through;	5 up;	8 text
3 on;	6 call;	

2

1 line;	3 signal;	5 text
2 busy;	4 coverage;	

DEVELOPING CONVERSATIONS
Explaining where people are

3

1 on business;	3 sick;	5 from home;
2 a meeting;	4 visiting a client;	6 the factory

4

1 b, a, c; 2 c, b, a; 3 c, a, b; 4 b, c, a

5

1 f; 2 a; 3 c; 4 d; 5 h; 6 e; 7 b;
8 g

LISTENING

6

Tina Morrison called about your meeting next <u>Tuesday</u>. She's going to be away on <u>holiday</u> that day, so can you change the meeting to <u>Thursday</u>? <u>Two o'clock</u> at her office. If there are any problems, please call her mobile on <u>08857678548</u>.

7

Tina Morrison called about your meeting next Thursday. She's going to be away on business that day, so can you change the meeting to Friday? Three o'clock at her office. If there are any problems, please call her mobile on 088976576548

GRAMMAR *yet, already, still* and *just*

8

1 just; 2 yet; 3 already; 4 still

9

1 I've just spilled my coffee.
2 I've already called him.
3 I haven't seen her yet.
4 We're still waiting for it.
5 I haven't spoken to them yet.
6 He's just gone out for a moment.
7 She's still looking for it.
8 They've already paid us.

READING

1

b

2

1 d; 2 g; 3 b; 4 c; 5 h; 6 a; 7 e;
8 f

3

1 the early 1990s;
2 because the signal wasn't always very good;
3 it fell dramatically;
4 teenagers in rich countries;
5 the way people do business and socialise
6 in the developing world

4

1 F; 2 T; 3 F; 4 T; 5 F; 6 T

5

1 the best market for their fish;	4 plan their work;
2 unnecessary waste;	5 farming methods;
3 local weather forecasts;	6 that we can't imagine yet

VOCABULARY Forming negatives

6

un-	wise, fortunate, happy, expected, fair, comfortable, common, natural, pleasant
im-	polite, practical, patient, possible
in-	appropriate, convenient
il-	legal
ir-	rational

7

1 unhappy;	5 unfortunate;	9 unexpected;
2 inappropriate;	6 unwise;	10 inconvenient
3 impolite;	7 impatient;	
4 illegal;	8 irrational;	

PRONUNCIATION Same or different?

8

1 D; 2 S; 3 D; 4 S; 5 S; 6 D

DEVELOPING WRITING Text and email – abbreviations

1

1 R;	5 4;	9 poss;	12 2;
2 ASAP;	6 l8r;	10 c;	13 u;
3 docs;	7 msg;	11 txt;	14 yr
4 eve;	8 meet;		

2

Answers may vary. Example answer:
From: Brian Dufriss
Subject: This evening's meeting
Date: 14 January 2015
To: Steve Zizek
Dear Steve,
Thanks for your messages. Are you coming to the meeting this evening? If so, could you please bring the documents that we discussed?
Please let me know if this is possible as soon as you can.
See you soon,
Brian

VOCABULARY Reporting crimes

3

1 came;
2 kicked;
3 threatening;
4 hitting/kicking;
5 kicking/hitting;
6 having;
7 making;
8 grabbed;
9 ran;
10 bought;
11 got;
12 hacked;
13 stole
14 follow;
15 crashed;
16 texting

LISTENING

4

1 a bank;
2 four;
3 check your bank balance;
4 three;
5 four;
6 approximately 12 minutes

5

1 a new account;
2 is important;
3 will be available;
4 training purposes;
5 high volume of;
6 more convenient

GRAMMAR Reporting speech

6

1 were helping;
2 hadn't seen;
3 had phoned;
4 were going;
5 had seen;
6 hadn't heard

7

1 She said Anna had posted the letter on Tuesday.
2 You said you were sending me the books today.
3 You said you hadn't been to the office all day.
4 You said you hadn't brought your notes with you.
5 They told us they hadn't delivered the letters yet.
6 You said you were going to the post office right now.

8

1 said
2 asked
3 told
4 asked
5 told/asked
6 said

VOCABULARY BUILDER QUIZ 12

1

1 d;   2 a;   3 f;   4 b;   5 c;   6 e

2

1 coverage;
2 inconvenient;
3 resend;
4 irrational;
5 unexpected;
6 initially

3

1 T;   2 F;   3 F;   4 T;   5 F;   6 T;
7 F;   8 T

4

1 transfer;
2 campaign;
3 continuously;
4 relatively;
5 threatening

UNIT 13

VOCABULARY Films

1

¹S	C	I	E	N	C	E	F	I	C	T	I	O	N

²H	I	S	T	O	R	I	C	A	L	D	R	A	M	A

³A C T I O N

⁴T H R I L L E R

⁵C O M E D Y

⁶M A R T I A L A R T S

2

1 a horror;
2 special effects;
3 past;
4 predictable;
5 martial arts;
6 romantic

3

1 A;   2 C;   3 A;   4 B;   5 A;   6 B;
7 B;   8 C

LISTENING

4

1 c;   2 a;   3 b

6

1 C;   2 A;   3 B;   4 C;   5 B;   6 A

7

1 T;   2 F;   3 F;   4 T;   5 T;   6 F

DEVELOPING CONVERSATIONS *supposed to*

8

1 d;   2 a;   3 e;   4 f;   5 b;   6 c

9

1 What are you doing;
2 Would you like;
3 is supposed to;
4 really talented;
5 amazing;
6 Why don't you;
7 are supposed to;
8 do you fancy

GRAMMAR -ed / -ing adjectives

10

1 bored;
2 interesting;
3 excited;
4 shocked;
5 disappointing;
6 annoying;
7 tiring;
8 confused

11

1 annoying;
2 surprised;
3 worried;
4 disgusting;
5 boring;
6 amazing

GRAMMAR Noun phrases

1

1 film cameraman;
2 fashion industry;
3 film director;
4 photo of my family;
5 works of art;
6 cinema audience

2

1 film cameraman;
2 cinema audience;
3 works of art;
4 film director

3

1 fashion industry;
2 film director;
3 works of art;
4 cinema audiences;
5 photo of my family;
6 film cameraman

4

1 b;   2 a;   3 a;   4 b;   5 b;   6 a;
7 a;   8 b;   9 b;   10 b

PRONUNCIATION -ed

5

/ɪd/	/d/
excited	bored
disappointed	tired
interested	starred
treated	amazed
directed	played
recorded	surprised

Reading

8

1 B;   2 C;   3 A

9

1 B;   2 A;   3 B,C;   4 A;   5 B,C;   6 C

10

adjective	verb
moving	move
exciting	excite
disappointing	disappoint
amazing	amaze
shocking	shock
surprising	surprise
upsetting	upset

Vocabulary Music, art and books

1

1 instruments;
2 composer;
3 albums;
4 concert;
5 singer;
6 portrait photographer;
7 sculptures;
8 exhibition;
9 landscape;
10 paintings;
11 novel;
12 comedy;
13 crime fiction;
14 authors;
15 poetry

Grammar Present perfect continuous

2

1 for;   2 for;   3 since;   4 since;   5 for;   6 for

3

1 been acting, starred;
2 directed, been working;
3 started, has held;
4 has been playing, has had;
5 known, have been going;
6 become, published

4

1 has been playing;   3 has recorded;   5 has been
2 has gained;   4 has worked;   touring

Developing writing Blog entry – a book review

5

1 moving;   2 interested;   3 surprising

6

1 c;   2 a;   3 b

Vocabulary Builder Quiz 13

1

1 in;   3 of;   5 in
2 on;   4 at;

2

1 composers;   4 explosion;   7 wealthy;
2 social;   5 leading;   8 conductor
3 unpredictable;   6 director;

3

1 rehearsing;   3 Festival;   5 depressing;
2 promote;   4 talent;   6 source

4

1 e;   2 a;   3 f;   4 b;   5 d;   6 c

UNIT 14

Vocabulary Things in the house

1

2

1 mop and bucket, a;   3 dustpan and brush, d;
2 needle and thread, c;   4 hammer and nails, b

Developing conversations Explaining where things are

3

1 A: Can I borrow a hairdryer?
   B: There's one on the bathroom wall.
2 A: Where do you keep the plasters?
   B: There's a first aid kit in the kitchen cupboard.
3 A: Have you got any snacks?
   B: Yes, there are some in the fridge.
4 A: Have you got a needle and thread?
   B: There's a sewing box on the shelf.
5 A: Can I make a drink?
   B: Yes, the coffee is on the shelf.
6 A: Have you got today's paper?
   B: It's on the table by the TV.

4

1 next;   3 at;   5 under;   7 on;
2 in;   4 on;   6 in;   8 in

Grammar Relative clauses

5

1 where you can keep fit;
2 who prepares food in a restaurant;
3 which cleans carpets;
4 who make things from wood;
5 where you can watch the latest movies;
6 which helps you to get dry;
7 where horse racing takes place;
8 which hold water

6

1 who;   3 who;   5 who;   7 who;
2 where;   4 when;   6 where;   8 when

7

1 which;   3 who;   5 which
2 which;   4 who ;

LISTENING

8
The following should be ticked:
Clean carpets in lobby; Clean marble floor in dining room; Wipe mirrors; Put up picture

9 & 10
1	A vacuum cleaner	Under the stairs
2	A mop and a bucket	In the cupboard behind the reception area
3	A cloth	In the drawer in the staff room
4	A hammer and some nails	In the cellar

11
A torch

VOCABULARY Containers

1
1	shampoo;	4	butter;	7	crisps;
2	bread;	5	cheese;	8	eggs
3	fish;	6	sausages;		

2
1 e; 2 c; 3 b; 4 d; 5 a; 6 f

READING

3
b

4
1 In an empty shop in Oxford Street, London;
2 10;
3 7,227;
4 *Break Down*;
5 consumer society;
6 his cat;
7 He felt an incredible sense of freedom;
8 He has become one of the most respected artists in the UK.

5
1 T; 2 F; 3 F; 4 F; 5 T; 6 F

6
1 Why do you think that?
2 It was so wasteful!
3 I think he made a good point.
4 We all have too many possessions these days.
5 But he could have given them to charity.
6 You're always going shopping.

GRAMMAR *must, mustn't*

7
1 c; 2 b; 3 a

8
1	You must;	6	You must;
2	You mustn't;	7	You don't have to;
3	You must;	8	You don't have to;
4	You mustn't;	9	You mustn't;
5	You don't have to;	10	You mustn't

GRAMMAR Verbs with two objects

1
1	for;	3	to;	5	to;	7	to;
2	to;	4	for;	6	to;	8	for

2
1 He gave me the books.
2 I bought a cup of coffee for you.
3 He poured me a glass of milk.
4 I sent a postcard to you.
5 She made me a sandwich.
6 He read the report to them.
7 They lent us their car.
8 We cooked them dinner.

PRONUNCIATION /g/ and /k/, /b/ and /p/

3
1	class;	6	could;
2	gave;	7	ban;
3	bin;	8	pad;
4	pair;	9	goal;
5	gold;	10	pouring

LISTENING

4
1 T; 2 T; 3 F; 4 T; 5 F; 6 F

WRITING

5
a 3 b 4 c 1 d 2

VOCABULARY BUILDER QUIZ 14

1
1	rid;	3	sack;	5	spilt;
2	clue;	4	shame;	6	consumed

2
1 T; 2 F; 3 F; 4 T; 5 T; 6 F; 7 F

3
1	reduction	3	consumers;	5	in efficient
2	guilty;	4	dispose;	6	recycling

4
1	clue;	3	exhausted;	5	jam;
2	petrol;	4	soap;	6	plaster

UNIT 15

VOCABULARY The economy and quality of life

1

C	O	T	D	E	R	U	K	A	E	W	N	P	U
X	Y	O	O	A	O	N	I	D	Q	W	X	Y	L
W	C	L	C	B	T	E	S	C	E	T	N	T	E
T	N	L	X	T	I	M	E	O	F	F	P	I	V
A	E	U	I	Y	N	P	K	S	A	L	A	R	Y
S	R	E	N	A	W	L	Z	T	M	H	J	U	T
Z	R	T	F	I	Q	O	V	O	I	C	E	C	R
Q	U	A	L	I	T	Y	O	F	L	I	F	E	O
S	C	M	A	K	L	M	B	L	Y	A	R	S	P
T	R	I	T	E	U	E	M	I	R	C	H	B	S
Y	P	L	I	C	I	N	Z	V	Q	D	U	J	N
P	W	C	O	I	W	T	P	I	Y	F	G	J	A
U	L	O	N	S	T	R	O	N	G	O	W	A	R
Q	I	M	A	V	E	R	A	G	E	R	S	A	T

2

1 unemployment;   4 quality of life;   7 inflation;
2 pace of life;   5 climate change;   8 salary
3 job security;   6 weak;

LISTENING

3

1 Yes, she does.
2 It's doing better than before.
3 She and Miguel want to get married, and she wants him to try living in Prague for a while so that he can understand her culture.

4

1 higher;   3 cheaper;   5 higher;
2 lower;   4 expensive;   6 happier

5

1, 3, 4, 6

GRAMMAR Time phrases and tense

6

1 e;   2 f;   3 a;   4 b;   5 g;   6 h;
7 d;   8 c

7

1 The government used to spend more on education.
2 Yesterday they opened a new shopping centre on the ring road.
3 She's going to start a new job in advertising next week.
4 He's had three jobs in the last two years.
5 The economy is improving at the moment.
6 She's had three loans from the bank in the last five years.

8

1 Unemployment has risen over the last few months.
2 The average salary used to be higher when I was at school.
3 Inflation has fallen since last year.
4 The price of petrol has risen again in the last few weeks.
5 The cost of living is falling at the moment, and prices are lower.
6 I think the economy will improve next year.

DEVELOPING CONVERSATIONS Comparing prices

9

1 cheaper;   4 cheaper;
2 cheaper than (it is);   5 the same;
3 more expensive;   6 slightly lower than

10

1 they cost €300,000 in Faroland.
2 it costs €20,000 in Celtonia.
3 whereas it costs €1 in Celtonia.
4 whereas they cost €1,000 in Faroland.

READING

1

1 an Economics teacher at university
2 the Grameen Bank.
3 the Nobel Peace prize.

2

1 F;   2 T;   3 T;   4 T;   5 F;   6 T;
7 T;   8 F

3

1 interest;   3 micro-credit;   5 borrowed;
2 lend;   4 pay back;   6 loan

VOCABULARY Money verbs

4

1 owed;   3 won;   5 left;   7 lose;
2 borrowed;   4 gave;   6 save;   8 plays

5

1 credit card;   3 back;   5 attention;   7 interest
2 bill;   4 to do it;   6 paid;

LISTENING

6

1 paying bills online;   3 at first he is worried, then he
2 easy;   likes it

7

1 c;   2 a;   3 b;   4 a;   5 b;   6 b;
7 c;   8 a

PRONUNCIATION

8

/aɪ/ bill;   /əʊ/ owl;   /aʊ/ through;   /eɪ/ said

GRAMMAR Time clauses

1

1 I'll pay back the money I owe you as soon as **I'm able to/ I can.**
2 Call me after **you transfer** the money. OK?
3 **I'll lend** you the money until you get paid.
5 When I find a job, **I'm going to/I'll** open a savings account.
7 As soon as **I get** confirmation of payment, I'll let you know.
8 When **I have** enough money, I'll buy a new car.

2

1 when;   3 until;   5 after;
2 as soon as;   4 before;   6 as soon as

3

1 will cancel;   4 recovers;   7 take out, check;
2 have;   5 won't invest, falls;   8 finish, will come
3 won't fall;   6 win, will take;

VOCABULARY Dealing with banks

4

1 take out;   4 charge;   7 transfer;
2 cancel;   5 make;   8 change
3 open;   6 pay;

5

1 I will transfer some money to him/my brother.
2 I will pay some money into my account.
3 I will charge them some money/a fee for the translation.
4 I will take out a mortgage.
5 I will open an account.
6 I will cancel my credit card.

DEVELOPING WRITING
Email – giving information and advice

6

1 cost of living;   3 cost;   5 expenses;
2 pay;   4 charges;   6 spend

7

£170: rent/accommodation per week
£13: lunches in the university canteen
£210–220: minimum total spending per week

8

1 c;   2 a;   3 b

9

Example answer:
From: Marita Bland
To: Paco Mendoza
Subject: re: social life in Lisbon
Dear Paco,
You asked about the social life in Lisbon. Lisbon is a very exciting, lively city, but it is quite expensive, so as a student here, you'll need to budget carefully.
There are ways that you can save some money. The college student centre offers free films and parties, and discount prices at the bar. Also, the local cinema and theatre offer student discounts, and entry to the art gallery is free. However, some sports facilities are expensive. The cheapest is probably the swimming pool. Also, restaurants are usually expensive here, but don't worry, my mum's a good cook!
We look forward to welcoming you here. Don't hesitate to write again if you have any more questions.
Best wishes,
Marita

VOCABULARY BUILDER QUIZ 15

1

1 T;   2 T;   3 F;   4 T;   5 F

2

1 It's an old motorbike, so it **isn't worth** much.
2 Our **insurance policy covers** fire and flooding.
3 It cost us €10,000 to **repair the damage** to the house.
4 In times of recession, people want more **job security**.
5 She decided to **buy shares** in the company.

3

1 loan;   3 owed;   5 charity
2 popularity;   4 currency;

4

1 c;   2 e;   3 d;   4 b;   5 a

5

1 up;   3 down;   5 into
2 down;   4 out;

UNIT 16

VOCABULARY Describing parties and events

1

1 reception;   3 surprise;   5 housewarming
2 launch;   4 leaving;   6 dinner

2

1 c;   2 h;   3 e;   4 g;   5 a;   6 b;
7 f;   8 d

3

1 host;   4 general;
2 comfortable and convenient;   5 full;
3 backward;   6 past

DEVELOPING CONVERSATIONS Linked questions

4

1 Did you have a good time?
2 What time did you leave?
3 And what was the venue like?
4 Was there anything to eat?
5 Or did you hang out with your friends?
6 Was anyone I know there?

7 Is he the person you went to school with?
8 What's he like?

LISTENING

5

d

6

Kind of party	21st birthday
Atmosphere	Fun and noisy
Venue	Converted warehouse
Food	Cold buffet
Music	DJ
End time	3.00 – 4.00 am

7

1 What kind of party is it going to be?
2 What sort of venue do you want?
3 Have you got any suggestions?
4 Can you think of anywhere else?
5 And are you going to serve any food?
6 What kind of music would you like?
7 What time do you want the party to finish?

PRONUNCIATION

8

1 With lots of people?   ↗
2 Oh, yes, at least a hundred.   ↘
3 How about a cold buffet?   ↘
4 Yeah, a cold buffet's good.   ↘
5 Shall we say three to four in the morning?   ↗
6 Yeah, that's great.   ↘

9

1 Where did you go last night?   ↘
2 Did you see what she was wearing?   ↗
3 Why were you so rude to him?   ↘
4 Have you been here before?   ↗
5 How many people here do you know?   ↘
6 Are you going to eat something?   ↗
7 Who's that man in the sunglasses near the bar?   ↘
8 Do you have the time?   ↗

VOCABULARY Historical events

1

¹E	M	P	I	R	E				
	²R	U	L	E	S				
³I	N	D	E	P	E	N	D	E	N	T
	⁴O	C	C	U	P	Y			
⁵E	S	T	A	B	L	I	S	H	
	⁶K	I	L	L					
		⁷I	N	V	A	D	E		
		⁸C	I	V	I	L	W	A	R

2

1 independent;   3 Empire;   5 Republic;
2 established;   4 occupied;   6 invaded

3

1 Civil;   3 lasted;   5 king;
2 Union;   4 ruled;   6 killed

READING

4

3

5

500	*The first settlers arrived.*
1778	*Captain Cook visited the islands.*
1779	*Captain Cook was killed.*
1805	*King Kamehameha established a monarchy*
1820	*Christian missionaries arrived.*
1893	*American businessmen seized power in a revolution.*
1898	*Hawaii became a territory of the USA.*
1941	*Japan attacked Pearl Harbor.*
1959	*Hawaii became the 50th state of the USA.*
1961	*Barack Obama was born.*

GRAMMAR Articles

6

1 the, -;
2 The, -;
3 -, the, -;
4 A, -, the, a, a;
5 -, the, the;
6 The, the, the;
7 -, the, -;
8 a, -, a

7

1 ~~the~~ civil war;
2 ~~the~~ people, ~~the~~ refugees;
3 ~~the~~ oil;
4 ~~the~~ farming;
5 ~~the~~ unfair taxation;
6 a war, ~~the~~ Germany;
7 ~~the~~ 2011, ~~the~~ 28,000;
8 ~~the~~ power;
9 ~~the~~ soldiers;
10 ~~the~~ Queen Victoria

8

1 the;
2 the;
3 -;
4 the;
5 The;
6 a;
7 the;
8 -;
9 -;
10 A;
11 the;
12 the;
13 the;
14 the

DEVELOPING WRITING

1

The Normans sailed across the English Channel.
The Normans established a camp.
The Normans and the English fought a battle.
King Harold was killed.
William marched to London.
William was crowned king.

2

1 1066 is the year that the Normans invaded Britain.
2 William was the first in a line of kings and queens which includes Queen Elizabeth II.
4 Meanwhile = at the same time as

LISTENING

4

1 T;   2 F;   3 T;   4 F;
5 F;   6 T;   7 F;   8 T

GRAMMAR Verb patterns (-*ing* or infinitive with *to*)

5

1 I forgot to post the letter. I remember telling her to go home early.
2 He spent two weeks doing nothing. She decided to review all the work.
3 They hated going to the theatre. They persuaded us to play tennis.
4 I'd like to help my parents with their business. I don't feel like watching TV this evening.
5 She enjoyed taking her brother to school. She asked me to help with her assignment.
6 Her new boss offered to help her sort out the accounts. The new job stopped her spending so much time at home.

6

1 Yes. I hate taking the bus.
2 No. I stopped smoking last year.
3 I'd like to go to Hawaii.
4 No, thanks. I feel like watching TV at home.
5 Because I forgot to pay my bill.
6 I remember seeing my brother's face.
7 I spent a year working for my father's business.
8 Yes. I managed to speak to her yesterday.

VOCABULARY BUILDER QUIZ 16

1

1 settled;
2 converted;
3 venue;
4 unique;
5 ceremony;
6 independent

2

1 impressive;
2 religious;
3 shortage;
4 economic;
5 leader;
6 persuade

3

1 F;   2 T;   3 F;   4 F;   5 T;   6 T;   7 T

4

1 colony;
2 parade;
3 region;
4 rule;
5 bowl;
6 agriculture

Outcomes Pre-intermediate
Student's Book / Workbook Combo Split B

Hugh Dellar and Andrew Walkley

Publisher: Gavin McLean

Publishing Consultant: Karen Spiller

Development Editor: Clare Shaw

Editorial Manager: Claire Merchant

Head of Strategic Marketing ELT: Charlotte Ellis

Senior Content Project Manager: Nick Ventullo

Senior Production Controller: Eyvett Davis

Cover design: emc design

Text design: Alex Dull

Compositor: emc design

National Geographic Liaison:
    Wesley Della Volla / Leila Hishmeh

Audio: Tom Dick & Debbie Productions Ltd

DVD: Tom Dick & Debbie Productions Ltd

Student's Book and Workbook Split B ISBN: 978-1-337-56109-9

National Geographic Learning
Cheriton House
North Way
Andover
UK
SP10 5BE

Cengage Learning is a leading provider of customized learning solutions with employees residing in nearly 40 different countries and sales in more than 125 countries around the world. Find your local representative at **www.cengage.com**.

Cengage Learning products are represented in Canada by Nelson Education Ltd.

Visit National Geographic Learning online at **ngl.cengage.com**
Visit our corporate website at **www.cengage.com**

STUDENT'S BOOK CREDITS

Printed in Greece by Bakis SA
Print Number: 01   Print Year: 2017

© Monkey Business Images/Shutterstock.com; 82 © supertramp88/Shutterstock.com; 83 © Delmonte, Steve/Cartoonstock; 84–85 © Chris Howey/Shutterstock.com.

Cover: © Johnathan Ly.

Illustrations: 54 Phil Hackett; 8, 52, 96, 97 KJA Artists; 80 Mark Draisey.

Acknowledgements

The publisher and authors would like to thank the following teachers who provided the feedback and user insights on the first edition of Outcomes that have helped us develop this new edition:

Rosetta d'Agostino, New English Teaching, Milan, Italy; Victor Manuel Alarcón, EOI Badalona, Badalona, Spain; Isidro Almendarez, Universidad Complutense, Madrid, Spain; Isabel Andrés, EOI Valdemoro, Madrid, Spain; Brian Brennan, International House Company Training, Barcelona, Spain; Nara Carlini, Università Cattolica, Milan, Italy; Karen Corne, UK; Jordi Dalmau, EOI Reus, Reus, Spain; Matthew Ellman, British Council, Malaysia; Clara Espelt, EOI Maresme, Barcelona, Spain; Abigail Fulbrook, Chiba, Japan; Dylan Gates, Granada, Spain; Blanca Gozalo, EOI Fuenlabrada, Madrid, Spain; James Grant, Japan; Joanna Faith Habershon, St Giles Schools of Languages London Central, UK; Jeanine Hack; English Language Coach.com, London, UK; Claire Hart, Germany; David Hicks, Languages4Life, Barcelona, Spain; Hilary Irving, Central School of English, London, UK; Jessica Jacobs, Università Commerciale Luigi Bocconi, Milan, Italy; Lucia Luciani, Centro di Formaziones Casati, Milan, Italy; Izabela Michalak, ELC, Łódź, Poland; Josep Millanes Moya, FIAC Escola d'Idiomes, Terrassa, Catalonia; Rodrigo Alonso Páramo, EOI Viladecans, Barcelona, Spain; Jonathan Parish, Uxbridge College, London, UK; Mercè Falcó Pegueroles, EOI Tortosa, Tortosa, Spain; Hugh Podmore, St Giles Schools of Languages London Central, UK; James Rock, Università Cattolica, Milan, Italy; Virginia Ron, EOI Rivas, Madrid, Spain; Coletto Russo, British Institutes, Milan, Italy; Ana Salvador, EOI Fuenlabrada, Madrid, Spain; Adam Scott, St Giles College, Brighton, UK; Olga Smolenskaya, Russia; Carla Stroulger, American Language Academy, Madrid, Spain; Simon Thomas, St Giles, UK; Simon Thorley, British Council, Madrid, Spain; Helen Tooke, Università Commerciale Luigi Bocconi, Milan, Italy; Chloe Turner, St Giles Schools of Languages London Central, UK; Sheila Vine, University of Paderborn, Germany; Richard Willmsen, British Study Centres, London, UK; Various teachers at English Studio Academic management, UK.

Authors' acknowledgements

Thanks to Karen Spiller and Clare Shaw, and to Dennis Hogan, John McHugh and Gavin McLean for their continued support and enthusiasm.

Thanks also to all the students we've taught over the years for providing more inspiration and insight than they ever realised.

And to the colleagues we've taught alongside for their friendship, thoughts and assistance.

WORKBOOK CREDITS

Although every effort has been made to contact copyright holders before publication, this has not always been possible. If notified, the publisher will undertake to rectify any errors or omissions at the earliest opportunity.

Text

Page 113: Different Strokes is a charity set up by Younger Stroke Survivors. Different Strokes helps stroke survivors to optimise their recovery, take control of their own lives and regain as much independence as possible by offering information, advice and rehabilitation services. For more information about Different Strokes please visit www.differentstrokes.co.uk.

Photos

The publisher would like to thank the following sources for permission to use their copyright protected images:

110 © carlosseller/Fotolia.com; 111 © sonorian/iStockphoto; 112 © epa european pressphoto agency b.v./Alamy Stock Photo; 114 (l) © matka_Wariatka/Fotolia.com; 114 (m) © matka_Wariatka/Fotolia.com; 114 (r) © Perkmeup/Bigstock.com; 116 (l) © AnneMS/Shutterstock.com; 116 (r) © Mr Pics/Shutterstock.com; 117 (t) © monkeybusinessimages/iStockphoto; 117 (b) © Dmitry Naumov/Shutterstock.com; 118 © PhotoAlto/Eric Audras/Getty Images; 120 © Andreas Karelias/Fotolia.com; 123 © Luke Miller/iStockphoto; 124 © Xavier ROSSI/Gamma-Rapho/Getty Images; 126–127 © paul prescott/Shutterstock.com; 128 © Timo Darco/Fotolia.com; 129 © Izabela Habur/iStockphoto; 130 (l) © David Wells/Alamy; 130 (r) © Aga & Miko (arsat)/Shutterstock.com; 132 © Timo Darco/Fotolia.com; 135 © stephanie phillips/iStockphoto; 137 (l) © icholakov/Bigstock.com; 137 (r) © Creations/Shutterstock.com; 141 © Roman Milert/iStockphoto; 142 © Paul Grover/REX; 143 © kipuxa/iStockphoto; 144 © Bardofthebroch/Bigstock.com; 144–145 © Kenneth William Caleno/Shutterstock.com; 146 © al_ks/iStockphoto; 147 © Petrovich9/iStockphoto; 148 (t) © jeremy sutton-hibbert/Alamy; 148 (b) © Philippe Lissac/Godong/Corbis; 150 © David R. Frazier Photolibrary, Inc./Alamy; 152 © Lynne Carpenter/Shutterstock.com; 153 © JLGutierrez/iStockphoto; 154–155 © Mariusz Blach/Fotolia.com; 155 © GeorgiosArt/iStockphoto; 156 © duncan1890/iStockphoto.

Illustrations by Mark Draisey and Clive Goddard.